Reflections
on
Revelation
Part II – The Seven Seals

Reflections

on

Revelation

Part II – The Seven Seals

A Study Guide
Ray Ruppert

Tex Ware
Everett, WA

Unless otherwise noted, all Scriptures are taken from the Holy Bible King James Version.

Scripture references marked (KJV) are taken from the King James Version of the Bible.

The Bible text designated (ESV) is from THE HOLY BIBLE, ENGLISH STANDARD VERSION™ Copyright © 2000, 2001 by Crossway Bibles.

The Bible text designated (NIV®) is Scripture taken from the Holy Bible, NEW INTERNATIONAL VERSION®, NIV® Copyright © 1973, 1978, 1984 by Biblica, Inc.® Used by permission. All rights reserved worldwide.

The Bible text designated (NASU) is from THE NEW AMERICAN STANDARD BIBLE UPDATE. Copyright © 1960, 1962, 1963, 1968, 1971, 1972, 1973, 1975, 1977, 1995, by The Lockman Foundation.

The Bible text designated (NASB) is from THE NEW AMERICAN STANDARD BIBLE. Copyright © 1960, 1962, 1963, 1968, 1971, 1972, 1973, 1975, 1977, by The Lockman Foundation.

The Bible text designated (NKJV) is from THE NEW KING JAMES VERSION, Copyright © 1982, Thomas Nelson, Inc.

The Bible text designated (NLT) is from HOLY BIBLE, NEW LIVING TRANSLATION ® Copyright © 1996, 2004 by Tyndale Charitable Trust.

The Bible text designated (RSV) is from the REVISED STANDARD VERSION OF THE BIBLE, Copyright © 1946, 1952, 1971 by the Division of Christian Education of the National Council of the Churches of Christ in the USA.

ISBN-13: 978-1-935500-55-1

Contents

Foreword vii

Introduction ix

Lesson 1 – Revelation 4:1-6a 1

Lesson 2 – Revelation 4:6b -11 15

Lesson 3 – Revelation 5:1-5 25

Lesson 4 – Revelation 5:6-14 39

Lesson 5 – Revelation 6:1-17 59

Lesson 6 – Revelation 7:1-17 81

Lesson 7 – Revelation 8:1-13 99

Lesson 8 – Revelation 9:1-21 121

Lesson 9 – Revelation 10:1 – 11:3 137

Lesson 10 – Revelation 11:4-19 157

Lesson 11 – Revelation 12:1-17 175

Lesson 12 – Revelation 13:1-18 195

Lesson 13 – Revelation 14:1-20 217

Other Books by Ray Ruppert 241

Foreword

Mr. Ruppert has produced an effective study of the Book of Revelation as his use of questions followed by answers engage the student or group studying Revelation. He emphasizes the key principle of what the text meant THEN before what it means NOW, which I believe are crucial to understanding Revelation. The outline he used for the messages to the 7 churches is the same as I used when I taught Revelation at Northwest University. While I did not do an exhaustive evaluation of his studies, his interpretation corresponds to mine in areas such as the first seal in chapter 6 and the two witnesses in chapter 11.

I commend Mr. Ruppert for the research, time and I'm sure, prayer that he has put into these three study guides, which I believe can lead one, whether a new believer or an "old-timer" in the faith like me, to desire to study this book that deals with lessons for today's church and *events leading up to Christ's 2nd Coming, God's final Judgments, and the New Heavens and the New Earth*! If he is able to present this class at our church, I for one would attend it.

Shalom good friend and *Maranatha, even so come LORD Jesus!*

Dr. Dwaine Braddy – Retired professor of Bible and Pastoral Ministries for 26 years at Northwest University, Kirkland, Washington.

Introduction

By now, you should have finished the study of the first three chapters of Revelation. In one sense, these chapters were the easiest because the symbols and theology was quite evident. Many fail to continue on in the book of Revelation because it is more difficult. This study will delve into the description of heaven before the tribulation starts, work through much of the tribulation, and an interlude tying in some historical events.

As with Part I, the prophecies and symbols will be studied in conjunction with the rest of the Bible so that you will learn from the Bible what God has to say in the book of Revelation. The objective of this study is to bring you closer to Jesus and give you hope for the future. In doing this, you will know Him more and will be able to serve Him better regardless of your circumstances. This study is not designed to tell you when, where, or why some country is going to invade Israel. It will not tell you when the rapture is going to occur, but it will give you enough Scripture to understand the different views.

Room is provided to write your answers to the questions in boxes. Look up the suggested verses, work through them, and answer the questions before you read what I have to say. You will gain a better understanding and will more likely be able to take it to heart than by simply reading my answers.

In addition, if you rely on what I have said, your Bible's study notes, or commentaries, then you are relying on the words of men instead of the Word of God. We all have biases and we are susceptible to error. While you may gain some understanding about the passage you will not be training yourself to rely on the Holy Spirit when you study the Bible (1 John 2:27).

Compare your answers and make notes where you agree or disagree with my conclusions. Make sure all your thoughts are based on Bible verses.

A good concordance (the ones in the back of most Bibles are usually too limited) and a Bible with chain references are all that is needed to do this study. Computer software and internet Bible reference sites provide good concordances. The Thompson Chain Reference is a remarkably good reference and is now online at http://www.studylight.org/concordances/tcr/.

May you be blessed as you study God's Word.

Lesson 1 – Revelation 4:1-6a

After these things I looked, and behold, a door standing open in heaven, and the first voice which I had heard, like the sound of a trumpet speaking with me, said, "Come up here, and I will show you what must take place after these things." Immediately I was in the Spirit; and behold, a throne was standing in heaven, and One sitting on the throne. And He who was sitting was like a jasper stone and a sardius in appearance; and there was a rainbow around the throne, like an emerald in appearance. Around the throne were twenty-four thrones; and upon the thrones I saw twenty-four elders sitting, clothed in white garments, and golden crowns on their heads. Out from the throne come flashes of lightning and sounds and peals of thunder. And there were seven lamps of fire burning before the throne, which are the seven Spirits of God; and before the throne there was something like a sea of glass, like crystal. (NASU)

Summarize the first three Chapters of the book of Revelation. Note any significant divisions and the purpose of each division.

How is this fourth chapter of Revelation significantly different from the previous three?

The opening of chapter four is a major division in the book of Revelation. The first chapter was the first division and introduced us to Jesus, who He is and what He has done to save us. The second division included chapters two and three, which showed us how Christian churches were fairing in the world from Jesus' viewpoint. I didn't capitalize church here because these are organizations, not congregations where everyone is a believer. In Part I of this study I included a lot of teaching about how we can live as individuals as well as the way the Church really should be. We got a lot of practical stuff out of these two divisions. Now, we enter into the part of the book that few people study because there are many symbols and varied views of how to interpret them. However, by neglecting the remainder of the book we also run the risk of reducing our understanding of Jesus as well as the spiritual forces of evil. We need to know these things because our Father has given them to us to help us in our walk with Jesus, as well as to tell us what will happen in the end times. They haven't been written simply to give bored theologians something to do.

From this point in Revelation, it is important to start asking many questions about everything that is going on. Does the command to John to come up here apply symbolically to the church? Does it signify the rapture, or is it just an invitation to him so that God can give him His viewpoint? Most times the simplest answer is the right one. The same thing applies to some of the many symbols that appear. The simplest answer can be found when the symbol is explained in other parts of Scripture.

What Must Take Place after These Things

> John is about to be show some things that are in the future. What is the time frame of the things he will be shown?

"After this" are two key words that signal that a significant change in the book has taken place. They can be understood in various ways.

Up to this time, Jesus was seen walking among the churches. The first three chapters have often been seen as representing the age of the Church. The words "after this" signify that something new or different has arrived. Jesus says that what John is about to see is what must take place after this Church age, which has just been discussed. The big question for us to answer is whether the Church age is limited to the time John wrote the book or if it extends to the present and the future.

> Write the things which you have seen, and the things which are, and the things which will take place after this. (Rev 1:19 NKJV)

To answer part of the question about "after this", we need to go back and see what Jesus had in mind. John has already written what he has seen, the description of the glorified Savior, so that part of his instruction has been completed. The things, which are, refer to the description of the churches and His message to them. So "after this" is referring to a time after the messages are delivered.

We have several options to understanding this and each has its own interpretive problems:

1. The simplest understanding is to say that these things are to happen right after the dictation of the letters. All that is written in the book has already taken place in the first century. This is called the **preterist** or the contemporary historical view. The primary rational supporting this view is that it is the way the original recipients would have understood it.[1] This view generally results in either a postmillennial (Christ returns after the millennium) or amillennial (the millennium is symbolic) view. This relegates most of the rest of the book to our history. A version of this is supported by Hank Hanegraaff[2] of the Christian Research Institute.

2. One common view that keeps changing as time goes on is the **historicist** approach. It originally was a forecast of the history of Western Europe during the Middle Ages and Reformation. Since this is now history to us, the approach has been abandoned. However, it is essentially the precursor to many modern predictions of world events including Russia and the

---

[1] Andreas J. Köstenberger, L. Scott Kellum, and Charles L Quarles, *The Cradle, the Cross, and the Crown* (Nashville: B & H Publishing Group, 2009), 23150-23152, Kindle.

[2] Thomas Ice, "Book Review of the Apocalypse Code: Find Out What the Bible Really Says About the End Times... and Why It Matters Today. by Hank Hanegraaff," *Chafer Theological Seminary Journal* 13, no. 1 (Spring 2008): 95, accessed April 26, 2017, http://chafer.nextmeta.com/files/v13n1_6hanagraff_the_apocalypse_code.pdf.

reestablishment of the nation of Israel. The interpretive problem is that it relies on current events and disregards the relevance for the first century churches. [3] This most often results in a pretribulation, premillennial view. The obvious problem with this is that the interpretation changes from year to year as countries are associated with symbols but they rise and fall without the return of Jesus. It also focuses on the Western Church and ignores both the plight and strength of the Third World Church in predicting the state of the world and Jesus' return.

3. There is also the **idealist** approach, which considers Revelation to be timeless. The idealists view Revelation only as a symbolic battle between good evil with no regard to past or future events. While this view can therefore relate the events symbolically to all churches for all time, it must also deal with the very literal messages to the seven churches. It also fails to deal with Jesus' return and judgment on earth.[4] It necessarily results in an amillennial view.

4. Whether they know it or not most evangelicals adhere to what is called the **futurist** position. There are two broad divisions. Early Christian writer such as Justin Martyr (100-165) espoused dispensationalism. It fell out of favor and gave way to allegoric views but was reinstituted in the sixteenth century. Current adherents were and are D. L. Moody, C. I. Scofield, C. Ryrie, and T. LaHaye. It separates Israel and the Church and uses strict literal interpretations of the Bible. Their interpretation inevitably leads to a pretribulation return of Jesus and is therefore a premillennium (Jesus returns before the millennium) view. This applies most of Revelation to the Church of today. **Modified futurist** position is also called historical premillennialism. These do not hold to the strict literalism of dispensationalism. This system often results in a posttribulation view. This makes the application to the modern Church even more applicable than does the strict literalism.[5]

We could say that these things will take place after the rapture, or after the promises and warnings that Jesus gave the churches have been fulfilled. If we try to get too specific about when they will occur, we are in danger of limiting our understanding in the rest of the book because we will have to interpret them in light of what we have already decided. We could also consider "after this" to be in John's future at some undisclosed time. This is safer to assume since it places no limitations and is literally what it means. If, as we read and study, we can see some things that shed light on the time of the rapture or Jesus' return, we can go back and add that detail without the problem of having to fit it into our understanding of this verse. What I am advocating is that we don't settle on one of the above-mentioned views because each one locks us into a presupposed solution that will limit our ability to get the most out of Revelation. This approach is called an **eclectic blend**, which is what recent commentators use.[6] I decided on this approach long before I heard of it because it makes the most sense.

---

[3] Köstenberger, 23182-23193.
[4] Köstenberger, 23194-23212.
[5] Ibid., 23213-23277.
[6] Ibid., 23278-23279.

Heaven

Have you ever wondered what heaven is like? How would you describe heaven?

If you asked the average person in America, he would probably talk about standing around on clouds and playing harps. Everyone there would have wings and look like angels. Get ready, because the visions of heaven have some of these elements but also blow away the myths that most people believe.

It is important to see that Jesus invited John to see this vision. This is not something that John has willed or sought after. It is the Sovereign Lord who has decided to give him a vision. When John does go up it is in the Spirit. It is not bodily. Anyone who has had a true vision of heaven could only have it based on God's provision. The first thing that John sees is a throne with someone sitting on it.

His Throne

What image do you think most people have of God? What do you imagine when you think of God being exalted on His throne?

In the year that king Uzziah died I saw also the Lord sitting upon a throne, high and lifted up, and his train filled the temple. (Isa 6:1)

We will come back to this verse several times because of the appearance of the Lord, His throne, and the creatures that are there with Him. Isaiah says he saw the Lord high and exalted. Just what do you imagine when you think of God being exalted? Webster's Dictionary defines exalt as: 1. To raise on high: lift up; elevate. 2. To raise in rank, character, honor, etc. 3. To glorify or praise; pay honor to. 4. To fill with delight, pride, etc. 5 To increase the force or intensity of, as colors.[7] If we take each meaning and think about God's appearance, we can see how our Lord is exalted.

He is on a throne that is physically above us so that we may see Him clearly and without distraction. He has the highest rank that is possible in all of the physical or spiritual realms. There is none greater than our Lord. His character is the purest that can be. He is honored above all creation because He has made all things. We are to give Him praise and honor when we exalt Him. We are to be filled with delight and pride that He is our God when we see Him. There is no way to increase the force or intensity of our God because He is all powerful, but when we see Him exalted, we may begin to understand to a greater degree, His power, majesty, and glory.

As we look at the description in Revelation, this is the view that we need to have. Yes, He is our Father and our spirit cries, "Abba" (Rom 8:15), but in light of the end

---

[7] *Webster Comprehensive Dictionary International Edition*, s.v. "Exalt." (Chicago: J. G. Ferguson Publishing Company, 1984)

times that are being revealed, His power, majesty and justice will strike fear into the heart of the unbelievers.

> How can this vision of God help us when we face trials?

Your eyes will see the king in his beauty; they will behold a land that stretches afar. Your mind will muse on the terror: "Where is he who counted, where is he who weighed the tribute? Where is he who counted the towers?" You will see no more the insolent people, the people of an obscure speech which you cannot comprehend, stammering in a tongue which you cannot understand. (Isa 33:17-19 RSV)

Isaiah gives us a hint of what might go through our minds when we come face to face with the Lord. We will see His beauty and maybe, for a split instant, we will wonder about all the evil people that had brought terror to the earth as the Judah's enemies did when they destroyed and plundered Jerusalem. But our attention will turn back to the beauty of the Lord and they will be utterly forgotten. We need to be so absorbed in His beauty that evil does not bother us or distract us from our mission now. If we have a vision of our Sovereign Lord as we see Him in Revelation, this can occur.

Your throne, O God, endures forever and ever. You rule with a scepter of justice. (Ps 45:6 NLT)

The LORD has made the heavens his throne; from there he rules over everything. (Ps 103:19 NLT)

This is what the LORD says: "Heaven is my throne, and the earth is my footstool. Could you build me a temple as good as that? Could you build me such a resting place? (Isa 66:1 NLT)

> What do these verses bring to your mind about the throne of God?

His throne is a symbol of His everlasting nature. From it, He dispenses justice. This is very important to remember every day, not just as we study the book of Revelation. He will always be around and He does dispense justice. He has established His throne in heaven; however, we need to allow Him to be on the throne of our lives so that He is the center of all we think, do, and become. God is even bigger than a throne, for all of heaven is His throne. Our Lord fills all of everything. Nothing escapes His notice.

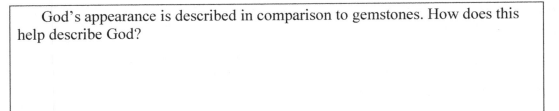

God's appearance is described in comparison to gemstones. How does this help describe God?

The appearance of God on the throne is cloaked in terms that are hard to explain. Many versions of the Bible translate some of the words differently. Jasper seems to stay the same but carnelian is also called sardine. Bible dictionaries don't help a lot; they only explain that they don't know precisely what John was talking about when he tried to explain what he saw.

> Over the heads of the living creatures there was the likeness of a firmament, shining like crystal, spread out above their heads. (Ezek 1:22 RSV)

You can continue to read all of Ezekiel's vision with references to gems, fire, and rainbows. Ezekiel saw something that he had trouble explaining as well. The problem is that both John and Ezekiel were witnessing something that was totally unknown to either of them. This was something that was so marvelous that they tried to explain it in terms of jewels and other things of great value or beauty. From these visions, it becomes evident that the appearance our God, the one who cares about us as individuals as well as nations and even the universe, is far beyond our capabilities to explain. It is only possible from these verses to inspire within us a sense of awe at His presence and who He is.

Do you have any problem accepting the impossibility of describing God? What are some of the other mysteries of God that you have trouble accepting or describing?

It is interesting that we can accept the physical impossibility to describe God's appearance, but we become frustrated when we try to explain His methods or His attributes. Perhaps we should learn to accept some of the mysteries of God without completely needing to understand them as well. As an example, there are numerous references to God's election in the Bible as well as many references in which we see God giving us choices. How can both be true? They are true, yet many people spend endless hours trying to explain away one or the other. Others try to explain how both can be true but end up like John and Ezekiel, using terms and theories that give us a glimpse of the infinite mind of God, but are woefully inadequate.

The Rainbow

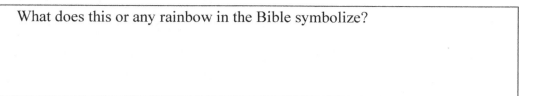

What does this or any rainbow in the Bible symbolize?

The rainbow that appears in the cloud, even though it is described in Revelation as looking like an emerald, is symbolic of God's promises. He used the rainbow in Genesis 9:13-16 as a specific promise not to destroy the earth with a flood again. When we see the rainbow around Gods throne, we can be assured that it is always in His presence. This reveals that it is His nature never to forget His promises. If this one promise was so important that He would always have a rainbow around Him, what of His other promises in the Word? He has just given seven promises to the churches. All of these involve eternal life.

Twenty-Four Elders

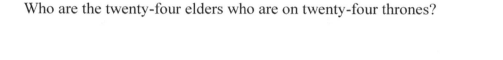

Who are the twenty-four elders who are on twenty-four thrones?

The twenty-four elders are generally believed to represent all believers. This is mainly due to the description of their clothes. They are all dressed in white, which is promised for believers in Revelation 3:5 and they have crowns, which are also promised to us. It could also be said that the number twenty-four stands for the twelve tribes of Israel and the twelve apostles. Revelation 21:12-14 describes the wall around the New Jerusalem with twelve gates. Each gate has a name of one of the tribes of Israel, while there are twelve foundations, each with a name of one of the apostles. This would then represent those who came in faith from the Old Testament and those who came in faith from the New Testament.

> And the four living creatures, each one of them having six wings, are full of eyes around and within; and day and night they do not cease to say, "HOLY, HOLY, HOLY, *IS* THE LORD GOD, THE ALMIGHTY, WHO WAS AND WHO IS AND WHO IS TO COME." And when the living creatures give glory and honor and thanks to Him who sits on the throne, to Him who lives forever and ever, the twenty-four elders will fall down before Him who sits on the throne, and will worship Him who lives forever and ever, and will cast their crowns before the throne, … (Rev 4:8-10 NASB)

What appears to be the main occupation of the twenty-four elders? How can we be like them?

One thing is certain, these elders only appear in the book of Revelation, and they are constantly worshiping the Lord. In Revelation 4:10 we see them falling before the throne every time the creatures give glory and honor to God. In verse 8, it says that the creatures never stop saying how holy God is. This is a never-ending circle of worship and praise. Wouldn't it be wonderful if we, too, could always be in a state of worship before God regardless of what we are doing? We should try doing just that.

They also acknowledge the sovereignty of God by laying down their crowns before Him. Even though Revelation 3:26 tells us He will give us authority to rule with Him, we will still be under Him. Revelation 5:8, 14, 7:11, 11:16, 19:4 are all verses where they again fall at the feet of God. It is an inspiration to think about the fact that elders, those we respect and admire, have absolutely no second thoughts about falling down before God. In shedding their crowns, they are removing all pride, holding nothing back from Him. Indeed, they represent not only all believers, and even more importantly what we should be like in our worship.

Lightning and Thunder

> As I looked, I saw a great storm coming from the north, driving before it a huge cloud that flashed with lightning and shone with brilliant light. There was fire inside the cloud, and in the middle of the fire glowed something like gleaming amber. From the center of the cloud came four living beings that looked human. (Ezek 1:4-5 NLT)

> Above this surface was something that looked like a throne made of blue lapis lazuli. And on this throne high above was a figure whose appearance resembled a man. (Ezek 1:26-27 NLT)

> A great brightness shone around him, and burning coals blazed forth. The LORD thundered from heaven; the voice of the Most High resounded. He shot arrows and scattered his enemies; his lightning flashed, and they were confused. Then at the command of the LORD, at the blast of his breath, the bottom of the sea could be seen, and the foundations of the earth were laid bare. (2 Sam 22:13-16 NLT)

> My heart pounds as I think of this. It trembles within me. Listen carefully to the thunder of God's voice as it rolls from his mouth. It rolls across the heavens, and his lightning flashes in every direction. Then comes the roaring of the thunder— the tremendous voice of his majesty. He does not restrain it when he speaks. God's voice is glorious in the thunder. We can't even imagine the greatness of his power. (Job 37:1-5 NLT)

> Then a voice spoke from heaven, saying, "I have already brought glory to my name, and I will do so again." When the crowd heard the voice, some thought it was thunder, while others declared an angel had spoken to him. (John 12:28b-29 NLT)

List the things that appear when God manifests His presence.

> What is your reaction as you think about these things? Are you afraid? Why or why not?

Lightning, thunder, smoke, clouds, and the four living creatures are some of the things that appear to show that the Lord is near. Never do we see a clearly defined figure of God. We see a figure like that of a man. In Exodus 19:16-19, 20:18 God manifests His presence in lightning and thunder. The people were so overcome by these manifestations that they trembled and stayed at a distance. As believers, we have the opportunity to come into His presence (Ps 100:1).

Lightning and thunder convey images of His judgment in these verses. That's one of the reasons the Israelites were afraid. Since Jesus has taken the judgment of our sins upon Himself, we need not fear His judgment (Heb 4:16, Jude 24).

Thunder also represents the voice of God as Elihu tells of His might and wonder in Job 37. Elihu is the only one of Job's friends who isn't rebuked by the Lord. When he finishes his discourse, God Himself speaks to Job. I gather from this, that Elihu knew the Lord very well. I think that Elihu's heart pounded, not because he was afraid, but because he was thrilled to hear God's voice.

When God actually speaks some know exactly what He has said as Jesus did. Others who do not know Him can only hear thunder. Perhaps the closer we are to God, the easier it is to distinguish His voice from noise or even an angel speaking.

While we do not need to fear God's judgment, there is a danger today whereby Christians do not have a healthy respect for God. Some speak of a reverential fear of God, but make no mistake about these manifestations of God, they would most likely cause any of us to shake in our boots.

> How might the clouds and lightning that surround God demonstrate His provision or protection?

The clouds that surround the Lord can also be seen as His provision to protect us from His wrath. If He were to appear unhidden, we would die. If He appeared clearly in all His glory, the brilliance of His radiance would consume us.

Think of the lightening as energy that radiates from God to uphold all things. The amount of energy that is in a bolt of lightning is immeasurable with our instruments because the instrument would be burned up. Whenever lightning strikes, we say that it is an act of God. How true it is, for only He can control it. The fact that lightening is so immeasurable and that it is so far from our control demonstrates the power and glory of our Lord.

The radiance and light that surround Him always symbolizes His holiness and purity. Things are refined by fire and light. Sunlight shining on a steam of water can kill germs and purify it. He gives us enough of His light to cleans us but not so much to kill us.

Seven Lamps

In Revelation 1:4, we dealt with the seven spirits of God so we won't address that again.

> Some scholars say that the seven lamps before the throne represent the raptured church. Explain how this is or is not an accurate analysis.

There are some who would say that these lamps are also the lamps that appear in Revelation 1:12 and 19, which are the seven churches addressed in Revelation 2 – 3. These scholars believe the church has been raptured before the beginning of chapter four since these lamps are now standing before the throne in heaven. I like that idea; however, this is not the plain and simple teaching of Revelation 4:5. In chapter 1 the Word plainly says that the lampstands on earth are the churches and this verse very plainly says that the lamps in heaven are the spirits of God. To say anything else is to make the scripture fit what you want.

Sea Of Glass

The sea is figurative of many things in the Bible but most often relates to people and nations.

> But let him ask in faith, with no doubting, for the one who doubts is like a wave of the sea that is driven and tossed by the wind. (James 1:6 ESV)

> Daniel declared, "I saw in my vision by night, and behold, the four winds of heaven were stirring up the great sea. And four great beasts came up out of the sea, different from one another." (Dan 7:2-3 ESV)

> How and why are the seas in these verses different from the one described in Revelation 4:6?

A person who doubts is like a wave of the sea. A person who doubts is unsure of God's will and therefore cannot align himself with it. But in heaven, we see a sea of glass with nary a wave in sight expressing an absolute calmness. Before the Lord there will be no doubts and no unrest. Unrest is caused by sin, which occurs when we want to do our thing instead of what the Lord wants. When we fight against God there is only one result, personal turmoil. Not until we rest in His forgiveness and perfect holiness can we have a heart that is like a sea of glass.

In Daniel's verses, the sea is churned up by the winds and four beasts come up out of it. In this case, the sea represents the people of the earth who are restless and never content. The beasts are nations or leaders of nations who come from or are a product of the nations (Dan 7:17).

> In my vision at night I looked, and there before me was one like a son of man, coming with the clouds of heaven. He approached the Ancient of Days and was led into his presence. (Dan 7:13 NIV®)

> What is the difference between those who follow the beasts (or kings) in Daniel 7:2 and us who follow Jesus who is described in Daniel 7:13?

The difference is that our rest comes with Jesus because He brings holiness and righteousness where there was none before. He doesn't come from the sinful sea of mankind but He comes from above, sinless and pure.

In Revelation 12:17-13:4 we again see a beast that comes from the sea. There, the message is clear that Satan will give his power to this ruler in a way that he has never done before. It can be seen from this and Matthew 4:8-9 that Satan has been given authority and power over earthly kingdoms as he directs and guides this beast and makes him a mighty ruler. But, since God is sovereign, even Satan's plans fit into the scheme of things and these prophecies will come true.

The main point is that Satan can pull up from a sinful, dissatisfied world people who will follow and be used by him. But Jesus can clean up and make a sinful person satisfied in Him. In Him we have rest.

> I know how to get along with humble means, and I also know how to live in prosperity; in any and every circumstance I have learned the secret of being filled and going hungry, both of having abundance and suffering need. (Phil 4:12 NASU)

Contrast this unrest with Paul who learned to be content with and in all things. When we find discontentment in things, whether it is a job, church, marriage, or any other task or situation, we open ourselves up to Satan's leading. I'm not talking about seeing a problem that has to be resolved, but an attitude of complaining. When I was in the Navy, people always grumbled no matter what they were doing; they could always find something wrong that was someone else's fault.

> They shall not hurt nor destroy in all My holy mountain, For the earth shall be full of the knowledge of the Lord As the waters cover the sea. And in that day there shall be a Root of Jesse, Who shall stand as a banner to the people; For the Gentiles shall seek Him, And His resting place shall be glorious. It shall come to pass in that day *That* the Lord shall set His hand again the second time To recover the remnant of His people who are left, From Assyria and Egypt, From Pathros and Cush, From Elam and Shinar, From Hamath and the islands of the sea. NKJV (Isa 11:9 NKJV)

What additional things can we learn about the sea of glass from these verses?

The knowledge of the Lord will cover the earth like a sea. Politics and philosophies claim solutions to man's problems. They claim that if everyone would adhere to the conservative, liberal, ideological, or religious values they expound, we would all be at rest. But we will have rest only when everyone has a saving knowledge of the Lord. Even our Christian differences are overcome when we gain this all-encompassing knowledge. That rest will only take place before the throne of God.

This world will be a place of rest when all the nations come to Jesus. As the banner of Jesus is raised, all nations will come to Him. It will happen as He reaches out His hand and brings people to Himself from the whole world.

What is the symbology of the sea being like glass and crystal?

The sea is clear as crystal and may very well refer to the holiness of those who stand before God. Crystal was any clear, colorless, hard material like quartz. Crystal is transparent and represents our need to be transparent before God and with each other. When sin separates us from God, we are the ones who cannot see Him and we try to hide our sin from Him. In reality, we are always transparent because He can see through us. We only become transparent when we stop trying to fool ourselves and others.

1 John 2:12-14 talks of knowing Jesus and knowing the Father. The Greek word for knowing expresses the idea of being aware of, feeling, perceiving, being sure, and understanding.[8] When we are transparent with people, we know them this way. We can see when they are hurting or happy without them having to say a word because we know them. This is the way we should know the Father. Without Him saying a word, we should be able to determine His will. This is only possible when His Holy Spirit lives in us. We don't need Him to say a word because we have already hidden His Word in our hearts and this is the way we come to know Him.

How is the Church – redeemed people of all ages – symbolized by the colorless quality of crystal?

He did this to present her to himself as a glorious church without a spot or wrinkle or any other blemish. Instead, she will be holy and without fault. (Eph 5:27 NLT)

---

[8] *Biblesoft's New Exhaustive Strong's Numbers and Concordance with Expanded Greek-Hebrew Dictionary*, s.v. "NT:1097", (Seattle: Biblesoft and International Bible Translators, Inc. 2006).

The crystal is colorless to indicate that it is without flaw. The sea of glass could then represent all believers whether dead, alive in the state that we should be now, or the way we will be forever in His presence.

May we exalt our Lord in every aspect of our lives, knowing Him better and remembering His promises so that we may be at peace in His presence. That is a witness that will shake the world.

Lesson 2 – Revelation 4:6b -11

And around the throne, on each side of the throne, are four living creatures, full of eyes in front and behind: the first living creature like a lion, the second living creature like an ox, the third living creature with the face of a man, and the fourth living creature like an eagle in flight. And the four living creatures, each of them with six wings, are full of eyes all around and within, and day and night they never cease to say, "Holy, holy, holy, is the Lord God Almighty, who was and is and is to come!" And whenever the living creatures give glory and honor and thanks to him who is seated on the throne, who lives forever and ever, the twenty-four elders fall down before him who is seated on the throne and worship him who lives forever and ever. They cast their crowns before the throne, saying, "Worthy are you, our Lord and God, to receive glory and honor and power, for you created all things, and by your will they existed and were created." (ESV)

What is the purpose of the four living creatures?

My first thoughts were to view the four living creatures in two ways. They could symbolize the attributes that we should have before God since we, like them, are beings that continually live before God. They could also symbolize the characteristics of God since they have often been seen when He is seen. Then it occurred to me that they don't have to be symbolic of anything. It is possible that God created these beings for His own pleasure and to declare His holiness to all creation.

Like A Lion

Scripture says a lot about lions and what they represent. Read these verses.

What is sweeter than honey? What is stronger than a lion? (Judg 14:18b NIV®)

Then even the bravest soldier, whose heart is like the heart of a lion, will melt with fear, for all Israel knows that your father is a fighter and that those with him are brave. (2 Sam 17:10 NIV®)

You are a lion's cub, O Judah; you return from the prey, my son. Like a lion he crouches and lies down, like a lioness — who dares to rouse him? (Gen 49:9 NIV®)

What could the creature like a lion represent?

15

The lion is obviously symbolic of strength, courage, and ferocity. The ferocity of the lion is even used to describe Satan's hatred and desire to destroy Christians (1 Peter 3:8). It also symbolized Israel (Nu 24:9) and Jesus (Rev 5:5).

> Woe to those who go down to Egypt for help *And* rely on horses, And trust in chariots because *they are* many And in horsemen because they are very strong, But they do not look to the Holy One of Israel, nor seek the LORD! (Isa 31:1 NASU)
>
> For thus says the LORD to me, "As the lion or the young lion growls over his prey, Against which a band of shepherds is called out, *And* he will not be terrified at their voice nor disturbed at their noise, So will the Lord of hosts come down to wage war on Mount Zion and on its hill." Like flying birds so the Lord of hosts will protect Jerusalem. He will protect and deliver *it*, He will pass over and rescue *it*. (Isa 31:4-5 NASU)

What does the lion represent in these verses and how should we apply this to our lives?

They represent God in His protection of his people. Think about these verses for a few minutes in relation to a time of trouble and confusion coming on the world when people are turning everywhere except to the Lord. This has happened throughout history and will be completed in the end times. The mighty God of heaven is waiting to help any who turn to Him. Instead we turn to others for help. The Israelites turned to the Egyptians for help. People today turn to psychiatrists, mediums, self-actualization classes, drugs, alcohol, and various other "wise things" of man. But these things are not God's intention. These things can even happen to a church when they turn to the world's methods of trying to "sell" the Gospel. They may even decide to use worldly money raising techniques to fund their operations or capital improvement plans. When they do this, they will eventually see the hand of God turned against them. On the other hand, think of the comfort of having the Lord God Almighty protect His people and not letting the clamor of the world take them away from Him.

Like An Ox

> So Moab said to the elders of Midian, "Now this company will lick up everything around us, as an ox licks up the grass of the field." (Num 22:4a NKJV)

How might the ox demonstrate our spiritual determination or God's character?

This showed the relentless eating habits of oxen. They would continue eating in a pasture until all the grass was consumed. Nothing would be left. This is the attitude we need in our spiritual life. Like an ox, we must carefully consume all of the Word of God. We need to look at all He has said to us.

As an attribute of the Lord, this could show that He is patient and steady. In the cosmic battle between good and evil, He will leave nothing of wickedness behind but will consume it all.

Oxen were also animals of sacrifice. Jesus sacrificed Himself for us.

> Then Jesus said, "Come to me, all of you who are weary and carry heavy burdens, and I will give you rest. Take my yoke upon you. Let me teach you, because I am humble and gentle at heart, and you will find rest for your souls. For my yoke is easy to bear, and the burden I give you is light." (Matt 11:28-30 NLT)

Jesus is also identifying Himself with some other qualities of an ox. He is gentle and humble and in His strength, He carries our burdens for us. God is also a jealous God who wants His people to turn to Him. When we do, we receive comfort and rest. He has already carried the burden of our sin, so why not let him carry all the other burdens as well?

Like A Man

> How does the creature with a face like a man represent our relationship with God?

> Then God said, "Let us make man in our image, after our likeness; and let them have dominion over the fish of the sea, and over the birds of the air, and over the cattle, and over all the earth, and over every creeping thing that creeps upon the earth." (Gen 1:26 RSV)

The third creature had a face like a man. This shows that the living creatures are like us in that they are created beings. The word "image"[9] in the Hebrew means a representative figure. The work "likeness" in the Hebrew means "resemblance."[10] Man is created to resemble God and to be a representative figure of Him. In doing this He has given us some of His attributes. We possess intelligence, having the ability to think, make choices, and show emotion. As God is holy, and these creatures are living in His presence, they, too, are holy. God originally created us to be holy and to live in His presence. We need to use our intelligence to choose to be holy. Our ability to think also lets us know that we aren't holy and that the only way we can become holy is by the means that God has revealed.

> For assuredly He does not give help to angels, but He gives help to the descendant of Abraham. Therefore, He had to be made like *His* brethren in all things, that He might become a merciful and faithful high priest in things *pertaining* to God, to make

---

[9] *Strong's*, s.v. "OT:6754."
[10] Ibid., s.v. "OT:1823."

propitiation for the sins of the people. For since He Himself was tempted in that which He has suffered, He is able to come to the aid of those who are tempted. (Heb 2:16-18 NASB)

This also shows us that God identifies with us. When we come before the throne of God, this creature should be a constant reminder to us that God knows our weakness and won't forget that He has made atonement for our sins through Jesus our Lord. (Actually, I doubt we will ever forget when we see Jesus in heaven; however our Lord often speaks to us in many ways just to make sure we don't forget.) This is the only way we can become holy – through the blood of Jesus.

Like an Eagle

What can we learn from eagles regarding our relationship to God and His attributes?

Even youths shall faint and be weary, and young men shall fall exhausted; but they who wait for the LORD shall renew their strength; they shall mount up with wings like eagles; they shall run and not be weary; they shall walk and not faint. (Isa 40:30-31 ESV)

This is the picture of one who puts his hope in the Lord. In time of trouble and hardship, He will renew us. The eagle is shown as a tireless creature that can soar and continue for hours without rest. In the presence of the Lord, we too, will not grow weary. When we are tempted to give up or become depressed, we need to go into the throne room of the Lord to be renewed. We need to be reminded of this over and over again. No matter what the problem is, no matter how bad the circumstances, our Lord is sovereign and He will renew us and give us strength.

You yourselves have seen what I did to Egypt, and how I carried you on eagles' wings and brought you to myself. (Ex 19:4 NIV®)

The symbol of an eagle is associated with the Lord's divine protection. When Israel was brought out of Egypt, it was totally by the will and power of the Lord. Later in the book of Revelation we will see another time when a woman is saved by giving her two wings of a great eagle (Rev 12:14).

He found him in a desert land, And in the howling waste of a wilderness; He encircled him, He cared for him, He guarded him as the pupil of His eye. Like an eagle that stirs up its nest, That hovers over its young, He spread His wings and caught them, He carried them on His pinions. (Deut 32:10-11 NASU)

I watched a You Tube videos where eagles are flying beside and above others. According to the makers, these are young eagles learning to fly with the adult.[11] Apparently, the air currents from the adult make it easier for the young to learn; it appears as if the adult is carrying them. Others have said that eagles actually kick the young out of the nest and then swoop down and catch them until they learn to fly. (This isn't documented by any researchers that I could find on the web.) However, they have been seen to fly over the nest to lure the young to take their first flight.

The Lord is alongside of us at all times as well as hovering over us, leading us in His paths. He also has to stir up our nests at times to get us moving on to where He wants us to go. Unlike the eagle, God does actually carry us. The Christian walk is not a walk that seeks the comfort of *status quo*, but one that involves stretching to make us grow.

> Now my days are swifter than a runner; They flee away, they see no good. They pass by like swift ships, Like an eagle swooping on its prey. (Job 9:25-26 NKJV)

This verse relates the swiftness of the eagle to the shortness of our lives. Think also about the swiftness of judgment that comes from the Lord. To the eagle's victim, it comes out of the blue (up to 190 miles per hour), and is seldom anticipated except for a split second, if at all. The Lord's vengeance will come upon the earth in the same way. In the expanse of history, seven years of tribulation will seem very swift. Because people at that time will be so calloused, they will be like an eagle's victim and wonder from where it came.

Covered With Eyes

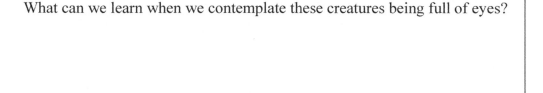

What can we learn when we contemplate these creatures being full of eyes?

> Your eye is a lamp that provides light for your body. When your eye is good, your whole body is filled with light. (Matt 6:22 NLT)

These creatures dwell in the presence of the living Lord and have eyes all over them. It is possible that they only have eyes for God, and so should we. In the presence of God these beings are fully flooded with the light of the Lord. They are full of light just as we can be if we are truly focused on Him.

> Having the eyes of your hearts enlightened ... (Eph 1:18 RSV)

It shouldn't be surprising to think of creatures with eyes all over them, since we refer to having eyes in our hearts. These are eyes that see spiritual truth. These are eyes by which we gain understanding of the Lord.

---

[11] Unfortunately there are many eagle videos and I was unable to locate one that was a real proof of this.

For since the creation of the world His invisible attributes, His eternal power and divine nature, have been clearly seen, being understood through what has been made, so that they are without excuse. (Rom 1:20 NASB)

We gain understanding by what we see, and we can see His nature in what He has created as well as when we use our eyes to read His word.

Let us fix our eyes on Jesus, the author and perfecter of our faith, who for the joy set before him endured the cross, scorning its shame, and sat down at the right hand of the throne of God. Consider him who endured such opposition from sinful men, so that you will not grow weary and lose heart. (Heb 12:2-3 NIV®)

We need to fix our eyes on Jesus to see His response to opposition and pain. We always need to remember that the book of Revelation is a book of pain and sorrow for many, but those who have their eyes fixed on Jesus will see the end, which is the joy that He has provided for us. When our eyes are full of Jesus, we will not grow weary and lose heart.

The eyes of the creatures represent their total concentration on God.

Six Wings

Above him stood the seraphim. Each had six wings: with two he covered his face, and with two he covered his feet, and with two he flew. (Isa 6:2 ESV)

Jesus said to him, "The one who has bathed does not need to wash, except for his feet, but is completely clean. And you are clean, but not every one of you." (John 13:10 ESV)

What three things does the creatures' use of their wings remind us about ourselves?

In Isaiah, the creatures covered their feet with their wings. As the creatures hide their feet we are reminded that our feet come in contact with the dirty part of the world. The unholiness of the world should not be brought before the Lord. He is too holy to look upon that. Of course, we also know that since He made the provision for us to come to Him complete and in confidence, this is only symbolic and must remind us that the blood of Jesus must cover our sin. They also cover their faces showing that He is also so holy we can't look directly at Him. Thanks be to God that He has also provided the covering of His righteousness so that through Jesus, we may see Him. The creatures also use their wings for movement, which represents our ability to serve Him.

Keep me as the apple of the eye; Hide me in the shadow of Your wings From the wicked who despoil me, My deadly enemies who surround me. (Ps 17:8-9 NASU)

How precious is Your lovingkindness, O God! And the children of men take refuge in the shadow of Your wings. (Ps 36:7 NASU)

Be gracious to me, O God, be gracious to me, For my soul takes refuge in You; And in the shadow of Your wings I will take refuge Until destruction passes by. (Ps 57:1 NASU)

What are God's attributes symbolized by wings?

God's protection, comfort, and shelter are all symbolized in wings. The shelter is sometimes only until the disaster has passed. He doesn't promise escape from the disaster but shelter so that we may endure it. What He wants us to do is to come to Him to cope with our problems of life. Alcoholics and other dysfunctional families learn to cope in non-biblical ways and many times never learn the truth. Only by seeking refuge in Him can we truly cope. After the disaster has passed, we come out from under the wings and are on the front lines, stronger than ever.

Never Stop Saying Holy

The four living creatures never stop saying holy, holy, holy is the Lord God Almighty. What does this tell us about God?

And one cried unto another, and said, Holy, holy, holy, is the LORD of hosts: the whole earth is full of his glory. (Isa 6:3)

When Isaiah saw these creatures, they were declaring the holiness of God and His glory. When John saw them, they were still declaring God's holiness. Day and night, they never stop, most likely from eternity past to eternity future. Doesn't this tell us something unique about God's holiness? We may refer to holy angels or holy saints, but the holiness of God is so amazing and beyond our comprehension that these creatures have never stopped declaring it. He is a loving God and He has demonstrated it by sending Jesus to die for us, but the creatures don't cry "loving" day and night. We could recite the same argument for each of His attributes and discover that it is only His holiness that is declared forever. When I read the first few books of the Bible, I see His great concern for holiness. If we ever doubt His holiness or attribute to Him any kind of evil thoughts or intent, we have maligned the most important attribute of God.

But as He who called you is holy, you also be holy in all *your* conduct, because it is written, "*Be holy, for I am holy.*" (1 Peter 1:15-16 NKJV)

If we don't have a concern for personal holiness, then we have missed a significant aspect of our lives in Christ.

The creatures also use the phrase "Lord God Almighty," which describes His authority, position, power, and everlasting nature. John explains in verse 9 that this is giving glory, honor, and thanks to God. How often do we forget that our words are often the only way that others can know that we are giving God glory, honor, and thanks? I love that song that says, "With our hands lifted high to the sky, And the world wonders why We'll just tell them we're loving our King"[12] Our hearts may very well express it, but for others to see it and know what it is, it must become verbal. John picks up on the last verse of what the creatures say and emphasizes it two more times. God lives forever and ever. No matter how long it takes for these things to take place, the same God is in control. We don't have to deal with a new administration every four or even a hundred years.

He Is Worthy

> What do the elders demonstrate when they fall down and cast their crowns before the throne? What does this imply for us?

The elders fall down before the throne every time the creatures declare God's holiness. I can only picture them continually on their faces. The creatures never stop crying holy so they must be there in a constant state of worship. When we discussed the crowns in Revelation 2:10, several were listed that we will all receive when we get to heaven. If the elders' crowns are representative of the crowns we are to receive, then they are showing that all we have in the way of righteousness, joy, love, compassion, or anything else is owed to our Lord and God.

The elders then take up the praise and are vitally concerned with God's worthiness to receive that glory, honor, and power. The King James Version says they were created for His pleasure. God would not will into being something that was not made for His pleasure and anything made for His pleasure is good because He is a holy God.

> And God saw every thing that he had made, and, behold, it was very good. And the evening and the morning were the sixth day. (Gen 1:31)

God made all things for His pleasure and they are good but that doesn't rule out the fact that sin has entered this world causing corruption and that has grieved our Lord.

As we continue into the book of Revelation, we will always want to remember these attributes of God, for it is because of His holiness that the end of sin must come. Since He does live forever, He can see the big picture, which gives Him the ability to judge fairly. By the end of the book He will have allowed man to try every way he can to save himself and shown that they are all in rebellion against God. So at the end, if any do not come by His way, by faith in Jesus, then He can say that He has seen it all and still men have rebelled. Because He is worthy both from the standpoint of having paid the price for sin, and having created all things, He has the right to carry out the judgment. Because He is all-powerful, He has the ability to carry out the judgment.

---

[12] Kaan, "We Will Worship the Lamb of Glory Lyrics - Dennis Jernigan," elyrics.net, October 1, 1998, accessed May 19, 2013, http://www.elyrics.net/read/d/dennis-jernigan-lyrics/we-will-worship-the-lamb-of-glory-lyrics.html.

May you be inspired by His holiness and worthiness to worship Him in holiness and truth. May His holiness and worthiness enable us to trust Him for all things and live a holy life in Jesus.

What did you find in Revelation 4 that helped you understand God or yourself better?

How has this helped you in your Christian walk?

Lesson 3 – Revelation 5:1-5

Then I saw a scroll in the right hand of the one who was sitting on the throne. There was writing on the inside and the outside of the scroll, and it was sealed with seven seals. And I saw a strong angel, who shouted with a loud voice: "Who is worthy to break the seals on this scroll and open it?" But no one in heaven or on earth or under the earth was able to open the scroll and read it. Then I began to weep bitterly because no one was found worthy to open the scroll and read it. But one of the twenty-four elders said to me, "Stop weeping! Look, the Lion of the tribe of Judah, the heir to David's throne, has won the victory. He is worthy to open the scroll and its seven seals." (NLT)

God's Right Hand

> What does God's right hand symbolize for wicked people?

Your hand will find out all your enemies; your right hand will find out those who hate you. You will make them as a blazing oven when you appear. The Lord will swallow them up in his wrath; and fire will consume them. (Ps 21:8-9 RSV)

Be exalted, O Lord, in thy strength! We will sing and praise thy power. (Ps 21:13 RSV)

This is a fitting start to look at the right hand of God. It is a symbol of His strength and justice. When He appears in the last times it will be for judgment against His enemies. The scroll that He has in His right hand contains the details of the punishment that He will inflict upon the earth. We will actually sing and praise His might as it happens just as David rejoiced when he anticipated His coming in this psalm.

Does it seem strange to you to think that we will actually be singing and praising someone who is killing billions of people? Doesn't it seem to go against everything that Jesus taught? After all, didn't Jesus protect the woman caught in adultery? Doesn't He tell us to turn the other cheek? Don't most people ignore the Old Testament because they abhor the way God had Israel ruthlessly kill off other nations? Aren't we champions of the unborn who are murdered by the millions each year? Doesn't our faith teach us that it is wrong to take a life?

> Have you ever asked these questions or have you been asked? How would you answer them?

Questions like these have led many people to believe that we should altogether eliminate capital punishment. Many people, Christians included, have gotten the idea that it is wrong to think that the wicked should be punished by death or even worse, a sentence of eternal suffering and pain. But from the beginning of the Old Testament to the end of the Bible, God has shown His displeasure with wickedness and the need to curb it and in the end, eliminate it. We indeed need to praise Him for the strength that it takes to stand up to evil and do something. We don't rejoice that billions die, but that justice is finally accomplished. It is from this lack of praise and an inability to look at things from God's perspective that people then allow themselves to be caught up in a doctrine that denies the existence of hell and Satan.

Those who do not understand God's provision for the punishment of evil either condemn capital punishment or demand it without mercy. The Christian walk recognizes the need for governments to curb evil with appropriate punishment (Rom 13:1-6). Contrary to modern thinking, capital punishment is a deterrent to crime because that is what God has said (Deut 19:19-20, 21:21). Personally, we need to remember that we are not the ultimate judge and that we need to forgive and not seek revenge (Rom 12:17-21). We must not confuse our role as a Christian to tell of God's forgiveness with God's role as sovereign Judge.

> What does God's right hand symbolize for Christians?

For not by their own sword did they win the land, nor did their own arm save them, but your right hand and your arm, and the light of your face, for you delighted in them. (Ps 44:3 ESV)

There is no fear for God's people at His right hand. It is a symbol of strength for protection and love as He cares for His own. It was with His right hand He delivered Israel. Likewise, the deliverance that comes in the book of Revelation will rid all evil influences in the world. We need to come to the realization that just as there were many in the Old Testament who perished, there are many who will perish today and even more in the last times. It is necessary for the Lord God Almighty to finish His plan. The seriousness of this is demonstrated in the fact that page after page of the book of Revelation is devoted to describing that destruction. Hell-fire and brimstone preaching has its place. It is there because it is in the Word and for some it is the only way that they will acknowledge God.

> What does God's right hand symbolize for the Church?

Kings' daughters are among Thy noble ladies; At Thy right hand stands the queen in gold from Ophir. (Ps 45:9 NASB)

My soul clings to Thee; Thy right hand upholds me. (Ps 63:8 NASB)

While Psalm 45 was a wedding song, we can also see the symbolism of the position of the Bride of Christ, the Church, at His right hand. There are fears and uncertainty at every turn of our lives. If we are honest with ourselves, we have to admit that we don't know from moment to moment what will happen to us. We like to feel in control of things, or at least think that the law of averages will work in our favor so that we will be able to accomplish our goals. However, the only hope for real security is that His right hand upholds us when we cling to Him. As members of His Church, when we cling to our God with all that we are, with all our being, He tells us that He is upholding us with His right hand. It doesn't matter what will happen or how we perceive it – good or bad – because God is upholding us. The gates of hell will not prevail against the Church (Matt 16:18). As members of His Body, we are eternally secure at His right hand. This is the most secure position anyone can have.

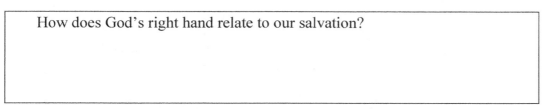

How does God's right hand relate to our salvation?

Sing to the LORD a new song, for he has done marvelous things; his right hand and his holy arm have worked salvation for him. (Ps 98:1 NIV®)

"Yes, it is as you say," Jesus replied. "But I say to all of you: In the future you will see the Son of Man sitting at the right hand of the Mighty One and coming on the clouds of heaven." (Matt 26:64 NIV®)

Salvation comes because Jesus died on the cross to take our sins, yet there are several places in the Bible that refer to God working salvation by His right hand. No wonder Jesus is at His right hand, for in that sense, Jesus is God's right hand.

The Scroll

What does the sealed scroll written on both sides represent?

The Word of God has been recorded on scrolls since Moses started to write it down. This scroll could very well represent the unchanging and sure Word of God. The idea that it is written on the outside and inside symbolizes that for some, it is clear but to others, the prophecies are hidden.

Read the Scriptures following this question. What are some reasons that John may have started weeping other than that no one was found worthy to open the scroll?

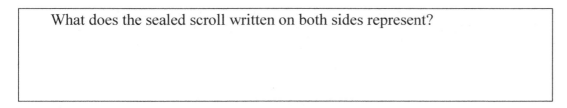

> The entire vision will be to you like the words of a sealed book, which when they give it to the one who is literate, saying, "Please read this," he will say, "I cannot, for it is sealed." Then the book will be given to the one who is illiterate, saying, "Please read this." And he will say, "I cannot read." (Isa 29:11-12 NASU)

A sealed scroll of pending disaster was presented to people in Isaiah's time. They should have been able to understand its meaning. But they made excuses for not reading it. It was God's warning and the real reason they couldn't read it was that they weren't about to heed what it said. They were rebelling against God. Is it possible that when John saw this scroll in heaven, he thought of these verses in Isaiah? Did he weep because he was afraid that no one would be able to open it and warn the people?

> Moreover He said to me, "Son of man, eat what you find; eat this scroll, and go, speak to the house of Israel." (Ezek 3:1 NKJV)

> But the house of Israel will not listen to you, because they will not listen to Me; for all the house of Israel *are* impudent and hard-hearted. (Ezek 3:7 NKJV)

> And go, get to the captives, to the children of your people, and speak to them and tell them, 'Thus says the LORD GOD,' whether they hear, or whether they refuse." (Ezek 3:11 NKJV)

Ezekiel was in a very similar situation as Isaiah. God's Word was presented to Ezekiel to pass along to the people, but will they listen? No, God tells him that they won't listen even though they are not a nation of obscure speech or a difficult language (vs. 6). In other words, it wasn't their inability to understand the message, but they lacked willingness to obey. Whether they listen or not, it is our duty to tell. The people that are the closest to us – family, relatives, and work associates – are sometimes harder to approach with the Gospel message than complete strangers are. Another point is that the scroll in heaven will be opened and many people who should be familiar with its contents don't know anything about it. How can we warn people of the coming disaster if we don't take the time to find out what is in it? Ezekiel was told to eat the scroll. The message became a part of him. Was John's concern that people wouldn't take the message to others or those that hear wouldn't heed the words of the scroll?

> But you, Daniel, keep this prophecy a secret; seal up the book until the time of the end, when many will rush here and there, and knowledge will increase. (Dan 12:4 NLT)

Daniel didn't understand what was put in his scroll because it was for a different time. This was not a warning of impending disaster for his time, but for the distant future, a time when global travel will be common to many and knowledge has increased. Does this sound like today? Perhaps John was anticipating the return of Jesus and he is weeping because none can open the scroll that reveals the end times. Perhaps he even believes that as a result, the return of Christ will not occur (it will occur). Surely, these are reasons to weep.

> Then I said, "Behold, I come; In the scroll of the book it is written of me;" (Ps 40:7 NASB)

David wrote this prophecy about Jesus, but it applied to his own life as well. He believed that the future was written on God's scroll and each person is included. The scroll in heaven will certainly affect the lives of billions of people, another reason to weep.

Scrolls were usually written on one side. What is the significance of this one having writing on both sides?

Then I lifted up my eyes again and looked, and behold, *there was* a flying scroll. And he said to me, "What do you see?" And I answered, "I see a flying scroll; its length is twenty cubits and its width ten cubits." Then he said to me, "This is the curse that is going forth over the face of the whole land; surely everyone who steals will be purged away according to the writing on one side, and everyone who swears will be purged away according to the writing on the other side. (Zech 5:1-3 NASU)

This scroll carried a curse over the whole land for those who do evil. It was written on both sides, so that no matter how you look at it, the answer for the wicked was the same. The same will be true for the scroll in heaven; no matter how you look at it, the prophecies spell doom for the wicked.

Now when I looked, there was a hand stretched out to me; and behold, a scroll of a book *was* in it. Then He spread it before me; and *there was* writing on the inside and on the outside, and written on it *were* lamentations and mourning and woe. (Ezek 2:9-10 NKJV)

These two instances of scroll with writing on both sides have the same purpose. If the scroll in God's right hand follows the same pattern, then it will not contain good news. As we proceed in the book of Revelation, this will be confirmed. Each seal will reveal more woes to come upon the earth.

What might be the significance of the seven seals on the scroll?

In Jeremiah 32:9-15, Jeremiah redeems a piece of property from his cousin. The process is interesting because two deeds were written. One was sealed and put away in an earthen jar to persevere it. The other was an open deed for anyone to examine. It was a custom to write the conditions of the redemption of lost or sold properties on a scroll and seal it. Some have said that the scroll in God's hand is the title deed to the earth, man's original inheritance that was lost when Satan deceived Adam and Eve in the garden.[13] Like Jeremiah's sealed deed, this scroll in heaven is the one that is preserved and provides the conditions for the redemption of the earth.

> The men did as they were told and mapped the entire territory into seven sections, listing the towns in each section. They made a written record and then returned to Joshua in the camp at Shiloh. (Josh 18:9 NLT)

There is a parallel between the scroll in heaven and the time that seven tribes of Israel had delayed in taking possession of the Promised Land. Joshua had them map out the land and write it in a scroll with seven parts.

The scroll has seven seals. Since the number seven is associated with God and His perfection, this could indicate many things. One is that since there are seven seals only someone who has the perfection of God can open them.

> For whoever keeps the whole law but fails in one point has become guilty of all of it. (James 2:10 RSV)

If a person has committed only one sin, then that person is not worthy to open even one seal. Later we will also see that the seven seals represent the completeness of the judgment of God, for when the last seal has been opened and God's wrath has been completely poured out, the end will have come. Jesus will then be in control of the earth. All the condition for the redemption of the earth will have been met.

Who Is Worthy

What is needed to be worth to open the scroll?

Why aren't angels worthy to open the scroll?

Why isn't man worthy?

The angel asks who is worthy to break the seals and look at the Word of God. It is more than just looking at the Word but is also the idea that the person who takes the scroll must also be able to carry out what it says. This is a dramatic emphasis of the fact that no man or any other created being is worthy. For even the angels in heaven do not venture forth to take the scroll. While the angels don't have the power to do it, man is even less worthy.

[13] Robert Jamieson, A. R. Fausset, and David Brown, *A Commentary Critical, Experimental, and Practical on the Old and New Testaments*, (Seattle: Biblesoft, 2006), Rev 5:1, Electronic database.

Then the LORD saw that the wickedness of man was great on the earth, and that every intent of the thoughts of his heart was only evil continually. (Gen 6:5 NASB)

For all of us have become like one who is unclean, And all our righteous deeds are like a filthy garment; And all of us wither like a leaf, And our iniquities, like the wind, take us away. And there is no one who calls on Thy name, Who arouses himself to take hold of Thee; For Thou hast hidden Thy face from us, And hast delivered us into the power of our iniquities. (Isa 64:6-7 NASB)

These verses point out that sin has overtaken everyone. There isn't a single person who can claim that they have never sinned. If they do, then they are calling God a liar. A new heart has been given to us when we accept Jesus as our Lord and Savior, but there are always inclinations to sin creeping in. From Isaiah, we see that even Christians can blow it and turn away from God. The verse says, "have become" indicating that it is not the way they were in the first place. Verse 7 says that He has hidden His face, which means that at some time before, His face had shown upon them. There is no doubt that no man could have the perfection necessary to take the scroll, even a man redeemed by Jesus. Whoever takes the scroll must be totally worthy and the first part of worthiness is to be without sin.

The second part of being worthy is the receptive side of worthiness. The person must be worthy to receive praise, honor, glory, and power. Whoever takes it will be worshiped (therefore, sinless angels are excluded). He will execute the power and receive glory and praise. This certainly leaves out any other created beings.

And he said to him, "All these I will give you, if you will fall down and worship me." Then Jesus said to him, "Be gone, Satan! For it is written, "'You shall worship the Lord your God and him only shall you serve.'" (Matt 4:9-10 ESV)

Then I fell down at his feet to worship him, but he said to me, "You must not do that! I am a fellow servant with you and your brothers who hold to the testimony of Jesus. Worship God." For the testimony of Jesus is the spirit of prophecy. (Rev 19:10 ESV)

Jesus made it clear that only God is to be worshiped. Satan will accept worship because he is totally sinful. Any creature that is holy will not accept worship but will point it in the direction it belongs.

The Lion of the Tribe of Judah

How do we know that this Lion is Jesus?

Judah, your brothers will praise you; your hand will be on the neck of your enemies; your father's sons will bow down to you. You are a lion's cub, O Judah; you return from the prey, my son. Like a lion he crouches and lies down, like a lioness — who dares to rouse him? The scepter will not depart from Judah, nor the ruler's staff from between his feet, until he comes to whom it belongs and the obedience of the nations

> is his. He will tether his donkey to a vine, his colt to the choicest branch; he will wash
> his garments in wine, his robes in the blood of grapes. (Gen 49:8-11 NIV®)

The Lord gave us a major clue about the Messiah in these verses. From this prophecy, the symbol of Judah became a lion. The prophecy also has other, more subtle clues. His brothers (that includes us) will praise and bow down to Him. He has power over enemies. Eternal rule will be passed to Him. He will wash His robes in the blood of grapes indicating the vengeance of the Lord, which will appear later in the book of Revelation.

> I, Jesus, have sent My angel to testify to you these things for the churches. I am the
> root and the descendant of David, the bright morning star. (Rev 22:16 NASU)

The root of David refers to the fact that Jesus came from the tribe of Judah but also that Jesus is the Lord of David since He predates him. Jesus referred to this when He asked the Pharisees whose son the Christ would be (Mat 22:41-46). Jesus made it clear that He is the one who is to receive the promises that Jacob talked about in Genesis. Jesus has authority to take the scroll based on His unique perspective of being from David and also the Lord of David. He is the only one worthy of worship because He is God. Only God could both predate and be an offspring of David.

His Triumph

Jesus is worthy to take the scroll because He has triumphed.

Over Death

> How has Jesus triumphed over death? What does that mean for us?

> The sting of death is sin, and the strength of sin *is* the law. But thanks be to God, who
> gives us the victory through our Lord Jesus Christ. (1 Cor 15:56-57 NKJV)

In 1 Corinthians 15:42-55, Paul explains that Jesus came and won a spiritual battle. His body died just as Adam's died. But the result was a new body that is not perishable, one that will live forever. Because He was raised, not like Lazarus, to die again, but with an immortal body, He has conquered death. The reason that it had to be this way is explained also. Only the imperishable can inherit the kingdom of God, only the One who has gone through this is worthy to take the scroll. Paul also explained that we will also bear His likeness.

All of the "little god" preachers probably point to this and say "see, we will be gods because we will be like Him" but they fail to see that this points out that we will simply receive an immortal body so that we will be able to live in heaven in the presence of a holy and just God.

> There he will remove the cloud of gloom, the shadow of death that hangs over the
> earth. He will swallow up death forever! The Sovereign LORD will wipe away all tears.

He will remove forever all insults and mockery against his land and people. The LORD has spoken! (Isa 25:7-8 NLT)

Even before Jesus came, God gave us the promise that He would swallow up death. If we are to eventually die and receive an immortal body, we lose fear of death. Why then do we fear anything else that prevents us from laboring in the Lord?

Therefore, my beloved brethren, be steadfast, immovable, always abounding in the work of the Lord, knowing that in the Lord your labor is not in vain. (1 Cor 15:58 RSV)

Isn't it wonderful that Paul explained Jesus' victory over death, not only to tell us what we will become, but also to reassure us that our Christian work is not useless?

Over Temptation

How has Jesus triumphed over temptation and how does that help us?

Then Jesus was led up by the Spirit into the wilderness to be tempted by the devil. (Matt 4:1 NASB)

Then the devil left Him; and behold, angels came and *began* to minister to Him. (Matt 4:11 NASB)

For we do not have a high priest who cannot sympathize with our weaknesses, but One who has been tempted in all things as *we are, yet* without sin. Let us therefore draw near with confidence to the throne of grace, that we may receive mercy and may find grace to help in time of need. (Heb 4:15-16 NASB)

Jesus triumphed over temptation giving us hope and a pattern to follow to do likewise. If He had yielded, then it would have proven that He had sinned and therefore had to die for His own sins. His death would not have paid the penalty for our sins either, for only a pure sacrifice could do that. He would not have been worthy to open the scroll. His main temptation was to serve Himself and to avoid the cross. It started with Satan trying to get Him to satisfy His physical needs for food by "using" God to provide for His hunger when there was no need to do it. This escalated when Satan offered Him all the nations of the earth (which He will eventually get anyway) if He would worship Satan.

Satan continues to tempt us in the same ways. He wants us to satisfy our cravings and desires outside of God's timetable or prescribed means of living. We can look to Jesus for the strength to overcome those temptations because Jesus already has triumphed. We can draw near to God in times of temptation to get the help we need from Him.

Over Sin

> Jesus triumphed over temptations and never sinned. How did He triumph over sin?

For He made Him who knew no sin *to be* sin for us, that we might become the righteousness of God in Him. (2 Cor 5:21 NKJV)

All we like sheep have gone astray; We have turned, every one, to his own way; And the Lord has laid on Him the iniquity of us all. (Isa 53:6 NKJV)

And they made His grave with the wicked — But with the rich at His death, Because He had done no violence, *Nor was* any deceit in His mouth. (Isa 53:9NKJV)

Which of you convicts Me of sin? (John 8:46a NKJV)

Therefore, as through one man's offense *judgment* came to all men, resulting in condemnation, even so through one Man's righteous act *the free gift* came to all men, resulting in justification of life. For as by one man's disobedience many were made sinners, so also by one Man's obedience many will be made righteous. (Rom 5:18-19 NKJV)

Jesus knew sin only because God put our sins on Him. He made Jesus to be sin. That means that Jesus experienced sin without doing anything wrong. He experienced it not in the way we do, but in disgust and horror because He is holy; He experienced a loss of fellowship from His Father and all the other consequences of sin. Jesus didn't do anything that would cause any of the sins to be accounted to Him. His triumph over sin then is more than what we can do, which is avoiding sin. His triumph over sin is removing its eternal consequences and its power over us.

Over Men

> How has Jesus triumphed over men?

That is why the Scriptures say, "When he ascended to the heights, he led a crowd of captives and gave gifts to his people." (Eph 4:8 NLT)

Since the inclinations of our hearts are evil, the only way He can bring us to heaven is to make us captive or slaves to Himself. In this sense, He has triumphed over us. We talk a lot about the Father drawing us, being chosen, and even predestined (Eph 1:11). These terms really point out that He triumphs over us when we yield to Him. Make no mistake, there is only one way to heaven and that is through Jesus. We are either going to be saved as His slaves or perish as His enemies.

Over Satan

> How has Jesus triumphed over Satan?

> I will put enmity between you and the woman, and between your seed and her seed; he shall bruise your head, and you shall bruise his heel. (Gen 3:15 RSV)

> And he said to them, "I saw Satan fall like lightning from heaven. (Luke 10:18 RSV)

> Now is the judgment of this world, now shall the ruler of this world be cast out; and I, when I am lifted up from the earth, will draw all men to myself. (John 12:31-32 RSV)

It was predicted from the very beginning that Satan would be defeated. Even before the actual defeat of Satan on the cross, Jesus was able to see Satan's power broken on earth by His authority before His resurrection. These verses tie together both the defeat of Satan and the fact that Jesus will be taking people captive for Himself.

> Since then the children share in flesh and blood, He Himself likewise also partook of the same, that through death He might render powerless him who had the power of death, that is, the devil; and might deliver those who through fear of death were subject to slavery all their lives. (Heb 2:14-15 NASB)

This makes it abundantly clear the Satan has been defeated, and that the defeat occurred when Jesus died. As we continue in Revelation, it is clear that because Jesus died He is worthy.

> Whoever makes a practice of sinning is of the devil, for the devil has been sinning from the beginning. The reason the Son of God appeared was to destroy the works of the devil. No one born of God makes a practice of sinning, for God's seed abides in him, and he cannot keep on sinning because he has been born of God. (1 John 3:8-9 ESV)

> What works of the devil does Jesus give us the ability to overcome?

> There is no fear in love. But perfect love drives out fear, because fear has to do with punishment. The one who fears is not made perfect in love. (1 John 4:18 NIV®)

One of the works of the devil it to produce fear; fear of death is the greatest fear that we have. This is our comfort for any situation that we fear, not just death. The big reason people fear death is that they instinctively know that there will be a judgment and that they haven't lived a life worthy enough to escape that judgment. When we are saved, that fear is removed because we know we will not be judged by our works, but rather on the fact that God has accepted Jesus' punishment for our sins so that we don't have to pay the penalty. That is God's love for us.

These will wage war against the Lamb, and the Lamb will overcome them, because He is Lord of lords and King of kings, and those who are with Him *are the* called and chosen and faithful. (Rev 17:14 NASU)

The devil may be defeated, but unfortunately this passage reveals that he doesn't act like it. Satan's purpose is still to wreak havoc upon the saints and fight Jesus until he is permanently put away.

Nevertheless do not rejoice in this, that the spirits are subject to you, but rather rejoice because your names are written in heaven. (Luke 10:20 NKJV)

Satan's defeat is actually incidental. The main point is that we should rejoice because:

1. Our names are written in heaven.
2. Jesus draws men to Himself.
3. We are free from the fear of death.
4. Sin is destroyed for anyone who is born again.
5. We are followers of Jesus.

Over the Schemes of Men

How has Jesus triumphed over the schemes of men?

Once again they tried to arrest him, but he got away and left them. (John 10:39 NLT)

Jesus triumphed over the schemes of men when He walked away while they wanted to stone Him. At another time, people tried to throw Him off a cliff and he walked through the crowd and left (Luke 4:29-50). This shows that there is not a realm in which He is not sovereign. It doesn't matter what anyone says about free will or anything else. The very fact that Jesus could cause people not to do what they eagerly and forcefully wanted, proves that He is in control. One might argue that later they crucified Him and therefore did accomplish their will. But even then, Jesus made it clear to Pilate that it was only by the will of the Father that Jesus was being taken.

Jesus answered him, "You would have no power over me unless it had been given you from above; therefore he who delivered me to you has the greater sin." (John 19:11 RSV)

Over the Law

How did Jesus triumph over the Law?

When you were dead in your sins and in the uncircumcision of your sinful nature, God made you alive with Christ. He forgave us all our sins, having canceled the written code, with its regulations, that was against us and that stood opposed to us; he took it away, nailing it to the cross. And having disarmed the powers and authorities, he made a public spectacle of them, triumphing over them by the cross. (Col 2:13-15 NIV®)

See also Ephesians 2:14-16. Before Jesus came, salvation was still by faith in God, however that faith was supposed to be demonstrated by obedience to the Old Testament laws. It was impossible for any human being to live up to every law and the remedy was sacrificing animals – in faith. The religious rulers soon turned the laws into a system of salvation by works. Jesus abolished that, yet there are many religious leaders that have reverted back to salvation by works. Jesus freed us from that once for all.

Over the World

> What does Jesus give us because He has overcome the world?

These things I have spoken to you, that in Me you may have peace. In the world you have tribulation, but take courage; I have overcome the world. (John 16:33 NASB)

Jesus has overcome the world, but it is interesting to note that He didn't remove us from the world or remove the trouble. Instead, He has given us His peace. The way we can overcome the world is by letting His peace dwell in us.

> What is the ultimate purpose in Jesus' triumphs?

For our sake he made him to be sin who knew no sin, so that in him we might become the righteousness of God. (2 Cor 5:21 ESV)

In all of the areas that Jesus has triumphed, the bottom line is the conclusion of this verse. Whether He has triumphed over temptation, death, sin, or Satan, it is always for us that He has triumphed. That is humbling and also reassuring. It is no wonder that after declaring the worthiness of the Lamb, the elders fall at His feet and worship. What else can we do?

Let's remember that in Jesus, we are at the right hand of God the Father. We also have triumphed. It is only because He is worthy that we are in this position. Therefore, let's live, witness, and worship in accordance to what He has done.

Lesson 4 – Revelation 5:6-14

Then I saw a Lamb, looking as if it had been slain, standing in the center of the throne, encircled by the four living creatures and the elders. He had seven horns and seven eyes, which are the seven spirits of God sent out into all the earth. He came and took the scroll from the right hand of him who sat on the throne. And when he had taken it, the four living creatures and the twenty-four elders fell down before the Lamb. Each one had a harp and they were holding golden bowls full of incense, which are the prayers of the saints. And they sang a new song:

"You are worthy to take the scroll and to open its seals, because you were slain, and with your blood you purchased men for God from every tribe and language and people and nation. You have made them to be a kingdom and priests to serve our God, and they will reign on the earth."

Then I looked and heard the voice of many angels, numbering thousands upon thousands, and ten thousand times ten thousand. They encircled the throne and the living creatures and the elders. In a loud voice they sang:

"Worthy is the Lamb, who was slain, to receive power and wealth and wisdom and strength and honor and glory and praise!"

Then I heard every creature in heaven and on earth and under the earth and on the sea, and all that is in them, singing:

"To him who sits on the throne and to the Lamb be praise and honor and glory and power, for ever and ever!"

The four living creatures said, "Amen," and the elders fell down and worshiped.
(NIV®)

The Lamb

> Why didn't John see the Lamb before? Did He just magically appear?
>
>
> How does His sudden appearance here symbolize His appearance throughout the Bible?

Jesus didn't suddenly appear; He has been there all along. When we see the splendor and majesty of God we are unable to distinguish Jesus from God for He is God. It is only by His will that we are able to see Him apart from God. Just as God chose the time for Jesus to be born and to make the truth of the trinity visible, so here, God chooses the time to show John the Lamb who has been there all along. When He does reveal Himself, then we can see Him. Just as He was obscure in the Old

Testament, and then is seen plainly in the Gospels, He is also obscure, then seen plainly in many people's lives. It is also important to see that the book of Revelation brings together many of the promises of the Old Testament and the New. In the first three chapters, there were several places that emphasized Jesus is the Creator and the sovereign Lord who looks over His church. Here we see why He has been deemed worthy. The Lion is a symbol of power while the Lamb is a symbol of love. What good is a God who has power but not love, and vice versa?

The Trinity

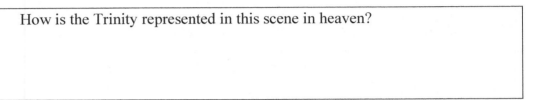

How is the Trinity represented in this scene in heaven?

John previously saw the Father on the throne, and then suddenly he sees the Lamb in the center of the throne with the Holy Spirit symbolized by the seven horns and eyes of the Lamb. This chapter provides us with a symbolic description of the trinity. There is one difference now, and that is that the Spirit, who was previously represented by the seven lamps before the throne is now represented by the eyes and the horns of the Lamb.

The Holy Spirit's Work

If the Spirit comes from the Father, why does Revelation say that the Spirit is the eyes and horns of the Lamb?

But the Helper, the Holy Spirit, whom the Father will send in My name, He will teach you all things, and bring to your remembrance all that I said to you. (John 14:26 NASU)

When the Helper comes, whom I will send to you from the Father, *that is* the Spirit of truth who proceeds from the Father, He *will* testify about Me. (John 15:26 NASU)

There are times when we tend to separate the persons of the Trinity too much. We have to understand the closeness of the Trinity and the number of times that the members are interchanged in various Scriptures. Read the book of Titus and you will see Paul mention Jesus our Savior, God our Savior, and our God and Savior Jesus Christ. He attributes our salvation to the regeneration and renewal by the Holy Spirit. The Holy Spirit is sent out into all of the earth yet He is also represented as being on the throne since He is a part of the Lamb. It is always a blessing to see that the Bible is truly consistent.

As a side note, this question about the Holy Spirit helped split the East and West Catholic Churches.[14] The East insisted that the Holy Spirit proceeds directly from the Father,[15] while the West believed that the Spirit proceeds from both the Father and the Son to maintain the equality of the members of the Trinity.[16] This is a prime example of what happens when we try to make litmus tests of orthodoxy based on minutiae of Scripture and preponderance of man's opinion. In addition to division, they miss the blessing and importance of what the Word is trying to tell us.

> How do the seven horns and eyes represent God's work to strengthen believers through the Holy Spirit?

For the eyes of the LORD run to and fro throughout the whole earth, to show Himself strong on behalf *of those* whose heart *is* loyal to Him. (2 Chron 16:9a NKJV)

They are the eyes of the LORD, Which scan to and fro throughout the whole earth. (Zech 4:10b NKJV)

The Lord showed Zechariah a lampstand with seven lamps. He told the prophet that this represented the might and power of the Holy Spirit, not man's abilities (Zech 4:1-6). These verses tie together the eyes, lamps, and the Holy Spirit who is sent into all the earth. Praise God, that one of the reasons His Holy Spirit is sent is to strengthen those whose hearts are fully committed to Him.

The LORD is my rock, and my fortress, and my deliverer, my God, my rck, in whom I take refuge, my shield, and the horn of my salvation, my stronghold. (Ps 18:2 RSV)

Horns are representative of several things in the Bible. Rulers, strength, and the source of salvation are among them. We commonly think only of Jesus as being the instrument of our salvation because He paid the price for our sins. Yet in Scripture each member of the Trinity is engaged in our Salvation.

But—"When God our Savior revealed his kindness and love, he saved us, not because of the righteous things we had done, but because of his mercy. He washed away our sins, giving us a new birth and new life through the Holy Spirit. 6 He generously poured out the Spirit upon us through Jesus Christ our Savior. Because of his grace he declared us righteous and gave us confidence that we will inherit eternal life." (Titus 3:4-7 NLT)

The Holy Spirit, as symbolized in the seven horns of the Lamb, is right in the middle of our salvation because He is the One who renews us and gives us new birth. He is also the one who convicts us of sin in the first place so that He can give us rebirth.

---

[14] J.A. Sheppard, *Christendom at the Crossroads: the Medieval Era* (Louisville: Westminster John Knox Press, 2005), Kindle 1761-1763.

[15] Ibid., 1903.

[16] Ibid., 1905-1908.

> How is the Holy Spirit's work demonstrated in Jesus in Luke 4:14-30?

And Jesus returned to Galilee in the power of the Spirit; and news about Him spread through all the surrounding district. And He *began* teaching in their synagogues and was praised by all. (Luke 4:14-15 NASB)

And all in the synagogue were filled with rage as they heard these things; and they rose up and cast Him out of the city, and led Him to the brow of the hill on which their city had been built, in order to throw Him down the cliff. But passing through their midst, He went His way. (Luke 4:29-30 NASB)

In Luke 4:14-30 we can see three manifestations of what the Holy Spirit does. This passage takes place right after the devil tempted Jesus in the wilderness. First, He was given power to preach with multitudes coming to listen to Him. Second, the conviction of the Holy Spirit is demonstrated in Jesus own hometown; however, this conviction didn't bring salvation but opposition. Third, the Holy Spirit also gave Him the ability to stall the plans of men and accomplish the work of God when He simply walked away from the crowd.

> How is the Holy Spirit's power demonstrated in believers?

But you will receive power when the Holy Spirit has come upon you, and you will be my witnesses in Jerusalem and in all Judea and Samaria, and to the end of the earth. (Acts 1:8 ESV)

The power of the Holy Spirit is not reserved only for Jesus as this passage and the text in Revelation 5:6 indicate. His Spirit is sent out into the entire world through believers to accomplish His will and purpose. The power mentioned here is to witness, not to get rich or accomplish our goals. God has decided to use us to accomplish His purpose, but thank God, He has also given us all that we need, His Holy Spirit.

After they prayed, the place where they were meeting was shaken. And they were all filled with the Holy Spirit and spoke the word of God boldly. All the believers were one in heart and mind. No one claimed that any of his possessions was his own, but they shared everything they had. With great power the apostles continued to testify to the resurrection of the Lord Jesus, and much grace was upon them all. (Acts 4:31-33 NIV®)

This Holy Spirit power was with the Apostles and all the believers enabling them to speak the Word boldly. This wasn't just for the Apostles, but all were filled with the Holy Spirit. It gave them the power to be of one heart and mind. This same power was given to Stephen and he spoke by the Holy Spirit so that no one was able to stand against what he was saying (Acts 6:8-10).

Just as Jesus was opposed, so was Stephen. The opposition didn't have a problem with what Stephen was doing as far as miracles or signs. His wisdom and what he said bothered them. We really don't need to be concerned with being able to answer all of the questions that a doubter or a skeptic raises. If we are faithful to the Word and are presenting it as the Holy Spirit leads us, then they will not be able to withstand the power of the Holy Spirit. This is the promise to all believers, regardless of their age in the Lord. The importance of knowing this is explained in 1 Corinthians 2:4-5:

> And my message and my preaching were not in persuasive words of wisdom, but in demonstration of the Spirit and of power, 5 so that your faith would not rest on the wisdom of men, but on the power of God. (NASU)

Even though the message of the Gospel makes logical sense when the facts are known and we come to believe, it isn't our logic that brings conviction and salvation. It isn't anything other than the power of the Holy Spirit that overcomes sinful man's resistance. Our faith must always rest on Him.

The Father Sees

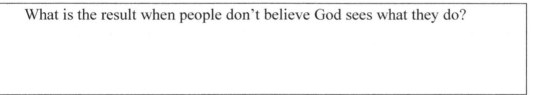

What is the result when people don't believe God sees what they do?

> Yet they say, The LORD shall not see, neither shall the God of Jacob regard it. (Ps 94:7)

This is taken from Psalm 94:1-11, which speaks of the vengeance of God upon the wicked. They think that the Lord doesn't see or hear what they are doing. However, the eyes of the Lord are upon everything. He knows what is happening with both the wicked and those who serve Him. The attitude of people in the last times will be based upon the idea that God does not see or care. It is a natural outcome of believing the theory of evolution. This is a stumbling point even for Christians when they attempt to make evolution palatable by saying that God started it with a big bang, but has let nature take its course. They believe that their god (lower case g) started things but doesn't see what is going on now. It eventually allows behavior that permits injustice and immorality because it denies individual responsibility and accountability to an eternal God who does care.

> You are of purer eyes than to behold evil, And cannot look on wickedness. Why do You look on those who deal treacherously, And hold Your tongue when the wicked devours A person more righteous than he? (Hab 1:13 NKJV)

The purity of the Lord is seen in His eyes. If the eyes of the Lord are throughout the earth in the form of the Holy Spirit in us, then why do we tolerate evil? We don't when we live holy lives and speak against it. That is when the Holy Spirit can use us to convict the lost. The important part of the horns and eyes representing the Holy Spirit is that He is sent out into all the earth.

Worthy Is the Lamb

In Revelation 4, we were shown the worthiness of God. It started with the voice of Jesus calling John to come up and see heaven. It included the presence of the Holy Spirit in the form of the lamps, and then went on to praise the Father. In our previous lesson we also saw the worthiness of Jesus as the Lion and we will now see His worthiness as the Lamb.

> How do we know that the Lamb is Jesus? What is the primary reason He is worthy to open the scroll?

The next day John saw Jesus coming toward him and said, "Look! The Lamb of God who takes away the sin of the world!" (John 1:29 NLT)

One of the elders told John that the Lion of the tribe of Judah was worthy to open the scroll. But when we look at who comes out to take the scroll it is a Lamb that is obviously alive but also bears the marks of having been slain. The Lamb is undoubtedly Jesus since He is the only sacrificial lamb that has ever been slain and is now alive. Previously, we discussed why the Lion of the tribe of Judah was worthy, but the fact that the Lamb appears points out one more reason why He is worthy. It is because Jesus gave up His rights to the point of death that He is counted worthy.

For the Son of man also came not to be served but to serve, and to give his life as a ransom for many. (Mark 10:45 RSV)

The Lamb has seven horns. The horn in the Old Testament represents a person or country that possesses power. Daniel 8:20-21 is a good example as it explains that the animals in Daniel's vision are nations and that the horns represent the kings of those nations.

And has raised up a horn of salvation for us In the house of David His servant —
(Luke 1:69 NASB)

In the New Testament, the word horn only appears in the book of Revelation and in this verse. In this verse, it is in the midst of praise to Jesus that is in this prologue to the prophecy of the ministry of John the Baptist. Jesus is worthy because He is the horn or power providing our salvation.

<u>Worthy of Worship</u>

The four living creatures and twenty-four elders worship Jesus as soon as He takes the scroll.

> What is the first way in which the elders worship Jesus? Why don't we worship as they do?

Worship in Posture

They fall down to start their worship. This is something almost foreign to the modern Church. I've seen some churches where people come up to the altar or front of the church and fall down. They are usually there to confess some sin or pray for healing. I don't know that I've ever seen people simply fall down on their knees or prostrate themselves in worship without a leader asking people to kneel. Certainly, there will be a day when all people will fall worship Jesus on their knees.

> Therefore God has highly exalted him and bestowed on him the name that is above every name, so that at the name of Jesus every knee should bow, in heaven and on earth and under the earth, and every tongue confess that Jesus Christ is Lord, to the glory of God the Father. (Phil 2:9-11ESV)

It is fitting that the elders initiate this kind of worship at the beginning of the book of Revelation. They are most likely the most highly honored men in heaven, yet they are not ashamed or self-conscious in the act of worship. We probably don't worship with the same abandon simply because we are too concerned with what people would say. Perhaps we won't really be able to worship in this way until we have our sin nature removed completely and are before the throne.

Worship with Music

> How would you describe acceptable worship music?

It has probably been going on since the beginning of the Church, but it shouldn't be happening. People complain about the worship music. It's too loud. It's too contemporary and doesn't honor God. It's not contemporary. It's has demonic rhythms. It doesn't move me. Complaining about worship music takes the emphasis off the One we worship and puts it on ourselves.

Biblical worship was often accompanied with musical instruments, yet some denominations have denounced and prohibit certain musical instruments in their worship because they aren't listed in the Bible. I can hear them now, "Since the twenty-four elders only had harps, that's the only instrument we should use."

> If King David invented a new musical instrument, would it be appropriate to use it to worship God? Explain why or why not.

If we invent new instruments, is it appropriate to use them to worship God? Explain why or why not.

[Woe to you,] Who sing idly to the sound of stringed instruments, And invent for yourselves musical instruments like David; (Amos 6:5 NKJV)

The people in this passage are condemned for singing idly instead of worshiping God. Their music was all for themselves, as is most of the world's music. However, that is a minor point in this study. This verse reveals that the instruments used in worship by David were invented by him. If David had only used existing instruments or ones that were listed in Scripture, he would have been limited in praise and worship of God.

I went to Pakistan on a mission trip. In a small slave village, we held a meeting for about forty-five slaves. They brought their own worship instruments – some were cooking pots. Their lack of sophisticated musical instruments didn't hinder their worship.

God has created us as beings that were made in His image. God is a creative God and we are a creative people. We often use that creative nature in ways that are displeasing to God. That is very evident in His command for us not to make carved images and bow down to them (Ex 20:4-5). This is clearly a prohibited use of our creativity. Some have taken this to mean that we shouldn't make any images, even paintings but this is a distortion of the original intent. If this were true, then God would not have commanded Moses to make two cherubim to overshadow the ark in the most holy place (Ex 25:18). The cherubim were there but not worshiped. They were instrumental in the worship of God.

In the same way, when we make musical instrument and use them in worldly music which is degrading and an insult to God, we have used our creative nature in a way that displeases Him. (I'm not saying all worldly music is degrading and an insult to God.) However, we can use those same instruments in godly worship to bring pleasure to Him.

Worship in the Bible was often spontaneous as it is with the twenty-four elders. Provide some examples of worship with music and the events that inspired them.

Then Moses and the people of Israel sang this song to the Lord: "I will sing to the Lord, for he has triumphed gloriously; he has hurled both horse and rider into the sea." (Ex 15:1 NLT)

46

> There the Israelites sang this song: "Spring up, O well! Yes, sing its praises! Sing of this well, which princes dug, which great leaders hollowed out with their scepters and staffs." (Num 21:17-18 NLT)

> After consulting the people, the king appointed singers to walk ahead of the army, singing to the LORD and praising him for his holy splendor. This is what they sang: "Give thanks to the LORD; his faithful love endures forever!" At the very moment they began to sing and give praise, the LORD caused the armies of Ammon, Moab, and Mount Seir to start fighting among themselves. (2 Chron 20:21-22 NLT)

> Around midnight Paul and Silas were praying and singing hymns to God, and the other prisoners were listening. (Acts 16:25 NLT)

In many places the Lord was worshiped and exalted for victory with the use of music. Moses did this in Exodus 15:1 and Miriam continued in Exodus 15:21. He is worshiped by Israel in Numbers 21:17-18 with singing as they gave thanks to Him for His provision. 2 Chronicles 20:21-22 tells of Judah's worship with music, which preceded victory, not just afterwards. How many of us can praise and worship our God in the face of seeming defeat as did Paul and Silas (Acts 16:25)?

The Lamb has demonstrated His victory by taking the scroll. Our response with music is to worship Him for the victory that He has provided as well as for all His provisions. Music is often at the heart of worship.

Worship with Prayers

How is worship with prayers like worship in the Old Testament?

When the Lord specified the method of sacrifice in the Old Testament, He called it a pleasing aroma (NIV®) thirty-seven times. Some of these sacrifices were required daily. Incense was also required as part of most offerings presented to the Lord.

> And Aaron shall burn fragrant incense on it; every morning when he dresses the lamps he shall burn it, and when Aaron sets up the lamps in the evening, he shall burn it, a perpetual incense before the LORD throughout your generations. (Ex 30:7-8 RSV)

The significance of this verse is that the incense must be burned regularly and for all generations. Our prayers should also be offered daily and never stop.

> Let my prayer be counted as incense before you, and the lifting up of my hands as the evening sacrifice! (Ps 141:2 ESV)

David portrays his prayers as being as pleasing to God as incense and the evening sacrifice. More than any other writer in the Old Testament, David pictures the Church in the New Testament. He has shown how believers will worship without the sacrifices and burning incense. Our prayers are like the pleasing aroma accompanying the sacrifices of the Old Testament.

In what other ways are our prayers a pleasing aroma to God?

> For we are a fragrance of Christ to God among those who are being saved and among those who are perishing; to the one an aroma from death to death, to the other an aroma from life to life. And who is adequate for these things? (2 Cor 2:15-16 NASB)

When we pray for someone's salvation, our prayers are like the aroma of Christ to God. How can we keep living lives that are also a fragrance of life to people who are being saved, but death to those who are rejecting Christ? It is by prayer! This too, gives glory to God and is a form of worship as we plead that the blood of the Lamb will save our lost friends, relatives, and even people we don't know.

The elders are pictured as having bowls of incense that represent our prayers. It is as if every prayer that we have ever said for salvations and for Jesus to come soon has been saved in time to be poured before the Lord all at once.

How can our prayers for help in times of trouble be prayers of worship?

> Answer me when I call to you, O my righteous God. Give me relief from my distress; be merciful to me and hear my prayer. How long, O men, will you turn my glory into shame? How long will you love delusions and seek false gods? Selah Know that the LORD has set apart the godly for himself; the LORD will hear when I call to him. (Ps 4:1-3 NIV®)

Many of our prayers are for relief from some situation and we want it now. We want God to hear us and answer right away. However, His answer is that we need to be right before Him before He will hear our prayers. If we are right before Him, we can rest on His promise that He does hear us.

I doubt that many of us have prayed as David did in Psalm 6:6-10 for deliverance from enemies, from Satan's trap, or even for the sins of our nation. However, many have. It is as if the tears that have been shed in prayer because of wickedness have been kept in the bowls that are now before the throne of God in heaven. When we see the Lord putting an end to sin and wickedness, it is as if He is saying, "Now I will turn these bowls of tears back upon the earth, they have been saved all these years for all who have cried for justice throughout history."

> For this cause everyone who is godly shall pray to You In a time when You may be found; Surely in a flood of great waters They shall not come near him. You are my hiding place; You shall preserve me from trouble; You shall surround me with songs of deliverance. (Ps 32:6-7 NKJV)

The comfort that we have when we pray is wrapped up in songs of deliverance. We see the scroll of destruction that has been handed to the Lamb. These prayers are before the altar and they bring forth a song of praise. This is very much like the worship churches have when we are called to a special time of worship and prayer. When we take our comfort in God instead of panicking, we bring glory and worship of our Lord.

> What are some of the things that will keep the Lord from answering our prayers?

If I had not confessed the sin in my heart, the LORD would not have listened. But God did listen! He paid attention to my prayer. Praise God, who did not ignore my prayer or withdraw his unfailing love from me. (Ps 66:18-20 NLT)

When we become Christians, the Holy Spirit comes to live in us and cleans us from sin. However, if we don't let Him do His convicting work in us, we may continue to hold sin in our hearts. If we are in this condition, then He will not listen. When we don't cherish sin the Lord hears us. If He hears us, why are our prayers not answered? He doesn't withhold His love from us, but He does know the timing and we must wait. In the case of our prayers for Him to come soon, the wait only adds to the incense in the bowls, to give Him glory at the appointed time.

You have heard that it was said, "You shall love your neighbor and hate your enemy." But I say to you, Love your enemies and pray for those who persecute you. (Matt 5:43-44 RSV)

The Lord's most desirable way of answering prayers for deliverance from injustice in the world is to bring to repentance those who are dispensing it. The difficulty for us is to wait for that time and not try to repay them with evil before it occurs. Corrie Ten Boom met a prison guard who had been her captor during World War II. He had turned to Christ and she told about the momentary struggle she had to accept him as a Christian brother.[17] While that would be difficult, it isn't as hard as it would be to show kindness and love to him if he had not become a Christian. When we don't love our enemies, our prayers will be hindered.

So when you spread out your hands in prayer, I will hide My eyes from you, Yes, even though you multiply prayers, I will not listen. Your hands are covered with blood. Wash yourselves, make yourselves clean; Remove the evil of your deeds from My sight. Cease to do evil, Learn to do good; Seek justice, Reprove the ruthless; Defend the orphan, Plead for the widow. (Isa 1:15-17 NASB)

---

[17] Corrie Ten Boom, and Jamie Buckingham, *Tramp for the Lord*. (Fort Washington: Christian Literature Crusade, 2008), 78.

If our prayers for justice are not from clean hands, if we are participating in injustice or the same sin as our enemies, we will not be heard. Our prayers will not be added to those in the bowls. They will add nothing and be useless.

Why doesn't God answer the prayers of those who see the United States sliding into sin and depravity?

Read Isaiah 1:15-17 again. The answer is that even Christians don't cease to do evil and our hands are covered in blood. We also don't do the things that are commanded regarding justice, orphans, and widows. We are caught up in the world's "isms," conservatism, liberalism, and socialisms so that we have become like the Pharisees.

As the selfishness of conservativism worked its way into the Church, the philosophy that God helps those who help themselves took over. When the Church stopped or slowed down its social work, the government naturally took over. Conservatives have become ruthless and heartless, denying justice and help to the oppressed because the government is doing it. Yet they do little if anything to resolve the problems. Like the Pharisees, I can see a conservative asking Jesus who is an orphan or a widow. Jesus will point to single moms and their children or the children of illegal immigrants.

Christians used to embrace more liberal viewpoints with a deep concern for people, but liberals have distorted that concern by claiming everything sinful from abortions to homosexuality as a "right." Because the Church has become afraid to proclaim the Gospel boldly and the consequences of rejecting it, it has allowed liberals to parade sin openly. Now, Christians don't express liberal help for the oppressed whether through the government or other sources out of fear of being linked to those who have distorted liberalism with blatant sin. Christians ought to be the most liberal people in the world by showing true love to others.

> Now the full number of those who believed were of one heart and soul, and no one said that any of the things that belonged to him was his own, but they had everything in common. (Acts 4:32 ESV)

> I do not mean that others should be eased and you burdened, but that as a matter of fairness your abundance at the present time should supply their need, so that their abundance may supply your need, that there may be fairness. (2 Cor 8:13-14 ESV)

The Church started out with a natural socialism based not on a person's rights but on a person's needs. Their attitude was that we are servants, not masters and when we see someone in need, we supply what they need. But Christians can't mention this today without being crucified as socialists or communists. Modern philosophy invaded the Church and individualism took over. The world reacted to the vacuum left by the Church and distorted this natural socialism. The world tries to legislate that which should come from the heart and produces a distorted version of socialism that is odious.

I am firmly convinced that the answers to our prayers for our nation's problems are not being heard by our Lord because we are praying for the wrong things – one of our "isms" to solve the problems. We are unwilling to do what is needed in the Church so that the government doesn't have to do it. We want to legislate morality. We don't want to share our wealth. If the Church does what it is supposed to do, our prayers would be answered.

Worship with a New Song

Why is this song in Revelation 5:9 new?

This is a new song and a type that hasn't been seen in the Bible before. We can find many songs of praises to the Lord, but this is the first song of praise to Jesus. It is a song that is giving Him praise for what He has done by His blood and by answering the prayers of the saints for the salvation of people. It is as if the incense in the bowls has now been poured out at the same time in this song of praise.

> Sing joyfully to the LORD, you righteous; it is fitting for the upright to praise him. Praise the LORD with the harp; make music to him on the ten-stringed lyre. Sing to him a new song; play skillfully, and shout for joy. For the word of the LORD is right and true; he is faithful in all he does. The LORD loves righteousness and justice; the earth is full of his unfailing love. (Ps 33:1-5 NIV®)

How are the elders following the instructions of the Psalmist and what should our response be?

The elders are following the instructions of this psalm as they sing the new song and use their harps. We are commanded to sing a new song to Him and shout loudly and with great joy. The instrumentalists are commanded to do so with skill, not sloppily. I'm glad He didn't make the same command regarding singing; otherwise I'd have to keep my mouth shut!

A mark of a dead or dying church can be seen in its music. They sing the same old hymns and have an idea that somehow these are the only holy songs that can be sung. The Lord has clearly commanded that we sing new songs. He has created us with the ability to look into His Word and life and find new things with which to praise Him. It is fitting that we should always be coming up with new words and music to praise Him. When we get into a routine, we stagnate. It appears to me that the Lord continually wants us to create new ways to study, pray, and praise Him. We can continue to do it because the earth is full of His unfailing love.

> What are some reasons to sing new songs?

> I waited patiently for the LORD; And He inclined to me and heard my cry. He brought me up out of the pit of destruction, out of the miry clay, And He set my feet upon a rock making my footsteps firm. He put a new song in my mouth, a song of praise to our God; Many will see and fear And will trust in the LORD. (Ps 40:1-3 NASU)

This psalm acknowledges that it is only the Lord who can give us a truly new song. New songs can come from the things we suffer. It is during the hard times that He teaches us new insights into His nature and we are able to sing new songs to Him. Also, since He has saved us, we have a new heart that can pour forth these praises.

Psalm 98 looks to the future, the time that we are about to see in the book of Revelation when salvation actually comes to the earth. We sing His praises for our current salvation which He has already provided but this is a song for the complete salvation of all things when even the curse on the earth is removed. Even the earth will be able to praise Him. The judgment of the Lord will then bring righteousness to all.

It has been refreshing to see in the Psalms the songs of praise for His sake, His salvation, His judgment as well as for physical victories He has provided.

> How does God react to our worship in song?

> Praise the LORD! Sing to the LORD a new song, And His praise in the assembly of saints. (Ps 149:1 NKJV)

> For the LORD takes pleasure in His people; He will beautify the humble with salvation. (Ps 149:4 NKJV)

John has been relating to us his vision before the assembly of the saints who are rejoicing in our Maker (Ps 149:2). The psalm goes on to say that when we do this, the Lord takes pleasure in us (Ps 149:4). This is not some solemn God that is frowning on the throne; this is the God who has made us for His pleasure. He is delighted as we sing and worship Him. He says that this is an honor for us to praise Him and we rejoice in this (Ps 149:5). It is also interesting to see that as we praise Him, He enables us to carry out His purpose beginning with carrying His Word (two-edged sword), which brings vengeance upon the nations (Ps 149:6-9). Even our praise of Him has purpose in bringing judgment in some inexplicable way and imparts honor to us as well (Ps 149:9.) Perhaps this refers to the time when we will be returning with Him.

Isaiah 42:10-13 is another proclamation to sing a new song from all parts of the earth. It is not something that only some of us do, it is something that all believers in all places are commanded to do. This command also ends with the Lord marching out to destroy His enemies. In these verses it says that He will stir up His zeal. As we praise Him, He gets excited and then He does the rest.

> Who is able to sing these new songs joyfully?

In Revelation 14:1-4 we will again we see a new song being sung by the 144,000 witnesses who might be the only believers on earth at this time; they could also be representative of the Church. We will address that when the time comes, but they are the only ones who can learn this new song. They are the redeemed. The songs of joy and praise that we sing cannot come from anyone that is not pure before the Lord. A non-Christian cannot sing these songs of joy. They may mouth the words, but the joy is not there.

> The new song declares that He is worthy because He was slain. Look up the following verses and explain why Jesus is worth of a new song of praise.
> - 2 Samuel 22:4
>
> - 1 Chronicles 16:25
>
> - Hebrews 3:3
>
> - John 1:18
>
> - Hebrews 7:25
>
> - Hebrews 9:28

He is worthy because He saves us from our enemies (2 Sam 22:4).
He is worthy because He is to be feared (1 Chron 16:25).
He is worthy because He is the Creator and Builder of the Church (Heb 3:3).
He is worthy because He has seen God (John 1:18).
He is worthy because He intercedes for us (Heb 7:25).
He is worthy because He has taken away our sins (Heb 9:28).

The Blood of Jesus

> The new song says that Jesus is worth because His blood has ransomed people for God. What do we learn about the blood of Jesus from the following verses:
> - Matthew 26:28
>
> - Acts 20:28, 1 Peter 1:18-19

- Romans 5:9

- Colossians 1:19-20

- Hebrews 9:14

- 1 John 1:7

- Revelation 7:14

Jesus knew that only blood would provide the sacrifice for sin (Matt 26:28). He also knew it was only His blood that would provide the once-for-all sacrifice for all sins. He said that His blood was poured out for many, not all people. Salvation only comes to those who accept His cleansing.

With His blood He purchased us (Acts 20:28, 1 Peter 1:18-19). We are not our own, we were on the auction block of slavery to sin and He used His own blood to buy us.

His blood has justified us (Rom 5:9). Synonyms for justify are: explain away, defend, vindicate, authenticate, certify, confirm, support, and vouch. These are all worldly terms that shed some meaning on what has happened through His blood but are inadequate to describe what has happened to us.

God has made peace with us through His blood (Col 1:19-20). Not only that, but all things are reconciled, brought back to the way they should be. We don't see this completely, but we will get a picture of the total reconciliation of all things before the end of the book of Revelation. However, we don't need to fear the wrath of God that will be demonstrated before the restoration occurs.

His blood cleanses our consciences (Heb 9:14). We don't need psychobabble. What is needed is to understand and accept what the blood of Jesus has already done. When we see this, and accept what God says and on His terms, we are then able to serve the living God with a clear conscience.

His blood purifies us from all sin (1 John 1:7). It is a paradox that blood, which stains our worldly clothes, will make us clean before the Lord.

Purification can only take place by immersing ourselves in the blood of the Lamb (Rev 7:14). The blood of Jesus is that which gives us power to overcome the world. This is not altering the fact of the power of the Holy Spirit, but it could certainly refer to the idea that as we meditate upon the blood of Jesus and what He went through, the Holy Spirit can use that to help us through any and all difficulties. If Jesus had loved His life here on earth, He would not have let His blood be shed. Then we would not have the promises recounted above.

Who will be ransomed by the blood and what will happen to them?

People who have been saved by His blood come from every possible division of people from as small a grouping as a tribe to as broad a group as a nation. Jesus knows no distinction and places no restrictions on those who can come to Him. He has brought us all together as one kingdom with one purpose, to serve Him as priests, priests that rule as they serve Him. It is emphasized that it is one kingdom, and everyone is a priest. This is in contrast to the Old Testament where only the Levites could be priests. Deuteronomy 33:8-10 indicates that from the tribe of Levi, the priests were to guard the covenant, teach the law, and offer sacrifices.

> You are coming to Christ, who is the living cornerstone of God's temple. He was rejected by people, but he was chosen by God for great honor. And you are living stones that God is building into his spiritual temple. What's more, you are his holy priests. Through the mediation of Jesus Christ, you offer spiritual sacrifices that please God. (1 Peter 2:4-5 NLT)

What is our function as priests in contrast to the Old Testament priests?

We are now a royal priesthood and offer spiritual sacrifices. Since Jesus offered the sacrifice for sin, the only thing we have to offer is praise, thanks, and ourselves. The Levites were mediators between man and God. A sinful person came to the priest to have him offer a sacrifice and the priests explained or taught the covenant to the people.

> All this is from God, who through Christ reconciled us to himself and gave us the ministry of reconciliation; that is, in Christ God was reconciling the world to himself, not counting their trespasses against them, and entrusting to us the message of reconciliation. So we are ambassadors for Christ, God making his appeal through us. We beseech you on behalf of Christ, be reconciled to God. (2 Cor 5:18-20 RSV)

We have a ministry that is like the priests of the Old Testament. We now have the message that people can come directly to God. The next time someone asks what you do, tell him or her you are a priest, a minister, or an ambassador. You may then have an opportunity to explain why.

Who Worships

How many angels are worshiping God?

What does their worship prove regarding the deity of Jesus?

> You are the LORD, you alone. You have made heaven, the heaven of heavens, with all their host, the earth and all that is on it, the seas and all that is in them; and you preserve all of them; and the host of heaven worships you. (Neh 9:6 ESV)

All the angels of heaven worship Him. How many angels are there? There are multitudes of beings in the heavens and they all worship Him. Daniel 7:10 and Hebrews 12:22 also mention that there are thousands upon thousands in heaven. If you multiply 1,000 by 1,000 and that by 10,000 by 10,000, then most calculators overflow (1 with 14 zeros following). It is mind boggling to consider how many angels there may be and that all with one voice and accord are stating or singing praise and worship to the Lamb.

Who says that Jesus is not God? All of the angels are worshiping Him. If He were a man, they certainly wouldn't. If He were another angel, they wouldn't. As they are singing they are attributing to Him the same honor as they previously gave to God in chapter four. Now they are even adding more by saying that the Lamb is worthy of receiving wealth, wisdom, and strength.

Why is Jesus' worthy to receive wealth and we aren't?

It struck me as odd that Jesus, who created all things, is being declared worthy of receiving wealth. Perhaps it is because none of us can truly manage wealth properly. Even the best of Christians struggle with wealth. Since wealth corrupts so easily, we can see that it is only God who can truly receive wealth. The same can be said about wisdom. How easy it is for us to become conceited when we know something. We think that others should know it also and we can become judgmental or proud. It is only our Lord who can handle these things without any problems.

Who else is worshiping God? Are there any clues as to when this worship takes place?

John went to great lengths to make sure we knew that all creatures were praising Jesus. He included every possible location of living beings and repeats that it is everyone in these places. There isn't any way to be more inclusive. It is also very interesting that this praise comes while there are still sinful people on earth. So, we have to ask some questions. Has this suddenly jumped in time to an even more distant future time (that is possible because we are in heaven and there are really no time restrictions) or is this something that portrays what should be and what will be eventually? Either way it shows that things in this book can be confusing if we are strictly literal and force the events to fit into our time sequence.

God's Honor and Glory

Why do you think God's honor and glory are mentioned in the praise in chapter four and again in the last two praises in chapter five?

This last song of praise is to both Jesus and the Father. In the last two songs of praise the words of honor and glory and power are repeated. In the book of Revelation, God's honor, glory, and power are on the line. If He doesn't judge in righteousness, then His honor is in question and it can be shown that He isn't really holy. If He doesn't execute judgment, then He isn't sovereign and someone else has more power than He does. If He doesn't rescue men from the curse of sin, then who will give Him glory? His ability to judge righteously and execute judgment while still saving people brings praise and glory to Himself. The "amen" of the four creatures and the songs of praise that have been offered affirm the belief of the multitudes that God is indeed who He says He is.

> All the ends of the earth will remember and turn to the LORD, And all the families of the nations will worship before Thee. For the kingdom is the LORD's, And He rules over the nations. (Ps 22:27-28 NASB)

> Turn to Me, and be saved, all the ends of the earth; For I am God, and there is no other. I have sworn by Myself, The word has gone forth from My mouth in righteousness And will not turn back, That to Me every knee will bow, every tongue will swear allegiance. They will say of Me, "Only in the LORD are righteousness and strength." Men will come to Him, And all who were angry at Him shall be put to shame. (Isa 45:22-24 NASB)

The Psalm speaks of a future time when all is restored and all know the Lord. They are willing to bow. In Isaiah, God appeals to people to give Him honor and glory now. He refers to the future time when all will bow before Him as an incentive to turn while it is a choice. Isaiah portrays a picture of two kinds of people. The righteous who, by their will and desire, come and bow down. All others will be forced to bow and confess. It will be to their shame however, not to their joy. Philippians 2:6-11 reminds us that Jesus gave up everything He had when He came and died on the cross. But now God has exalted Him back to His original place of honor so that all will bow and confess that He is Lord. Worship of Jesus brings glory to the Father. So then, when we worship Jesus, we worship the Father.

Let's join with the heavenly throng and give Jesus the worship that He is due. He is the Lamb who is worthy. He is God All Mighty. He is King of kings and Lord of lords.

Lesson 5 – Revelation 6:1-17

Revelation 6:1-8

I watched as the Lamb opened the first of the seven seals. Then I heard one of the four living creatures say in a voice like thunder, "Come!" I looked, and there before me was a white horse! Its rider held a bow, and he was given a crown, and he rode out as a conqueror bent on conquest.

When the Lamb opened the second seal, I heard the second living creature say, "Come!" Then another horse came out, a fiery red one. Its rider was given power to take peace from the earth and to make men slay each other. To him was given a large sword.

When the Lamb opened the third seal, I heard the third living creature say, "Come!" I looked, and there before me was a black horse! Its rider was holding a pair of scales in his hand. Then I heard what sounded like a voice among the four living creatures, saying, "A quart of wheat for a day's wages, and three quarts of barley for a day's wages, and do not damage the oil and the wine!"

When the Lamb opened the fourth seal, I heard the voice of the fourth living creature say, "Come!" I looked, and there before me was a pale horse! Its rider was named Death, and Hades was following close behind him. They were given power over a fourth of the earth to kill by sword, famine and plague, and by the wild beasts of the earth. (NIV®)

The First Six Seals

What does that fact that Jesus opens the seals reveal to us?

Each of the first four seals explicitly states that the Lamb opens the seals. For the last three seals it only says He. By that time, we know it is the Lamb who opens the seals. The importance of repeating who opens the seals is that we must recognize that God is in control. These things are not happening because of Satan's power. They are not happening from man's will. They occur because Jesus wills it.

We are again faced with a question of timing. Some people don't like to consider the book of Revelation in a sequential manner and with good reason. There are some parts that flash back in time to give a perspective of the past. There are others that race ahead to give an overview of the future. Other people like to see it sequentially in time. Therefore, some see the first six seals representing the course of history of the world while others see them representing the future. At first glance, we really don't know if we should be looking back in time to see if this started after John wrote it down or if it is referring to events that are in our future. On the other hand, it could represent both the past and the future in the same way we saw churches of today, church history in general, and churches of John's time in the first three chapters.

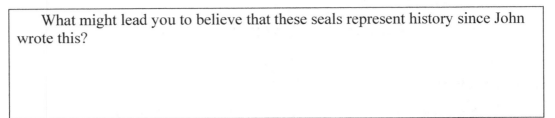

What might lead you to believe that these seals represent history since John wrote this?

When you hear of wars and rumors of wars, do not be frightened; those things must take place; but that is not yet the end. For nation will rise up against nation, and kingdom against kingdom; there will be earthquakes in various places; there will also be famines. These things are merely the beginning of birth pangs. (Mark 13:7-8 NASU)

To some degree, the first six seals represent the continuing cycles of life that Jesus referred to and can be seen repeated throughout history. We can see cycles of peace, war, famine, and reoccurring earthquakes. We need to remember that the end is still to come. In the fourth seal, we will see that a fourth of the mankind will be killed. This has come close to happening only once in history since the flood. But the end didn't come at that time. Jesus didn't tell us when the end would come but went on to tell of the persecutions that would occur before the end.

And the Gospel must first be preached to all the nations. (Mark 13:10 NKJV)

One thing that must occur before the end is that the Gospel must be preached to all nations. This is one reason I expect that the end could come very soon. There has been no other generation in which this has come closer than it has today. If the passages we have studied in Revelation had said that the Gospel had already been preached to all nations before the seals were opened, then we wouldn't have any doubt that the seals are opened at the very end of the age.

As a side note, the word translated, nations, is *ethnos* from which we get the word ethnic, referring to smaller groups of people. It is now believed by church growth experts that we have misunderstood Jesus' words. We should not expect the end until all ethnic groups have heard the Gospel.[18]

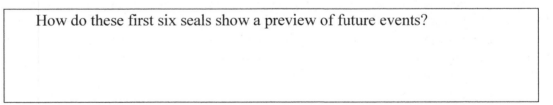

How do these first six seals show a preview of future events?

The first six seals may also represent a preview of the tribulation. As we read casually through them, we see a time of peace under a strong ruler. This time of peace is ended with one who makes war, followed by great economic trouble. As can be expected, famine and disease follow the war and economic trouble. Persecution of the saints is also promised. Lastly, we see the culmination of the ages as the Lord brings destruction on the earth, part of which includes a huge earthquake. Revelation 16:18

---

[18] A. Scott Moreau, Gary R. Corwin, and Gary B. McGee, *Introducing World Missions: a Biblical, Historical, and Practical Survey* (Grand Rapids: Baker Academic, 2004), 994-1005, Kindle.

also mentions an earthquake that is worse than any other in history. This makes the preview theory more plausible and if it is true, then we can look upon the events of the seventh seal to expand upon this outline. If not, then we must look at the remaining seal as a continuation of what has already happened.

One way or another, the first six seals represent a time on earth of immense problems. It is possible that these events occur so that the stage will be set for people to accept the leadership of the Antichrist or occur because he has already taken control.

Four Seals – Four Horses

> What is the significance of four horses of different colors? Where else in Scripture do we find this?

In a vision during the night, I saw a man sitting on a red horse that was standing among some myrtle trees in a small valley. Behind him were riders on red, brown, and white horses. I asked the angel who was talking with me, "My lord, what do these horses mean?" "I will show you," the angel replied. The rider standing among the myrtle trees then explained, "They are the ones the LORD has sent out to patrol the earth." (Zech 1:8-10 NLT)

The first chariot was pulled by red horses, the second by black horses, the third by white horses, and the fourth by powerful dappled-gray horses. "And what are these, my lord?" I asked the angel who was talking with me. The angel replied, "These are the four spirits of heaven who stand before the Lord of all the earth. They are going out to do his work." (Zech 6:2-5 NLT)

These are each a reference to four horses or teams of various colors. The connection is not that the colors mean anything special, but that the groupings of four are used to represent an action initiated by the Lord to go out into the entire world. In the first case, the action is a survey to determine the condition of the world. The second is sending God's Spirit. Drawing from these two examples, the use of four horses of different colors in Revelation 6 is a confirmation that the events depicted will befall mankind including all the world and not isolated parts. They are going at God's command to do His will. If there is any significance to the colors, we will have to draw that from the passage as we study it.

First Seal – White Horse

> What would be a good explanation for the symbology of the white horse?

There are very few references to a white horse in Scripture. One is Revelation 19:11, 14. The rider in this case is clearly described as Jesus and He is coming as a conquering King. His conquest will be quick and final. The others are in Zechariah above, none of which represent a conquering king. However, in extra-biblical symbolism, a white horse has been the symbol of a conqueror.[19] This would be the most likely symbol.

> What would be a good explanation for the symbology of the bow which the rider has?

> They lay hold on bow and spear, they are cruel and have no mercy, the sound of them is like the roaring sea; they ride upon horses, set in array as a man for battle, against you, O daughter of Zion! We have heard the report of it, our hands fall helpless; anguish has taken hold of us, pain as of a woman in travail. Go not forth into the field, nor walk on the road; for the enemy has a sword, terror is on every side. (Jer 6:23-25 RSV)

The bow has also been a symbol of warfare as in this case where the enemy is coming armed to attack Zion. I think the description of fear in this passage is appropriate to describe what will occur when the first horse and his rider is sent to the earth. As in Jeremiah, there isn't any attempt to fight back. This is the image that I see in Revelation 6:1-2. There is no mention made of fighting, but the rider is equipped so that others do nothing other than cave in to his control.

> The rider is given a crown rather than winning it. What does this mean?
>
> What is revealed by the phrase, "bent on conquest" used in the NIV® translation?

This indicates that he receives the leadership without a fight. The phrase bent on conquest indicates that this person is not a beneficial leader. His motive is conquest itself, not establishing peace.

> You are my King, O God; ordain salvation for Jacob! Through you we push down our foes; through your name we tread down those who rise up against us. For not in my bow do I trust, nor can my sword save me. But you have saved us from our foes and have put to shame those who hate us. In God we have boasted continually, and we will give thanks to your name forever. (Ps 44:4-8 ESV)

---

[19] Albert Barnes, *Barnes' Notes*, (Seattle: Biblesoft, 2005), Revelation 6:2, Electronic Database.

The Psalmist expressed the thoughts of a conqueror who did so at the bidding and guidance of the Lord. Rather than being bent on conquest, he recognized that the Sovereign Lord decrees any victory and he gives God the glory. Even though the white horse is sent from the Lord – signifying that it is His will that the rider is victorious, his attitude doesn't honor the Lord.

Even though He is bent on conquest, this rider appears to usher in a time of peace because the next rider is given the power to take peace away from the earth.

> What evidence shows that this rider is or is not Jesus and His conquest over sin?

Some suggest that the rider of this horse represents Jesus in His victorious conquest over sin or His enemies. They base this primarily on the fact that he is riding a white horse as in Revelation 19:11. He is given a crown, but it simply doesn't fit Jesus because he has an attitude that is bent on conquest.[20] Another problem with this view is that it doesn't fit the context. All the other seals are times of problems, a period when difficulties are set up and people are judged and even killed. We also know that when Jesus came the first time to conquer sin, it was humbly, on a donkey. We know that He will come in the air to take the church. We haven't established when this will occur. He will come to restore His kingdom but not before the wars and famine.

Everyone who comes in the name of peace or justice is not peaceful or just. It is easy to be deceived by outward appearances of lofty language and demonstrations of power.

> And Jesus answered and said to them, "See to it that no one misleads you. "For many will come in My name, saying, 'I am the Christ,' and will mislead many." (Matt 24:4-5 NASB)

These are the words Jesus spoke in answer to the disciple who asked Him when the end of the age would come. It is possible that the first rider represents all the false Christs, the ones whose motives are personal power and who use religion as a basis for power.

> What evidence would show this is or is not the Antichrist?

> And he shall confirm the covenant with many for one week: (Dan 9:27a)

---

[20] Daniel K. K. Wong, "The First Horseman of Revelation 6," *Bibliotheca Sacra* 153, no. 610 (April 1996): 214-16, accessed February 17, 2016, http://www.galaxie.com.ezproxy.liberty.edu:2048/article/bsac153-610-06.

The week is commonly recognized as a period of seven years. This first rider appears to bring peace even if it is out of fear. This rider has the qualities of the Antichrist. He is bent on conquest.

This probably represents the beginning of the tribulation when the Antichrist takes control in a peaceful manner but with evidence of great power. If so, then chapter six may be a quick overview of the rest of the book. There are many places in the book of Revelation that flash back in time, giving us a different perspective of the events of the end times as well as things that have happened even in our own past. It is too early in the study to make a definitive statement.

Second Seal – Fiery Red Horse

From the context of this passage, it is apparent that the red horse and rider symbolize war. Barnes agrees that this represents "carnage, discord, bloodshed" but says to see Zechariah 1:8 to back it up.[21] However, Zechariah 1:8-11 the red horse, along with the others, are sent to patrol the earth. They return to state that the earth remains at rest. This is a vastly different conclusion from carnage. This illustrates the need to be careful about applying symbols once they have been found and identified. As discussed before, there are very few references to red horses.

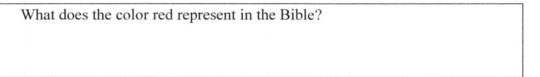

What does the color red represent in the Bible?

"Come now, let us reason together," says the LORD. "Though your sins are like scarlet, they shall be as white as snow; though they are red as crimson, they shall be like wool." (Isa 1:18 NIV®)

Red by itself symbolizes many things including sin. There are also times when it is associated with God's vengeance.

Who is this who comes from Edom, With garments of glowing colors from Bozrah, This One who is majestic in His apparel, Marching in the greatness of His strength? "It is I who speak in righteousness, mighty to save." Why is Your apparel red, And Your garments like the one who treads in the wine press? "I have trodden the wine trough alone, And from the peoples there was no man with Me. I also trod them in My anger And trampled them in My wrath; And their lifeblood is sprinkled on My garments, And I stained all My raiment. "For the day of vengeance was in My heart, And My year of redemption has come. "I looked, and there was no one to help, And I was astonished and there was no one to uphold; So My own arm brought salvation to Me, And My wrath upheld Me. "I trod down the peoples in My anger And made them drunk in My wrath, And I poured out their lifeblood on the earth." (Isa 63:1-6 NASU)

This is an interesting picture of God. Even when the Lord is bringing about His vengeance, He is robed in splendor. Many have criticized our God because of the way He has eliminated sinful nations in the Old Testament, yet He is able to do this and

---

[21] *Barnes*, Revelation 6:4.

retain His splendor. It is because of His great righteousness and His motivation is to save, not destroy. We can also see that when this vengeance takes place, God is alone. At the end of time, there will not be any nation standing for what is right. In the past, God used other nations to discipline those that needed it, but not now. Finally, there is this curious mixture of both vengeance and redemption. Clearly, our final redemption can't be completed until God's vengeance has been completed in order to remove sin.

> How do we see the effects of this rider's ability to make men kill each other – not including the obvious wars? What are some causes of this?

This last rider has power over peace and to make people slay each other. As we look at the way the U.S. is going, this phrase about making men slay each other makes more sense than ever before. Think about the number of times we hear in news that someone has walked into an office, school, restaurant, or other public place and has opened fire, killing many. It appears to be increasing in our country despite the campaigns to stop bullying and restrict firearms.

What makes people slay each other with such little regard for another's life? Sin, of course is the ultimate reason. However, the ever-increasing glorification of solving problems with violence in movies and video games contribute to this. Abortion even contributes because at the heart of it is the degradation of human life. The media and proponents of "women's rights" promote this concept over and over. Any person who believes it is OK to have an abortion for any reason has degraded human life in his own eyes. Deep down, people know that an unborn baby is a person. If it's OK to kill them, the only difference between killing the baby and any other person who inconveniences your life is a matter of what is "socially acceptable." Perhaps in the future, the Supreme Court will change the laws against murder so that it will be legal to kill others if you can prove that they potentially have an adverse effect on your life style. It will become justified homicide, just like self-defense. Hitler managed to do this.

> What does the sword usually symbolize in the Bible?

Whoever this person is or whatever his methods, he has the ability to cause people to kill each other. This is the reason it is primarily thought that this horse and rider represent war. The large sword indicates the ease with which he slays people. The sword is also a metaphor of constant strife and suffering through violence and war (2 Sam 12:10).

> Then Abner called to Joab and said, "Shall the sword devour forever? Do you not know that it will be bitter in the latter end? How long will it be then until you tell the people to return from pursuing their brethren?" (2 Sam 2:26 NKJV)

> Is this rider the Antichrist? Compare him to the king in Daniel 8:23-25 and Daniel 9:27.

At the end of their rule, when their sin is at its height, a fierce king, a master of intrigue, will rise to power. He will become very strong, but not by his own power. He will cause a shocking amount of destruction and succeed in everything he does. He will destroy powerful leaders and devastate the holy people. He will be a master of deception and will become arrogant; he will destroy many without warning. He will even take on the Prince of princes in battle, but he will be broken, though not by human power. (Dan 8:23-25 NLT)

The ruler will make a treaty with the people for a period of one set of seven, but after half this time, he will put an end to the sacrifices and offerings. And as a climax to all his terrible deeds, he will set up a sacrilegious object that causes desecration, until the fate decreed for this defiler is finally poured out on him. (Dan 9:27 NLT)

In this description of the Antichrist from Daniel, it is evident that his power will be supernatural. This seems to fit the brief description of the second rider and his ability to get people to kill each other and the devastation that will come upon the world. The most striking comparison to the Antichrist is that after the time of peace that the first rider established, peace will be taken away. It then appears that the rider of the first and second horses could be the same person – the Antichrist.

Third Seal – Black Horse

With the last two horses, we have gained the most insight for what the horse, rider, and other objects in the scene represented directly from the verses in which they appeared. Again, this will be the case with the black horse. Looking at how scales are used in the Bible only reveals that they are used as tools to measure things.

> What is the meaning of the symbols, scales, wheat, barley, oil, and wine, when the third seal is opened?

So again, by simply reading the passage we can discern that the balances are being used to weigh out basic foodstuff. The price is exorbitant. Yet the implication is that the price of wine and oil is left alone. These are the areas where people who have written end times books have a hay day. They can extrapolate for hours on the economy and trends and all sorts of things. These are fine, but the irony of this situation shouldn't be missed. Food will be scarce, but it will be easy to get drunk and try to escape reality with alcohol. It reminds me of Proverbs 31:6-7:

Give strong drink to him who is perishing, and wine to those in bitter distress; let them drink and forget their poverty, and remember their misery no more. (RSV)

Oil will be plentiful and is needed to keep our modern war machines operating and running. It will be a strange time of terrible injustice as the rich have what they want and the poor will only be able to get drunk. Perhaps it isn't all that strange since this is the situation in Russia for the last eighty years if not even longer. The common people have always had a plentiful supply of vodka while the elite (even under communism) have no problems. In the meantime, they manage to maintain an armed force with awesome destructive powers. However, if the scope of the first two seals is maintained, this condition will engulf the whole earth.

> Be on guard, that your hearts may not be weighted down with dissipation and drunkenness and the worries of life, and that day come on you suddenly like a trap; for it will come upon all those who dwell on the face of all the earth. But keep on the alert at all times, praying in order that you may have strength to escape all these things that are about to take place, and to stand before the Son of Man. (Luke 21:34-36 NASB)

When we are stressed by the cares of making a living in times of great inflation, or when many are out of work, the temptation is to escape. It is as if Jesus is saying that a sign of the times will be great numbers of people turning to alcohol and other drugs as never before. Many studies have shown that kids are turning to alcohol and drugs at an earlier age every year.[22] These kids may not get any more money than to buy their lunch, but they have an almost unlimited access to booze and drugs.

Fourth Seal – Pale Horse

> What are the ways in which the earth will be afflicted as the fourth rider is released? How do these already show up today reflecting what may happen in the end times?

In the fourth seal we see the effects of the first three seals multiplied. The wars cause economic problems and famine. In turn these problems cause plagues. If you study the famines and disease in the Sudan, you will find that they are not caused by natural disasters. They are caused by the war that went on for years. The war has been very one sided and an attempt by the government to eradicate Christianity. They purposefully restricted aid in order to kill as many as possible. The only way to get aid is to reject Christ and accept the Muslim faith.[23] If this is how governments behave now, how much more will these tactics be used when these seals are opened?

To add to this, the Lord increases the problem by allowing wild animals to kill more than they do now. Most animals naturally do not attack people. They usually

---

[22] National Institute on Drug Abuse, "When and how does drug abuse start and progress?" NIDA, October 2003, accessed November 02, 2017, https://www.drugabuse.gov/publications/preventing-drug-abuse-among-children-adolescents-in-brief/chapter-1-risk-factors-protective-factors/when-how-does-drug-abuse-start-progress.

[23] Nina Shea, "A War On Religion," Hudson Institute, July 31, 1998, accessed February 18, 2016, http://www.hudson.org/research/5986-a-war-on-religion.

have to be provoked. Perhaps this will result because of an increase of diseases like rabies or maybe the Lord will remove that natural restriction that now inhibits them. Another possibility is that the Lord will produce more animals like the killer bees, which have steadily increased and moved across many parts of the world. In the last few years, we've seen bands of monkeys attacking people when they run out of forest areas. The same thing has been happening with herds of elephants.

Another possibility has reared its ugly head in the last few years. Perhaps some genetically engineered animals have gotten out of control or had some unexpected side effects. We could also see plagues started from genetically altered viruses and bacteria.

> How many people will die as a result and how does this compare with past plagues and wars?

With the different methods of death, the problems on the earth will have increased to the point where a fourth of the population will die. Not even in WW I or WW II did this many people die. When the black plague swept through Europe in the 14th century, the population was reduced dramatically. It is estimated that 30 to 60% of the population died. But that only affected a small portion of the world. The total world population was reduced from 450 to a possible low of 350 million people, about 22%.[24]

As of March 12, 2012, the world population exceeded seven billion people. If a quarter of the people of the world were to die today, that would be over 1.75 billion people. Most of them would face an eternity without Christ.

While the plague may have killed nearly a quarter of earth's population, this rider can't be associated with that event because the events of the previous two seals didn't occur and the following ones did not come afterward. It is evident by now that this death being released on the earth isn't just history repeating itself or a recap of our past, but part of the end times.

> What does the personification of Death and Hades reveal?

The use of the terms Death and Hades lets us know that the power given to them is more than the removal of life. Since Hades is following death, my conclusion is that this is a description of the death of unbelievers and their ultimate relegation to hell.

> The rest of the dead did not come to life until the thousand years were ended. This is the first resurrection. (Rev 20:5 ESV)

---

[24] "Black Death," Wikipedia, May 19, 2013, accessed May 23, 2013, http://en.wikipedia.org/wiki/Black_Death.

> And the sea gave up the dead who were in it, Death and Hades gave up the dead who
> were in them, and they were judged, each one of them, according to what they had
> done. (Rev 20:13 ESV)

These verses link the death of unbelievers to Hades. The first resurrection is for believers. Hades does not hold them captive for a thousand years. Paul makes it clear that when a believer dies, he does not go to a place of unconsciousness, but to be with Jesus (Phil 1:21-25).

In contrast, Job 18:5-21, describes the death of the wicked, the person that does not know God. Look at just a few of these verses to get flavor for the whole text.

> The lamp of the wicked is snuffed out; the flame of his fire stops burning. (Job 18:5
> NIV®)

> He is torn from the security of his tent and marched off to the king of terrors. Fire
> resides in his tent; burning sulfur is scattered over his dwelling. (Job 18:14-15NIV)

> Surely such is the dwelling of an evil man; such is the place of one who knows not
> God. (Job 18:21NIV)

The last verse is a good definition of those who are evil. It isn't just the fact that they have done something deserving of punishment (we are all in this category), but they don't know God.

> Later the other virgins also came, saying, "Lord, lord, open up for us." But he
> answered, "Truly I say to you, I do not know you." Be on the alert then, for you do not
> know the day nor the hour. (Matt 25:11-13 NASU)

How true are the words of Jesus! The door will be closed for those who don't know God. Their dwelling will not be with God, but eternal torment.

What is the only way to know God?

> All things have been delivered to Me by My Father, and no one knows the Son except
> the Father. Nor does anyone know the Father except the Son, and the one to whom
> the Son wills to reveal Him. (Matt 11:27 NKJV)

There is only one way to know God. You have to know Jesus. Jesus isn't going to reveal the Father to anyone who denies that Jesus is who He said He is (God) and who rejects His sacrificial death on the cross for his sins. It's just as the bumper sticker says, "No Jesus, No Peace. Know Jesus, Know peace."

If you can't say, "I know Jesus and He knows me," then by all means, make the effort to get to know Him now. Once the lamp is snuffed out, it will be too late.

> Will Christian be raptured and escape these events of the end times?

Whether Christians will be caught up to heaven before or after these events start, still hasn't been made clear. One thing is clear and that is people will still be coming to Christ after these events. This will be made evident later in the book. What is abundantly clear is that God is in control and permits these things to happen. Whether we are facing global cataclysmic events as depicted here, national disasters, or personal disasters, we can face them with the confidence that our loving heavenly Father and the Lord Jesus (our Friend) know exactly what is happening to us. We don't need to fear these things. He will either take us out of the storm or enable us to ride out the storm. Either way He gets the glory.

> Grace be to you and peace from God our Father, and from the Lord Jesus Christ. Blessed be God, even the Father of our Lord Jesus Christ, the Father of mercies, and the God of all comfort; Who comforteth us in all our tribulation, that we may be able to comfort them which are in any trouble, by the comfort wherewith we ourselves are comforted of God. (2 Cor 1:2-4)

Revelation 6:9-17

> When he opened the fifth seal, I saw under the altar the souls of those who had been slain for the word of God and for the witness they had borne; they cried out with a loud voice, "O Sovereign Lord, holy and true, how long before thou wilt judge and avenge our blood on those who dwell upon the earth?" Then they were each given a white robe and told to rest a little longer, until the number of their fellow servants and their brethren should be complete, who were to be killed as they themselves had been.
>
> When he opened the sixth seal, I looked, and behold, there was a great earthquake; and the sun became black as sackcloth, the full moon became like blood, and the stars of the sky fell to the earth as the fig tree sheds its winter fruit when shaken by a gale; the sky vanished like a scroll that is rolled up, and every mountain and island was removed from its place. Then the kings of the earth and the great men and the generals and the rich and the strong, and every one, slave and free, hid in the caves and among the rocks of the mountains, calling to the mountains and rocks, "Fall on us and hide us from the face of him who is seated on the throne, and from the wrath of the Lamb; for the great day of their wrath has come, and who can stand before it?" (RSV)

Fifth Seal

> What does opening the fifth seal reveal about the past and the future of believers?

<u>Persecution</u>

The fifth seal is a reminder that many people throughout the ages have suffered because of their stand for God. It isn't just Christians who have been martyred, but it is also the Old Testament saints who died rather than compromise the Word of God. It is also a warning to all who seek to follow Jesus that many more Christians will be added to this select group of faithful saints during the last days before Jesus comes to rule in person.

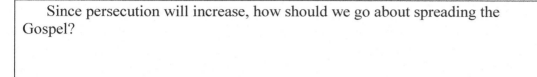

Since persecution will increase, how should we go about spreading the Gospel?

Look, I am sending you out as sheep among wolves. So be as shrewd as snakes and harmless as doves. But beware! For you will be handed over to the courts and will be flogged with whips in the synagogues. You will stand trial before governors and kings because you are my followers. But this will be your opportunity to tell the rulers and other unbelievers about me. When you are arrested, don't worry about how to respond or what to say. God will give you the right words at the right time. For it is not you who will be speaking—it will be the Spirit of your Father speaking through you.

A brother will betray his brother to death, a father will betray his own child, and children will rebel against their parents and cause them to be killed. And all nations will hate you because you are my followers. But everyone who endures to the end will be saved. When you are persecuted in one town, flee to the next. I tell you the truth, the Son of Man will return before you have reached all the towns of Israel. (Matt 10:16-23 NLT)

These passages suggest something that some modern day American Christians seem to forget in our luxury. We need to be shrewd when we bring the Word to others. Some feel that we should simply stand up in the market place, start proclaiming the Gospel, and let the chips fall where they may. I doubt that anyone who believes this has actually tried to proclaim the Word in a Muslim country. Because we can do this in the U. S., some have the attitude that our brothers and sisters in other places should be bolder. Since we haven't faced real persecution, we can philosophize easily. The truth is that we shouldn't bring upon ourselves unnecessary trouble by flaunting what we know whether here or overseas.

I was once in a Bible study at work. People knew about it, but we couldn't advertise it without losing the privilege of using a meeting room at lunch. We were innocent by finding out what company policy was, but we were shrewd by not demanding what some may have considered our rights to equal access to meeting rooms for non-business use.

There may also be times when we make mistakes and have to answer for our actions. I think there is a big difference between persecution and getting into trouble because we've done something stupid or even illegal. We can't call it persecution unless we have had to make a choice between obedience to God and obedience to the establishment. There are too many Christians claiming persecution in the workplace when the truth is that they are not doing their job but using work time to witness. God doesn't get glory when we patiently suffer for doing something wrong, only when we are doing something correctly (1 Peter 2:20).

When true persecution occurs, we don't have to worry because the Holy Spirit will provide our defense. We must realize, however, that the defense will probably provoke people to anger rather than let us escape unharmed (Acts 7:54-60). We will not always be able to avoid persecution because we are commanded to carry the Gospel to all people.

Note also, that it isn't just the establishment, but our families who are closest to us who are also likely to cause trouble. These are the people that we want to see come to the Lord most of all and at the same time pose the greatest risk to us because we trust them.

Instead of saying that we should not speak to persecutors, Jesus tells us that we should avoid becoming martyrs and flee the persecution. This accomplishes two things. It keeps us available to speak the message, and it spreads the message over greater areas than we would have normally gone. Martyrdom is something to expect, not to seek.

Vengeance

> What is the proper attitude we should have when persecuted?

Never pay back evil for evil to anyone. Respect what is right in the sight of all men. If possible, so far as it depends on you, be at peace with all men. Never take your own revenge, beloved, but leave room for the wrath of God, for it is written, "Vengeance is Mine, I will repay," says the Lord. "But if your enemy is hungry, feed him, and if he is thirsty, give him a drink; for in so doing you will heap burning coals upon his head." Do not be overcome by evil, but overcome evil with good. (Rom 12:17-21 NASB)

These verses outline the proper attitude to have as a Christian. We are to rest on the promise that the Lord knows what He is doing and that all we are to do is to leave the destruction of the unjust up to Him. In the meantime, we are to feed and give drink to our enemies. If we do not share the Gospel with them or they reject it, they will not be able to escape the destruction that will come upon them.

> Why should we be careful when we cry out to God for vengeance?

In Psalm 94, David calls out to the Lord to judge the earth. In verse three, he asks how long God will allow the wicked to enjoy their seeming dominance. Many people claim that God doesn't exist based on the evidence of the wicked and the appearance that they are getting away with it. But David has a different attitude, the same as those who have been martyred. He is asking the question, "how long," not requesting it to occur in his way or in his timing.

> He who disciplines the nations, does he not rebuke? He who teaches man knowledge— the LORD—knows the thoughts of man, that they are but a breath. (Ps 94:10-11 ESV)

We need to remember who God is, the One who made us, who knows our very thoughts, and also controls nations. We need to be very careful what we are asking and what our motives are. When we cry out for vengeance, He knows exactly why – whether it is because our feeling are hurt or because we see the true injustice in the world. We know that He never forsakes us and there will be a time when He will exercise His judgment (Ps 94:14-15). Until that time comes we need to be careful about our attitude and action.

When should we get involved with making sure justice happens?

> Who will rise up for me against the wicked? Who will take a stand for me against evildoers? Unless the LORD had given me help, I would soon have dwelt in the silence of death. (Ps 94:16-17 NIV®).

If we cry for justice, there may be times the Lord uses us to help in His judgment such as becoming involved in wars. There is the very real possibility that we will die just as the wicked. However, if we survive, it is only because of the Lord's help. This verse doesn't guarantee an escape from harm but the acknowledgement that survival is the Lord's will and decision. In such a time, we can slip and anxiety can easily overcome us if we don't lean upon the Lord (Ps 94:18-19). When we are the subjects of injustice, we need to learn that the Lord will repay; we must always wait upon Him and His direction. It is seldom, if ever that the Lord uses the same person as the victim, judge, jury, and executioner.

Read Deuteronomy 32:1-43. Pay careful attention to verses 21, and 36-37. What are some of the things you learned about God's vengeance from this passage?

In Deuteronomy 32:34-43 it is very clear that the Lord will avenge. He has set a time; He has sealed it up, and He will release His anger and wrath upon the earth. The Lord allows injustice to occur and uses it to bring His people back to Himself. When we put our trust in things other than God, He will methodically remove each of those things from our lives until we have nothing left except Him.

In verse 36 He is speaking of a future when they don't turn back and are all gone. He will then turn to those who have come against His servants and lift His hand against them. Does this mean that only when all the believers have been either martyred or raptured that the Lord will take His vengeance? That is an interesting thought. I'll leave it to you to ponder that possibility.

In verse 37, God asks them where their god is, the rock in which they take refuge. In Revelation 6:15 the people hide themselves in caves and ask the rocks to hide them. Don't miss the irony in this.

> They have made Me jealous with what is not God; They have provoked Me to anger with their idols. So I will make them jealous with those who are not a people; I will provoke them to anger with a foolish nation. (Deut 32:21 NASU)

This is God's promise to the Gentiles. Way back in time, He provided for us and will use us to make Israel jealous with the hope of bringing them back to Himself. Maybe Israel will realize this after the rapture occurs and there are no believers left.

Summarize what you have learned about vengeance.

The principal is this. It is all right to call out to the Lord when we have been wronged and to ask for His vengeance. However, it can't be for personal gain, but because the actions are unjust not only to ourselves but to others also. This is not speaking of asking for personal vengeance.

Also, things can happen to us that we deserve and there isn't any room for us to ask for vengeance because of these things (1 Peter 4:15-16). We are also to praise God for any time we suffer because we are Christians. In the Revelation passage, it is clear that these people were killed simply because they held on to their faith in Christ. In heaven, their personal motives are removed and they can clearly call on the Lord for vengeance. We can't call out for vengeance as long as we have anything other than the glory of God in mind. If self is in it, then we need to examine ourselves and wait. We need to remember that any persecutor who dies because of God's wrath or vengeance without coming to a saving knowledge of Jesus will be eternally lost. That is why we should follow the Scripture in Romans 12:17-21 and wait.

> However, for this reason I obtained mercy, that in me first Jesus Christ might show all longsuffering, as a pattern to those who are going to believe on Him for everlasting life. (1 Tim 1:16 NKJV)

We need to wait until the number has been completed. Who knows, maybe some of those who are the vilest persecutors will become Christians. If we ever doubt that someone could come to Christ, we only need to look at Paul and his testimony about himself. He was a murder and persecutor of the Church, but Jesus took him and turned him into one of the greatest evangelist of all time. Perhaps this ties back to Deuteronomy 32:36. When the Lord sees that there are none of His chosen left (either current believers or those He knows will come to Him), then He will feel free to take vengeance upon the world.

For God chose to save us through our Lord Jesus Christ, not to pour out his anger on us. (1 Thess 5:9 NLT)

He will not allow His people to face the wrath that He is about to place upon the earth. To get a better understanding of His wrath, consider that He will allow His people to be martyred, but He will not let them face His wrath. Since Christians suffer much throughout the world today, this can only mean that we really don't have a good concept about how horrible His wrath is. Whether the passage in Revelation describes the past, present or future, it doesn't matter. As long as there are Christians on the earth, there will be martyrs.

Sixth Seal

> What is the cause of these end times disasters that are described in the sixth seal?

This description of what will occur is a point of conjecture among all the end times experts. Many of the people who have recently written on the end times look at the terrible capability for destruction of our nuclear age and believe that this describes exactly what will happen as a result of global nuclear war. The earth will shake, the fallout will obscure the sun, and the moon and the stars will not be seen. The picture of a mushroom cloud rapidly expanding could be the description of the sky receding like a scroll. The stars falling could be the many warheads of missiles entering the atmosphere. One thing that this cause doesn't account for is that the mountains and islands will be removed. Another thing that this doesn't account for is the fact that people will recognize that this is the wrath of the Lamb being poured out and that they will want to hide from Him. The Lord may well use our own devices to bring about His will. Certainly, that is His pattern in the past, but there is also a supernatural element in this description.

> This is what the LORD says to his anointed, to Cyrus, whose right hand I take hold of to subdue nations before him ... I will go before you and will level the mountains ... so that you may know that I am the LORD ... who summons you by name. For the sake of Jacob my servant ... though you do not acknowledge me. I am the LORD, and there is no other; apart from me there is no God ... so that from the rising of the sun to the place of its setting men may know there is none besides me ... I form the light and create darkness, I bring prosperity and create disaster; I, the Lord, do all these things. (Isa 45:1-7 NIV®)

This is a fascinating passage that reveals much insight into our Lord and also the symbolism that may be in Revelation. God says that He will level the mountains before Cyrus. To my knowledge, there wasn't any mountain-leveling going on when Cyrus conquered Israel. I don't think the mountains and islands being moved in Revelation are only symbolic as used in Isaiah. In Revelation, they are accompanied by many other physical disasters, which leads me to believe that there is a catastrophic change occurring.

> What did you learn from Isaiah 45:1-7 about God that sheds light on the sixth seal in Revelation?

It is clear that God used Cyrus to punish Israel; God summoned Cyrus, even though he didn't acknowledge God. As the Antichrist works his evil in the world, as these wars depicted by the red horse become a reality, they are all summoned by God. It isn't because God has lost control or is unable to stop the disasters. On the contrary, our Lord owns up to the fact that the disasters are from Him. In the case of Cyrus, He used the prophet Isaiah to make it clear to Israel and to Cyrus that this was what was happening. It is likely that in the end times, whether it is by nuclear war, by natural disasters, or God's might, the knowledge of the end will be so well known that when it comes, even the rebellious will recognize it for what it is.

After Mt. Saint Helens blew up, I think many people may have revised their idea of what the end times scenario may be. Never in modern time has the eruption of a mountain been so well reported. The effect of that eruption could just as easily explain what John saw. Perhaps several dormant volcanoes around the world will erupt as a result of the great earthquake. The fact that the Bible says a great earthquake occurred leads credibility to the idea that this is entirely the Lord's work and He doesn't need to use our destructive forces. The sovereignty of God is forgotten when people think that all the destruction must be accounted for in mankind's destructive abilities.

> Read Isaiah 13:1-13. What is another possible cause for the destruction on the earth?

In this passage, the holy ones, the saints, and angels gather together to carry out the war of the Lord (Isa 13:3). He gathers them from all countries and from the ends of heaven. He calls them the weapons of His wrath (Isa 13:5). The reaction of the unsaved is terror; they simply do not know what to do (Isa 13:7-8). In many passages like this one, shaking the earth and heavens is mentioned. The book of Revelation is not the origin of this idea, it is simply agreeing with the rest of the Bible when it reports how the end will occur.

> For the LORD's indignation is against all the nations, And His wrath against all their armies; He has utterly destroyed them, He has given them over to slaughter. So their slain will be thrown out, And their corpses will give off their stench, And the mountains will be drenched with their blood. And all the host of heaven will wear away, And the sky will be rolled up like a scroll; All their hosts will also wither away As a leaf withers from the vine, Or as one withers from the fig tree. (Isa 34:2-4 NASB)

> What are three things found in these verses that parallel Revelation?

Again, this shows that the descriptions of what will occur have been given to us long before John saw it. In Revelation, we will see the armies of the nations gather together to do battle against God, but He will triumph. The phenomena in the skies are very similar to the descriptions in Revelation. The reference to the figs is in both.

> How might the reference to shriveled figs or falling figs be symbolic?

The fig tree has sometimes been used to symbolize Israel. In Mark 11:12-14, Jesus approached a fig tree without any fruit on it and cursed it. When He returned, it had dried up from its roots (Mark 11:20). Many explain the cursing and withering of the fig tree as a sign from Jesus because He came to the nation of Israel and found no fruit. The curse is that there will not be a harvest of souls that He desired from the nation. It is possible that the falling shriveled figs in Isaiah and in Revelation refer to those who in the end do not accept the Lord. If so, then they will be as numerous as the stars.

> What choices will unbelievers make in the end times regarding salvation?

Lift up your eyes to the heavens, and look upon the earth beneath: for the heavens shall vanish away like smoke, and the earth shall wax old like a garment, and they that dwell therein shall die in like manner: but my salvation shall be for ever, and my righteousness shall not be abolished. (Isa 51:6)

Think about material things that we count on being in place day after day vanishing. I could look out my window at work and see the Olympic Mountains and Mount Rainier. On the way home, I could see the Cascade Mountains and Mount Baker. Yet these mountains that seem so stable are going to wear out. Why do we put such importance on our material things that wear out even before our life does? This verse ends on the truly enduring things, God and His salvation and righteousness. The longer we wait for these things to come, the more people are tested until only unbelievers will be left, those who have placed all their trust in temporal things. They will then try to find permanence in the rocks as they are falling. They will have made their decision. It is the wrong decision, but it is the one they have made and it will be eternal.

Enter into the rock, and hide in the dust from before the terror of the LORD, and from the glory of his majesty. The haughty looks of man shall be brought low, and the pride of men shall be humbled; and the LORD alone will be exalted in that day. (Isa 2:10-11 RSV)

And men shall enter the caves of the rocks and the holes of the ground, from before the terror of the LORD, and from the glory of his majesty, when he rises to terrify the earth. (Isa 2:19 RSV)

What we see in the book of Revelation is what the Lord promised to do exactly as described long ago. Unbelievers will be brought to the place where they will have to hide to escape the splendor of the Lord. Hiding from God is nothing new. Adam and Eve started it all trying to hide from God as soon as there was sin in the world (Gen 3:8). They wanted to escape from the Lord because their sin was exposed by His presence. It is the desire of the natural man, the sinful part of us, to flee from Him who exposes our true nature (John 3:19-20).

Is it possible without going further in the book of Revelation to determine if the rapture has taken place after the sixth seal is opened? Explain why or why not.

Immediately after the tribulation of those days shall the sun be darkened, and the moon shall not give her light, and the stars shall fall from heaven, and the powers of the heavens shall be shaken: And then shall appear the sign of the Son of man in heaven: and then shall all the tribes of the earth mourn, and they shall see the Son of man coming in the clouds of heaven with power and great glory. And he shall send his angels with a great sound of a trumpet, and they shall gather together his elect from the four winds, from one end of heaven to the other. (Matt 24:29-31)

Jesus described the same events for the end as we find in Revelation 6:12-13. He also gives us some more clues as to the timing of these events. He says that this occurs immediately after the tribulation in those days. He says that all the nations and people will see Him coming and will mourn. Since believers will rejoice, it is the unsaved who will mourn. He will gather His elect (believers) from the four winds, from one end of heaven to the other.

"Immediately after the tribulation" is a powerful indicator that these events culminate after the seven years of tribulation. This would describe a post-tribulation rapture.

On the other hand, He isn't saying that He will take them from the earth. It is very possible that they have already died or been raptured. This would indicate that His wrath won't be revealed while there are any believers on the earth.

On the other, other hand, Scripture indicates that all unbelievers will be killed in God's wrath leaving living believers to repopulate the earth in the Millennium. However, there is also the possibility that He doesn't kill all unbelievers and leaves some to enter the Millennium. At this point, it is too early to make any definitive statement that the rapture has already happened.

Summary

Summarize what you have learned from Revelation 6.

Most evangelical Christians view the sixth seal as the beginning of the tribulation and the rapture must precede it because verse 17 indicates that the day of wrath has come. However this theory doesn't sufficiently account for the previous five seals.

This chapter looks more like a preview of coming attractions. At this point it appears that the overall view is a time of peace, but under a dictator. Following the peace will be a time of war, followed by economic disaster and then famine and disease. At this time, Christians will be persecuted more than any other time in history. The last scene is when the Lord brings His wrath upon the world and unbelievers. From here on out we will be getting more details of the events but may have to come back and revise this summary.

The one overwhelming fact of this chapter remains God's sovereignty and control of all events. It doesn't matter what kind of trials or troubles we are facing, we have to acknowledge that our Lord is in control. Are you facing illness, economic or natural disaster, enemies, war, demons, or anything else in creation? Does it seem like there is no way out? Remember that Jesus is our God and He is in control. We may join the martyrs in heaven sooner than we thought or even want to, but His timing is perfect. This is to bring us peace regardless of our situation!

Lesson 6 – Revelation 7:1-17

Revelation 7:1-8

Then I saw four angels standing at the four corners of the earth, holding back the four winds so they did not blow on the earth or the sea, or even on any tree. And I saw another angel coming up from the east, carrying the seal of the living God. And he shouted to those four angels, who had been given power to harm land and sea, "Wait! Don't harm the land or the sea or the trees until we have placed the seal of God on the foreheads of his servants." And I heard how many were marked with the seal of God—144,000 were sealed from all the tribes of Israel: from Judah – 12,000; from Reuben – 12,000; from Gad – 12,000; from Asher – 12,000; from Naphtali – 12,000; from Manasseh – 12,000; from Simeon – 12,000; from Levi – 12,000; from Issachar – 12,000; from Zebulun – 12,000; from Joseph – 12,000; from Benjamin – 12,000 (NLT)

In this chapter, it appears that we go back to the start of the tribulation, or maybe just before it. We then take another view of what will happen during the last times. Chapter six showed a quick view of the earth and unbelievers. This chapter is going to tell that even during that time, the Lord will have His servants spread the Word and that many will come to a saving knowledge of the Lord.

Four Corners, Winds and Angels

> What do the four corners of the earth represent?

It may seem obvious, but it must be emphasized that the four corners of the earth are used to make sure we know that what is about to happen will encompass the whole earth. In Ezekiel 7:1-4, the Lord spoke of disaster coming on the four corners of the land. He wanted to make sure that the nation of Israel knew that His judgment was coming against them and all parts of the nation would be affected. This chapter in Ezekiel is like the event in the end times. This is what I call Ezekiel's "doom chapter." It is filled with nothing but the predictions of the horror that will come upon the nation and the inability of anyone to escape. When the Lord said it would come upon the four corners of the land, it set the stage for the continued descriptions of the complete destruction that followed.

> Can we interpret the four winds as being either symbolic or literal?
>
> If symbolic, what do they represent? How does this affect us?

> If literal, what does this imply? What should be our response?

> And I will bring upon Elam the four winds from the four quarters of heaven; and I will scatter them to all those winds, and there shall be no nation to which those driven out of Elam shall not come. I will terrify Elam before their enemies, and before those who seek their life; I will bring evil upon them, my fierce anger, says the LORD. I will send the sword after them, until I have consumed them. (Jer 49:36-37 RSV)

In Jeremiah, the four winds represent every part of the earth and the four quarters of the heavens represent every part of heaven. It isn't as if we could go to some place and see where the winds start or see the angels holding back the wind. Rather, we again see the all-encompassing aspect of the events. The four winds in Jeremiah are destructive winds as are those in Revelation. However, in Jeremiah, it isn't the wind that is doing the destruction, but the foes and enemies of Elam. This clearly identifies these winds as symbolic.

> Daniel said, "I was looking in my vision by night, and behold, the four winds of heaven were stirring up the great sea. And four great beasts were coming up from the sea, different from one another." (Dan 7:2-3 NASB)

> These great beasts, which are four in number, are four kings who will arise from the earth. (Dan 7:17 NASB)

Wind seems to be random to us, but the Lord is the One in control of the wind. He uses this symbolism in Daniel several times in the Bible to show that all history turns out as He directs. This passage and the following verses show the correlation between the peoples of the earth and the sea. Envision the sea as the unorganized mass of humanity. Then God works to bring forth four nations.

When we see rulers changing in nation after nation only to bring about governments that are more opposed to Christianity or any religion, we can become anxious. We need to remember God's sovereignty. Even though we see from the following Scriptures that Satan is ruler of the earth and that the nations belong to him, it is still our sovereign Lord who guides and directs history.

> Again, the devil took him to a very high mountain and showed him all the kingdoms of the world and their glory. And he said to him, "All these I will give you, if you will fall down and worship me." (Matt 4:8-9 ESV)

> ... following the prince of the power of the air, the spirit that is now at work in the sons of disobedience ... (Eph 2:2b ESV)

If the land and the sea in Revelation are referring to the nations of the earth, then the winds should be interpreted as symbolic. Even if the land and sea doesn't represent the nations of the earth, the winds could be symbolic of God's wrath.

As we look into Revelation further, we can see that many disasters come from various directions harming the land, sea, and the vegetation on the earth. This brings up the possibility that these winds are not symbolic because the harm is going to come upon trees as well as land and sea. These are all things that can be severely affected by high winds. We could very well expect higher winds during the end times. The Lord may do this through natural means such as changing weather patterns (El Nino or La Nina).

If you look though history, the earth is continually becoming more arid in many places. The Sahara Desert is continually advancing. In many nations, people have cut trees for fuel (and other reasons) and the growth is not replaced. The result could be like the nation of Israel today. A lot of Israel would be a desert if it weren't for irrigation that makes it productive. In the times of David and before, the Lord called it a land flowing with milk and honey. It produced without irrigation and had large forestlands. Some of this can be blamed on our own misuse of the environment. It could simply be God's judgment upon sinful nations – very much like the drought and famine He brought upon Israel during the time of King Ahab. There are many disasters that could occur to the earth and people like to theorize about how it may occur, however this one is obviously declared to be in the power of the Lord.

We shouldn't become overly concerned with the direction that the earth is taking. We know it won't be here forever and that God will change it the way He wants to bring about these disasters. However, we certainly shouldn't be poor stewards of this planet either. We should do what we can to keep it looking good and functioning correctly – not poisoning it. That's one of our responsibilities God established after creation (Gen 2:15).

One way or another, symbolic or literal, the angels are currently holding back the winds and the implication is that they are about to let them go. The call from the angel coming from the east clarifies that the other four angels have power to harm, but haven't done it yet. It will not happen until the Lord gives His approval.

Fifth Angel

> What are two missions of this angel coming from the east?

> For then there will be great distress, unequaled from the beginning of the world until now — and never to be equaled again. If those days had not been cut short, no one would survive, but for the sake of the elect those days will be shortened. (Matt 24:21-22 NIV®)

Unless the days of disaster are cut short, no one will survive. The fifth angel has two missions. His first is to instruct the other four to hold the disaster. In this case he is doing it so that a special group of people may come to know the Lord. We aren't just talking physical survival, but eternal life.

His second mission is to bring the seal of the Living God. He is bringing the seal and in doing so, he is a participant in putting the seal on these people's forehead to mark them as God's chosen servants. Some say that because the rapture has already occurred there is no one to witness to these people; therefore, an angel must do it. But I ask, what about the Bible, books, tapes, and videos? Won't they be available to witness? Again, speculation can bring about any number of answers and theories.

> Who does God primarily use to bring people to salvation? How might angels participate in this?

While the Lord has left the mission of evangelism up to us (Matt 28:18-20), it is evident that angels have a part in this ministry as well. The angel says to wait until we put the seal on their foreheads. Just as this angel has a part in bringing people to Christ, we also have different jobs in bringing people to Christ. We won't know until we are in heaven how some of the things we have done in life have helped others come to Jesus. It is apparent that the Lord is using this angel to ensure that there will be enough time given so that all these people will come to Him. I wonder how many times unbelievers are spared from death by angels only because the Lord wants them to have another chance to repent from their sins and accept Jesus as their Lord and Savior.

Sealed Saints

> What is the seal that is placed on the foreheads of these believers?

I'm sorry to say that the cross on the forehead of believers that only other believers could see, which was purported to be this seal in the *Left Behind* series of books, is fantasy. These books are novels. Despite the author's claims to adhere to biblical accuracy, they are fiction and should not be used to interpret Scripture.

> Do not work for the food which perishes, but for the food which endures to eternal life, which the Son of Man will give to you, for on Him the Father, God, has set His seal. (John 6:27 NASU)

> If to others I am not an apostle, at least I am to you; for you are the seal of my apostleship in the Lord. (1 Cor 9:2 NASU)

The Father has placed His seal of approval upon Jesus. It was not a physical mark that could be seen, but it was demonstrated in the many miracles that Jesus performed. The seal of Paul's apostleship wasn't a physical mark either, but the numbers of people that came to Christ when he spread the Gospel.

> Now He who establishes us with you in Christ and has anointed us is God, who also has sealed us and given us the Spirit in our hearts as a guarantee. (2 Cor 1:21-22 NKJV)

> In Him you also trusted, after you heard the word of truth, the Gospel of your salvation; in whom also, having believed, you were sealed with the Holy Spirit of

promise, who is the guarantee of our inheritance until the redemption of the purchased possession, to the praise of His glory. (Eph 1:13-14 NKJV)

What does this seal mean to current believers?

God has done the work to make us stand firm in salvation. He is the One who makes us continue in Christ and it is because of His seal of ownership, His Holy Spirit, who guarantees it. We may die but He is forever and we will always be in Him. A partnership or sole proprietorship does not have a seal, but a corporation does. A corporation legally lives even if some of the owners die. A partnership is automatically dissolved when a partner dies. The Lord has a seal, a living seal, the Holy Spirit. Both the Lord and the seal live forever guaranteeing the permanence of our relationship with Him.

How does Ezekiel 9:3-6 prefigure this event in the book of Revelation?

Then the glory of the God of Israel rose up from between the cherubim, where it had rested, and moved to the entrance of the Temple. And the Lord called to the man dressed in linen who was carrying the writer's case. He said to him, "Walk through the streets of Jerusalem and put a mark on the foreheads of all who weep and sigh because of the detestable sins being committed in their city."

Then I heard the Lord say to the other men, "Follow him through the city and kill everyone whose forehead is not marked. Show no mercy; have no pity! Kill them all— old and young, girls and women and little children. But do not touch anyone with the mark. Begin right here at the Temple." So they began by killing the seventy leaders. (Ezek 9:3-6 NLT)

This occurred in a vision that was given to Ezekiel before the Lord destroyed Jerusalem because of its wickedness. When the actual battle came, people didn't have marks on their foreheads and there weren't six people doing the killing as the previous verses indicate. The man clothed in linen (priestly garb) is said to represent Christ in His priestly role as mediator. He is marking those upon whom He is having mercy to spare them from the calamity that is about to overtake Jerusalem. If we can see Christ in this vision, then the people are not limited to those in Jerusalem, but represent everyone down through the ages who have received God's mercy and salvation. The mark in this case would not be something visible on our foreheads, but as we have seen above, the Holy Spirit in our hearts and the fruit that He bears in our lives.

144,000 Jews

> Is this number being saved literal or symbolic? Are they really Jews or is this symbolic? Explain your reasoning.

Unless we can come up with something better, it appears that many people are about to be saved. They are not saved to start with because the angel had to stop the show for a while. If we take it literally, then there is a specific number of Jews who will be saved and as we will see later, for a very specific purpose. Many people argue that it cannot be taken literally because all of the genealogies have been lost. No one knows who is truly from which tribe anymore. The answer is just as obvious. The angels have direct access to God's records, so they know. Observe what the Lord has decreed.

> "I will strengthen the house of Judah, and I will save the house of Joseph. I will bring them back because I have compassion on them, and they shall be as though I had not rejected them; for I am the Lord their God and I will answer them. Then E'phraim shall become like a mighty warrior, and their hearts shall be glad as with wine. Their children shall see it and rejoice, their hearts shall exult in the Lord.

> "I will signal for them and gather them in, for I have redeemed them, and they shall be as many as of old. Though I scattered them among the nations, yet in far countries they shall remember me, and with their children they shall live and return. I will bring them home from the land of Egypt, and gather them from Assyria; and I will bring them to the land of Gilead and to Lebanon, till there is no room for them. They shall pass through the sea of Egypt, and the waves of the sea shall be smitten, and all the depths of the Nile dried up. The pride of Assyria shall be laid low, and the scepter of Egypt shall depart. I will make them strong in the Lord and they shall glory in his name," says the Lord. (Zech 10:6-12 RSV)

The Lord made this promise after the Jews (mainly from the tribe of Judah, Benjamin, and Levi) had already returned to Judah, so it can't be attributed to the restoration of Israel after the Babylonian captivity. It hasn't happened yet and is still waiting for its fulfillment. It will occur because He has compassion on them. Little verses like this always crop up when we think that God might respond to our pleas. He reminds us that it is because it is what He wants to do, because of His nature. It also shows that His restoration is perfect.

> Why or why not is the current state of Israel a fulfillment of this promise in Zechariah? How can this be applied to Christians?

Many people think that the current restoration of Israel is the fulfillment of this promise because Jews are returning from all over the world. This may be the start of it, but it hasn't been completed because the country is a secular state and hasn't returned to the Lord. When this is fulfilled, it will be as though He had never rejected them. (The same applies to us when we are saved – it is as if we had never been separated from Him.) This is the reason why the Jewish people to this day have been able to keep their identity. It is so that the Lord will have someone to bring back. It is also a good reminder to us. When we are among non-Christians, we should also remember Him and keep our identity. The Lord says He will signal them and bring them back. He doesn't need anyone to identify them, He knows who they are and He also knows who we are. He never forgets who His children are. The last verse needs to be emphasized, that they will walk in His name. Since the Messiah has already come once, the only way to walk in the name of the Lord is to walk in the name of Jesus. This obviously hasn't happened in Israel – yet!

Some suggest that the 144,000 should be taken symbolically and is representative of all believers. This is because there are twelve (apostles) times twelve (tribes) to form 144 and represent all Jewish and Gentile Christians. Ten is a number of completeness. Three is the number of God and 1,000 is ten to the third power indicating God's completion of salvation before His wrath is completed. All the math sounds neat, but it seems to me more man's desire to explain the numbers. As far as I've seen, this numerology doesn't have any Scriptural backing. On the surface, it would more likely to be symbolic of all Jews coming to Christ at the end time. Paul affirms that there will be a time when Israel will be saved.

> For I do not want you, brethren, to be uninformed of this mystery, lest you be wise in your own estimation, that a partial hardening has happened to Israel until the fulness of the Gentiles has come in; and thus all Israel will be saved; just as it is written, "The Deliverer will come from Zion, He will remove ungodliness from Jacob. And this is My covenant with them, When I take away their sins." (Rom 11:25-27 NASB)

What might be a problem with using this list of 144,000 Jews as representative of all Jews?

Dan is missing from the list of tribes in Revelation. The half tribe of Manasseh is included instead. (The descendants of Joseph were split into two tribes, Manasseh and Ephraim, his two oldest sons.) If we were to include the half tribes, then Ephraim is also left out, but Joseph is included. Hal Lindsey states that many scholars suggest that the reason for the substitutions is that the Antichrist will come from the tribe of Dan based on the following verse.[25]

> Dan shall be a serpent in the way, a viper by the path, that bites the horse's heels so that his rider falls backward. (Gen 49:17 ESV)

---

[25] Hal Lindsey, *There's a New World Coming*, (Santa Ana: Vision House, 1973), 121.

This seems like a stretch to me. It's also contradictory because Lindsey later identifies the Antichrist as Roman.[26] Scholars also think that Ephraim is left out because they led the way in splitting the kingdom of Israel in two. Lindsey also says that these two tribes were the first to lead Israel into idolatry. Some problems with these views are that Solomon revived the mess of idolatry with his many wives. Jeroboam, from the tribe of Ephraim, was the leader of the revolt against King Solomon's son; however, it was at the Lord's decree and as a result of Solomon's unfaithfulness near the end of his life. (See 1 Kings 11 and 12.) To use these things as a basis for tossing these two tribes out of the special Jews for Jesus task force is pure speculation as far as I'm concerned. Besides, Zechariah 10:7 refers to the Ephraimites and their return to Israel. If there is a reason for leaving out the names of these two tribes, it is well beyond me.

Read Revelation 14:1-5. What things in this passage about the 144,000 point to addressing them as literal or symbolic?

Then I looked, and there before me was the Lamb, standing on Mount Zion, and with him 144,000 who had his name and his Father's name written on their foreheads. And I heard a sound from heaven like the roar of rushing waters and like a loud peal of thunder. The sound I heard was like that of harpists playing their harps. And they sang a new song before the throne and before the four living creatures and the elders. No one could learn the song except the 144,000 who had been redeemed from the earth. These are those who did not defile themselves with women, for they kept themselves pure. They follow the Lamb wherever he goes. They were purchased from among men and offered as firstfruits to God and the Lamb. No lie was found in their mouths; they are blameless. (Rev 14:1-5 NIV®)

Arguments for these people being symbolic of all Jews or all believers can be made because they are going to learn a song that others can't learn. This fits a symbolic interpretation if those who can't learn it are people who reject Christ. Something that makes it hard to take this literally is that it appears that they are all single men and pure, not having had any sexual relationships with a woman.

What is it that makes a person defiled?

And He was saying, "That which proceeds out of the man, that is what defiles the man. For from within, out of the heart of men, proceed the evil thoughts, fornications, thefts, murders, adulteries, deeds of coveting and wickedness, as well as deceit, sensuality, envy, slander, pride and foolishness. All these evil things proceed from within and defile the man." (Mark 7:20-23 NASU)

---

[26] Ibid., 184.

But I say to you that everyone who looks at a woman with lust for her has already committed adultery with her in his heart. (Matt 5:28 NASU)

Based on Jesus' words, a person can be married and be undefiled by a woman. However, if they have ever had any immoral relationship with a woman, even in their mind, then they have been defiled because of what is in them. This makes it pretty tough to find 144,000 men anywhere in the world who could fit this picture before they become Christians. Also, they haven't ever lied. Wow! That makes it even tougher. We shouldn't be looking then for 144,000 single Jewish men who have kept themselves pure. Chapter 14 comes before Jesus' return to the earth, yet it says that He is standing on Mount Zion with these 144,000 and that they follow the Lamb wherever He goes. This has to be symbolic of people who are redeemed.

> Has your initial answer changed? Are then, the 144,000 symbolic of all people or only symbolic of Jews?

Even by a process of elimination, it is hard to say that these people are either symbolic of all Jews or a literal number of Jews. Again, with God, it would be possible for them to be a literal group. However, they could be symbolic of all men because they are offered as first fruits of those purchased from among men (all people), meaning that they are a symbol of all who are purchased by Jesus and His sacrifice. This fits with what we have been taught elsewhere in Scripture. All who have faith in Jesus are sons of Abraham – not just Jews.

Therefore, be sure that it is those who are of faith who are sons of Abraham. (Gal 3:7 NASU)

> If they represent all believers, then what promise can we claim for our own lives?

If we see that all believers are represented by the 144,000, then the beauty of this is that in the eyes of God, we are considered pure, undefiled, and not liars once we have come to know Him.

This includes you who were once far away from God. You were his enemies, separated from him by your evil thoughts and actions. Yet now he has reconciled you to himself through the death of Christ in his physical body. As a result, he has brought you into his own presence, and you are holy and blameless as you stand before him without a single fault. (Col 1:21-22 NLT)

For you died to this life, and your real life is hidden with Christ in God. And when Christ, who is your life, is revealed to the whole world, you will share in all his glory. (Col 3:3-4 NLT)

Doesn't this sound a lot like the 144,000 who are appearing with Jesus, blameless and appearing with Him Glory?

> After concluding that the 144,000 are symbolic, how might this change your conclusion about the winds and why?

At the beginning of the chapter, I waffled between interpreting the four winds as symbolic or literal without really landing on the side of either. I think that these elements need to be interpreted in context with the 144,000. The seal on their foreheads have been shown to be symbolic also. There isn't a break in the context to justify taking some things as literal and others as symbolic. In fact, the 144,000 are specifically tied to the winds because they must be sealed before the winds are released. Based on this, I would expect the destructive winds to be symbolic also.

> When do these people come to Christ? Do they all come before the rapture or do some come after?

They were commanded not to harm the grass of the earth, or any green thing, or any tree, but only those men who do not have the seal of God on their foreheads. (Rev 9:4 NKJV)

Chapter 8 of Revelation could be the beginning of God's wrath upon the earth. Since people are still being saved in chapter 9, it indicates that the 144,000 represent those who come to faith in Christ before and during the tribulation. The latter are present on the earth during some of the worst tribulation but are spared from suffering God's wrath. I still can't say for certain that this sealing occurs before or after the rapture of the Church. When the 144,000 appear on Mount Zion it would have to be in the spiritual realm since Jesus doesn't return physically until later. That could indicate that they will be raptured later, will be martyred, or it is all believers who are in Christ (Col 3:3-4). I guess we'll just have to stay tuned for more details.

> What has stood out to you in this part of the lesson?

Some things stand out in my mind:

- God is in control.
- God seals us forever, establishing our salvation.

- Our lives are hidden in Christ and our sinful lives are not seen. We are as if we had been pure from birth.

These things bring glory to our Lord and give us hope. It frees us from the guilt of the past and fear of the future. May you bask in these truths as you follow the Lamb.

Revelation 7:9-17

After this I looked, and behold, a great multitude which no man could number, from every nation, from all tribes and peoples and tongues, standing before the throne and before the Lamb, clothed in white robes, with palm branches in their hands, and crying out with a loud voice, "Salvation belongs to our God who sits upon the throne, and to the Lamb!" And all the angels stood round the throne and round the elders and the four living creatures, and they fell on their faces before the throne and worshiped God, saying, "Amen! Blessing and glory and wisdom and thanksgiving and honor and power and might be to our God for ever and ever! Amen."

Then one of the elders addressed me, saying, "Who are these, clothed in white robes, and whence have they come?" I said to him, "Sir, you know." And he said to me, "These are they who have come out of the great tribulation; they have washed their robes and made them white in the blood of the Lamb.

"Therefore are they before the throne of God, and serve him day and night within his temple; and he who sits upon the throne will shelter them with his presence. They shall hunger no more, neither thirst any more; the sun shall not strike them, nor any scorching heat. For the Lamb in the midst of the throne will be their shepherd, and he will guide them to springs of living water; and God will wipe away every tear from their eyes." (RSV)

Great Multitude

How do these verses and others dispel the claims of cults that it will only be a specific few or their members who will be saved, such as 144,000?

How do we know that even with multitudes not everyone will be saved?

Now when Jesus heard this, He marveled, and said to those who were following, "Truly I say to you, I have not found such great faith with anyone in Israel. And I say to you, that many shall come from east and west, and recline at the table with Abraham, and Isaac, and Jacob, in the kingdom of heaven; but the sons of the kingdom shall be cast out into the outer darkness; in that place there shall be weeping and gnashing of teeth." (Matt 8:10-12 NASB)

Jesus was obviously pleased with the faith exhibited by the Roman centurion. He used his faith as a point to start teaching them. Up to this time the Jews thought that they were the only ones who would be saved despite verses given to us as early as the following two.

> All the ends of the earth shall remember and turn to the LORD, and all the families of the nations shall worship before you. For kingship belongs to the LORD, and he rules over the nations. (Ps 22:27-28 ESV)

These promise a blessing and redemption to all nations. The only multitudes that the Jews expected to see in heaven were Jewish. This is also the claim of many cults today. On one hand, cults claim that only membership in their select group will guarantee salvation while on the other hand, other religions make the claim that any system of belief will provide salvation. Both are wrong as Jesus points out. He clearly indicates that it is by faith that people will be saved, but it isn't by misplaced faith, otherwise He wouldn't have warned the Jews of their impending eternal disaster.

> With so many in heaven, how do we know we won't be distant from Jesus?

> Such large crowds gathered around him that he got into a boat and sat in it, while all the people stood on the shore. (Matt 13:2 NIV®)

> For through him we both have access to the Father by one Spirit. (Eph 2:18 NIV®)

There were so many in the crowds that followed Jesus while He was on earth that He had to get into a boat to give a little distance between Him and them. When He was here physically, He couldn't minister to all their needs. The multitudes in heaven show us that there will be room for everyone and all our needs will be met. Even now, He has sent His Holy Spirit to us and we became part of Him (Col 3:3) so that there is no physical restriction hampering us from coming to Him. Ephesians 3:12 also tells us we can approach God with freedom and confidence. Hebrews 4:16, 10:19-20 also tell how we may approach God. It is only because of the blood of Jesus that we are able to do so. That blood has cleansed us from all sin so we can be in His very presence. Where the Father is, there is Jesus also. He will never be far away.

> We see a multitude in heaven, but on earth, is it safe to follow the multitudes? Will the majority of people be saved?

> Therefore when the people saw the sign which He had performed, they said, "This is truly the Prophet who is to come into the world." So Jesus, perceiving that they were

intending to come and take Him by force to make Him king, withdrew again to the mountain by Himself alone. (John 6:14-15 NASU)

The multitudes that came to Jesus to be fed and healed were looking for a king to save them, but Jesus didn't come to do that. His ministry was to prove to us that He is God by all that He said and did so that we would have faith in Him. Once He established His identity, He died for our sins and was raised giving the ultimate proof of His divinity. It is interesting to see that in heaven the physical care that He gives is precisely what the people wanted back then.

The problem is that they were unwilling to subject their spiritual life to Him. This is the reason that only a few will be saved. Jesus' classical answer that has been quoted often explains it clearly.

Then said one unto him, Lord, are there few that be saved? And he said unto them, Strive to enter in at the strait gate: for many, I say unto you, will seek to enter in, and shall not be able. (Luke 13:23)

Then shall ye begin to say, We have eaten and drunk in thy presence, and thou hast taught in our streets. But he shall say, I tell you, I know you not whence ye are; depart from me, all ye workers of iniquity. (Luke 13:26-27)

In God's perspective, only a few will be saved. In our eyes it will be a great multitude that we can't count. Jesus makes it clear that there will be many who try to get into heaven by their own devices. However, anything other than cleansing our robes in the blood of the Lamb is not enough. The joys of heaven and salvation are not automatic to anyone, especially those who by their deeds (especially their religious activities) hope to make it in. It isn't good enough to know about Jesus; the real criteria will be whether or not we know Him personally. If we know Him personally, He will know us and say, "Welcome, friend." To the chagrin of Jews of Jesus' day, many will make it, but not those that they expected. They will come from everywhere. There was a time in the United States, especially in the 50's, when many of the denominational churches felt the same. They knew it wasn't right but would come as close as possible to say that their denomination was right and all others were wrong. They wouldn't always say another denomination would not get into heaven but they certainly thought that they wouldn't be as close to Jesus. By the early 70's there were only remnants of this thinking. Now, the balance has swung past center so that most denominations are now saying anyone in any religion will get in. How contrary to His clear teaching that only a few will be saved.

Following the crowd is dangerous. Multitudes are fickle. See how they acted on Palm Sunday.

The next day a great multitude that had come to the feast, when they heard that Jesus was coming to Jerusalem, 13 took branches of palm trees and went out to meet Him, and cried out: "Hosanna! 'Blessed is He who comes in the name of the Lord!' The King of Israel!" NKJV (John 12:12-13)

On Palm Sunday, the people may have had Psalm 118 in mind as they waved their palm branches.

> Please, LORD, please save us. Please, LORD, please give us success. Bless the one who comes in the name of the LORD. We bless you from the house of the LORD. (Ps 118:25-26 NLT).

The author of the Psalm was looking forward to the day of salvation. Hosanna means to save now. The crowd on Palm Sunday thought salvation had arrived physically but didn't understand that it was about to be provided for their souls, not their bodies. Less than a week later, the same crowd was yelling to have Jesus crucified. They had no concept of Jesus' sacrifice but prophetically uttered these words:

> And all the people answered, "His blood be on us and on our children!" (Matt 27:25 RSV)

Ironically, they didn't understand that it is precisely because of the blood of Jesus shed for them and their children that they could be saved and that we are saved. The multitude in heaven has realized both the physical and spiritual salvation. The song they sing is similar to the shouts of joy on Palm Sunday and Psalm 118-25-26.

How do the angels, elders, and four living creatures respond to the multitude? How should we respond?

I really like Revelation 7:11-12. As the multitude thanks God for His salvation, the angels, elders, and four living creatures worship God for saving the multitude. When we think of God's salvation and the multitude that will include us, we should worship and have great joy. This scene in heaven is the fulfillment of what Jesus said.

> I say unto you, that likewise joy shall be in heaven over one sinner that repenteth, more than over ninety and nine just persons, which need no repentance. (Luke 15:7)

What is the significance that the multitude has robes made white in the blood of the Lamb?

We often mention what the blood of Jesus does for us. One thing that His blood does is to make us righteous. The white clothes that the multitude has are a symbol of this righteousness and the purity that can only be achieved by His blood that has been shed for us. The symbol of dipping robes into red blood and coming out white is lost on the world. They can't understand it, yet to us who have been cleansed by the blood of Jesus from all our sins and have our consciences cleansed from guilt, it provides an automatic recognition of the promises Jesus has given us.

> What are some of the other promises that are given to those who depend upon Jesus for their righteousness?

These believers have died before the end of the tribulation, yet the description of the care and position they receive before the throne affirms that believers who die will go to be with the Lord, not some other place of waiting or unconsciousness. Even more striking though, is the change of tense in verse 15. They are before the throne to serve Him day and night, but God will spread His tent over them. In the future they will never hunger.

> That makes sense, but why is the future tense kept in verse 17 to say that He will be their Shepherd?

I think that this has to do with the 1,000-year reign of Jesus that will follow the tribulation and also what will occur after the judgment. He will lead us into the New Jerusalem where the spring of living water flows. As we see those who have been cast into the burning lake of fire are missing, then is when He will wipe away our tears.

> And if children, then heirs; heirs of God, and joint-heirs with Christ; if so be that we suffer with him, that we may be also glorified together. (Rom 8:17)

First and foremost, we will be before His throne. We will also be co-heirs with Christ and we will be there reigning with Him. This is conditional on suffering with Him. Just as these who came out of the tribulation have suffered, we too, must be prepared to give up our lives to Him.

> And coming to Him as to a living stone, rejected by men, but choice and precious in the sight of God, you also, as living stones, are being built up as a spiritual house for a holy priesthood, to offer up spiritual sacrifices acceptable to God through Jesus Christ. (1 Peter 2:4-5 NASB)

We will also be serving Him. We are called to offer spiritual sacrifices, which is precisely what we do when we offer our lives to Him. As a result, in heaven we will continue to serve Him in some capacity that we don't really understand now. I really wish that there were more details on how we will do this. When we reign with Jesus during the 1,000-year reign we will all be assigned some duties. Also, there is the possibility that we are the armies in Revelation 19:14.

> Revelation 7:15 says that we will serve Him in His temple. Revelation 21:22 says there will be no temple because the temple is God and the Lamb. How then will we be able to serve in the temple?

I do not ask for these only, but also for those who will believe in me through their word, that they may all be one, just as you, Father, are in me, and I in you, that they also may be in us, so that the world may believe that you have sent me. (John 17:20-21 ESV)

If we are in Him and He is the temple, then we are also in the temple – even now! If this is true, then what ever we do, day and night, is in the temple. How much more then, should we be aware of whether or not our actions glorify the Lord?

In Revelation 7:15, a more literal translation of would say that He who sits on the throne will spread his tent over them.

> What promises does spreading His tent over the multitude give us?

"Who are you?" he asked. "I am your servant Ruth," she said. "Spread the corner of your garment over me, since you are a kinsman-redeemer." (Ruth 3:9 NIV®)

Ruth asked Boaz to spread the corner of his garment over her as a symbol that she was willing to come under his protection. When she did this, she was willing to hold up her end of the agreement, which was to become his wife.

"Then I passed by you and saw you, and behold, you were at the time for love; so I spread My skirt over you and covered your nakedness. I also swore to you and entered into a covenant with you so that you became Mine," declares the Lord God. (Ezek 16:8 NASU)

The Lord spread His garment over a young lady who was the symbol of Jerusalem. This custom was part of the betrothal ceremony. It was the symbol of promised protection. In Revelation 7:15 the Lord spreads His tent over the multitude showing that we are receiving His protection. In addition to that, we are betrothed to the Lord. This is a love relationship that goes well beyond any "if this then that" type of contractual agreements. Near the end of the book we will see the culmination of the betrothal period at the wedding supper of the Lamb.

> How does this preview of the wedding supper of the Lamb help us face death?

On this mountain the LORD Almighty will prepare a feast of rich food for all peoples, a banquet of aged wine — the best of meats and the finest of wines. On this mountain he will destroy the shroud that enfolds all peoples, the sheet that covers all nations; he will swallow up death forever. The Sovereign LORD will wipe away the tears from all faces; he will remove the disgrace of his people from all the earth. The LORD has spoken. In that day they will say, "Surely this is our God; we trusted in him, and he saved us. This is the LORD, we trusted in him; let us rejoice and be glad in his salvation." (Isa 25:6-9 NIV®)

The feast of the wedding supper will be beyond all imagination. However, it is not the central attraction. The feast will be consumed and it precedes the announcement that, in addition to His promise of taking care of those of us who have trusted in Him, the shroud of death will also be swallowed up for all people. Right now, we know that death holds no power over us because we have the promise of eternal life as well as a physical resurrection sometime in the future. These verses in Isaiah speak of a future when death will no longer have any power because there won't be any more death. That is the reality of what we only hope for at this time. We are looking forward to this time when all will know the presence of the Lord.

Yea, though I walk through the valley of the shadow of death, I will fear no evil: for thou art with me; thy rod and thy staff they comfort me. (Ps 23:4)

This verse has been quoted at many funerals. It brings us back from the hope of the future to the here and now. We are still living in a world that knows death. Every living soul knows that there will be a time to die and it is like walking through a deep dark valley. However, it is a valley that we need not fear because we know that Jesus has already conquered death and is raised. When we see the multitude in heaven, we know that those of us who know Jesus will be standing among them.

Surely goodness and mercy shall follow me all the days of my life: and I will dwell in the house of the LORD for ever. (Ps 23:6)

Until that time comes, we know that His goodness and love will be with us regardless of the circumstances. This gives us the power to live and continue through the valley until we reach the end. We don't just plod through either; we march through triumphantly. We can do this because we know that while we will be dwelling in His temple in heaven, He is now dwelling in His temple and we are His temple.

Do you not know that you are the temple of God and that the Spirit of God dwells in you? (1 Cor 3:16 NKJV)

How do we participate in the wedding supper of the Lamb even before it occurs?

So he sent other servants to tell them, "The feast has been prepared. The bulls and fattened cattle have been killed, and everything is ready. Come to the banquet!" (Matt 22:4 NLT)

And he said to his servants, "The wedding feast is ready, and the guests I invited aren't worthy of the honor. Now go out to the street corners and invite everyone you see." (Matt 22:8-9 NLT)

The picture of heaven that Jesus was drawing in this parable portrays the wedding supper of the Lamb. His servants, the prophets, had told Israel about the great feast which the Lord has prepared. But they rejected it. Because they rejected it, the invitation falls to us, the Gentiles, the multitudes that were not looking for God. We have also become the servants who go out to persuade others to come into the feast.

Jesus said to them, "I am the bread of life; he who comes to me shall not hunger, and he who believes in me shall never thirst." (John 6:35 RSV)

I am the living bread which came down from heaven; if any one eats of this bread, he will live for ever; and the bread which I shall give for the life of the world is my flesh. (John 6:51 RSV)

The message about the wedding supper that we deliver is always the same. Even though we have great promises of deliverance, protection, provision, and comfort, it comes only by partaking of the living bread, Jesus.

> Why do we need to recognize Jesus as our Chief Shepherd above our pastors and leaders?

Revelation 7:17 has one thing that shouldn't be overlooked. The Lamb is our Shepherd. There are times when we put too much emphasis on our church leaders to be our shepherds and expect them to be perfect. Sooner or later they will fail in one way or another. It may be something that they do or our expectations are not correct. We will have a problem with them. So, whether it is our problem or theirs, we become disappointed. But if we are looking to Jesus to be our Shepherd, we will never be disappointed because we know that He will never lead us astray. If we become disappointed because of our own misunderstanding of His will, even then, God will wipe every tear of disappointment away.

May you think about standing with this great multitude and joining them saying "Amen! Praise and glory and wisdom and thanks and honor and power and strength be to our God for ever and ever. Amen" (Rev 7:12 NIV®)! May His promises lift your burdens and give you strength to declare this every day!

Lesson 7 – Revelation 8:1-13

Revelation 8:1-5

And when he had opened the seventh seal, there was silence in heaven about the space of half an hour. And I saw the seven angels which stood before God; and to them were given seven trumpets. And another angel came and stood at the altar, having a golden censer; and there was given unto him much incense, that he should offer it with the prayers of all saints upon the golden altar which was before the throne. And the smoke of the incense, which came with the prayers of the saints, ascended up before God out of the angel's hand. And the angel took the censer, and filled it with fire of the altar, and cast it into the earth: and there were voices, and thunderings, and lightnings, and an earthquake. (KJV)

Seventh Seal

> Why is the half hour of silence in heaven significant? How does silence proclaim God's justice?

We have previously witnessed great shouts and songs of praise to God in the previous chapters of the book of Revelation. This silence is stunning in contrast. Can you imagine what was going through John's mind when the Lamb opens the seventh seal and there is nothing? There are no sounds, likely no motion, as all in heaven pause to see what comes next. Since we have read more, we know that this is ushering in the worst calamities ever to come on the earth since the flood. We can see that this silence is unusual because the Jewish custom is to mourn loudly at the announcement of such a disaster.

> Now we know that whatever the Law says, it speaks to those who are under the Law, that every mouth may be closed, and all the world may become accountable to God; (Rom 3:19 NASB)

The inhabitants of the earth are at their worst. The seventh seal appears to announce the final act of God's judgment and every mouth is silenced. The awesomeness of this moment is beyond anything that has ever happened before. When God appeared on Mt. Sinai and almost every other place, there was thunder and lightning (Ex 19:16). Instead of thunder and lightning, there is silence. It is this silent introduction to what is called the trumpet judgments that could be when the wrath of God comes.

If Christians are to be spared the wrath of God according to 1 Thessalonians 5:8, then the multitude in Chapter 7 who have come out of the great tribulation must be the raputured Church.

> "I will stretch out my hand against Judah and against all the inhabitants of Jerusalem; and I will cut off from this place the remnant of Baal and the name of the idolatrous

priests along with the priests, those who bow down on the roofs to the host of the heavens, those who bow down and swear to the LORD and yet swear by Milcom, those who have turned back from following the LORD, who do not seek the LORD or inquire of him." Be silent before the Lord God! For the day of the LORD is near; the LORD has prepared a sacrifice and consecrated his guests. And on the day of the LORD's sacrifice—"I will punish the officials and the king's sons and all who array themselves in foreign attire." (Zeph 1:4-8 ESV)

> Considering today's world, how is God's judgment on Judah like the one that will come in Revelation?

This tells of another time when the people were told to be silent before the Lord. It was a time of trouble and judgment to be brought upon Judah. Notice the indictment that the Lord brought against Judah. They were worshiping anything and everything except the Lord. Baal was the son of El, the father of the gods and the head of the Canaanite pantheon. He is also designated as "the son of Dagon" They were worshiping a god that was the son of a god yet the father of gods.[27] Does this sound familiar? The same thing is happening today as many in cults and even in mainline denominations distort Jesus' identity so that they no longer worship Jesus as the true Son of God. Other people were worshiping things of nature in the same way that much of the world does today. The most insidious correlation between Judah and the world of today is their worship of Molech (Milcom), a Semitic deity honored by the fiery sacrifice of children. Palestinian excavations have uncovered evidences of infant skeletons in burial places around heathen shrines.[28] We don't call him Molech today as he goes by many names such as "women's rights," "pro-choice", "embryonic research" and others.

Do you realize that some scientists are using human embryos for various research projects?[29] Each of these embryos has the full potential to become a living, breathing person. They never have a chance. Most abortions are done simply because the baby threatens the parent's lifestyle in one way or another.[30] The scientists are doing it in the name of bettering the human condition. We don't burn these children; we tear them apart in their mother's womb before they are born or toss them out from a Petri dish. Molech's real name is selfishness, that ugly monster within each of us that puts our own desire (rights) above the rights and needs of others. Society normally

---

[27] Merrill Frederick Unger, *The New Unger's Bible Dictionary*, s.v. "Gods, False," (Chicago: Moody, 1988), Biblesoft.

[28] Ibid.

[29] Erik Stokstad, "U.k. Researcher Details Proposal for Crispr Editing of Human Embryos | Science | Aaas," Sciencemag.org, January 13, 2016, accessed February 24, 2016, http://www.sciencemag.org/news/2016/01/uk-researcher-details-proposal-crispr-editing-human-embryos. "Niakan's research uses human embryos, created in fertility clinics, that are left over from in vitro fertilization (IVF) attempts and donated for research. After being studied, the embryos are destroyed when they are 7 days old."

[30] Lawrence B. Finer et al., "Reasons U.S. Women Have Abortions: Quantitative and Qualitative Perspectives," *Perspectives on Sexual and Reproductive Health* 37, no. 3 (September 2005): 110-18, accessed February 24, 2016, https://www.guttmacher.org/pubs/journals/3711005.html.

suppresses him with laws, rules, and regulations. The only real cure is to nail them to the cross when we accept Jesus as our Lord and Savior.

> I have been crucified with Christ and I no longer live, but Christ lives in me. The life I live in the body, I live by faith in the Son of God, who loved me and gave himself for me. (Gal 2:20 NIV®)

> The Lord commands all to be silent because He has roused Himself (Zech 2:13). What is one of the reasons He is bringing judgment as described in Zechariah 2:8?

> For thus says the LORD of hosts, "After glory He has sent me against the nations which plunder you, for he who touches you, touches the apple of His eye." (Zech 2:8 NASU)

> "Be silent, all flesh, before the LORD; for He is aroused from His holy habitation." (Zech 2:13 NASU)

The Lord declared to His people that He would protect them and bring destruction on those who have harmed them. Especially those who treat His people unjustly will need to be still before the Lord. The silence in heaven could be a prelude to the silence of the nations, as they won't have any defense to the charges that the Lord will bring against them. As the trumpets are sounded, we can see that God has roused Himself and will deal with all mankind in part based on how we have treated His people, but most importantly how we have related to one particular Jew, His Son.

Zechariah 2:8 says that the Jewish nation is the apple of God's eye. This brings up an interesting point that many commentators have made. Throughout history, nations have been called to bring punishment against the Jews. Assyria, Egypt, and Babylon are a few. In each case they did not do it in humility (see Jer 50) but were arrogant and enjoyed doing it. These nations were then punished. From then to now, no nation that has been anti-Semitic has stood the test of time. It is therefore thought that whoever befriends the 144,000 mentioned in chapter 7 will be spared death and will enter into the millennial kingdom. But the nations and people who persecute them will not be spared. Matthew 25:31-46 (reward or punishment is given according to the way a person has treated Jesus' brothers) is used to support this idea even though the context of these verses indicates that this is a final judgment and the reward is the final reward of eternal blessings, not just for a thousand years. I don't think this is an accurate interpretation, but is worth mentioning.

Seven Angels

> Briefly describe the celestial order of angels, names of angels, and their missions.

For some reason it appears that God has appointed a celestial order of angels. The seven angels that are in Revelation 8:2 are referred to specifically as "the" seven angels who stand before God. They are singled out from all the rest.

> And the angel answering said unto him, I am Gabriel, that stand in the presence of God; and am sent to speak unto thee, and to shew thee these glad tidings. (Luke 1:19)

Gabriel is one of these seven. He is especially privileged because he was assigned the once-in-history task of telling Mary that she would bear the Messiah. He also appeared to Daniel (Dan 8:16) and is possibly the one that appeared to him again in Daniel 10 and spoke of another angel, Michael, one of the chief princes. It could be that Michael is also one that stands before God.

> But the prince of the kingdom of Persia withstood me one and twenty days: but, lo, Michael, one of the chief princes, came to help me; and I remained there with the kings of Persia. (Dan 10:13)

There are also angels who are associated with little children (guardian angels) and always have the ability to see the face of God even though they don't necessarily stand in His presence in the same way the seven stand in His presence but have other missions as well. In my novel, *999 Years After Armageddon, The End of the Millennium*[31], I have the fun of speculating how this and other angelic activities function.

> Take heed that you do not despise one of these little ones, for I say to you that in heaven their angels always see the face of My Father who is in heaven. (Matt 18:10 NKJV)

Then there are some angels that do not stand in His presence. Rather, they come at appointed times to report.

> Now there was a day when the sons of God came to present themselves before the LORD … (Job 1:6)

Cherubim and seraphim are also mentioned many times in the Bible. It isn't always clear whether they are angels or other created celestial beings. Their duties are various as are their descriptions. Cherubim were appointed to guard the way back into the Garden of Eden (Gen 3:24) and images of them were made to be on the lid of the Ark of the Covenant, worked into the curtains of the tabernacle, engraved on the walls of the temple, and two that were to overshadow the place of the Ark in the Holy of

---

[31] For information about availability go to http://www.rayruppert.com/999-years-after-armageddon.html.

Holies. While some of these looked very much like angels, as we understand them, the ones supporting God's throne in Ezekiel 10 are described like the living creatures in Ezekiel 1. They are also similar to the seraphim in Isaiah 6.

These angels that stand before the Lord are each given a trumpet to blow and announce a new phase in God's judgment of the earth.

> For the Lord himself will come down from heaven with a commanding shout, with the voice of the archangel, and with the trumpet call of God. First, the Christians who have died will rise from their graves. (1 Thess 4:16 NLT)

When the Lord comes and raptures the Church we will also hear the voice of an archangel as one of the three ways that He will announce this event. Arch means chief. It may be that one of these seven angels will also have the privilege of proclaiming the rapture. All this is to point out the seven highest angels are used so that we know that what is about to happen is extremely significant. The importance of their previous announcements has shaken the very foundations of man's history. What comes next will certainly be profound.

Another Angel

> Is the angel that offers incense with the prayers of the saints the Angel of the Lord – Jesus? Explain your answer.

Another angel appears and offers incense mixed with the payers of the saints. Because of the prayers that are mixed with the incense, some think that this is Jesus in His role as Intercessor. Most people believe that when the Angel of the Lord appeared in the Old Testament it was the pre-incarnate vision of Jesus. This is also used to help justify identifying this angel as Jesus. Therefore, we need to look at least one of these encounters in the Old Testament.

> And Mano'ah said to the angel of the Lord, "What is your name, so that, when your words come true, we may honor you?" And the angel of the Lord said to him, "Why do you ask my name, seeing it is wonderful?" So Mano'ah took the kid with the cereal offering, and offered it upon the rock to the Lord, to him who works wonders. And when the flame went up toward heaven from the altar, the angel of the Lord ascended in the flame of the altar while Mano'ah and his wife looked on; and they fell on their faces to the ground. The angel of the Lord appeared no more to Mano'ah and to his wife. Then Mano'ah knew that he was the angel of the Lord. And Mano'ah said to his wife, "We shall surely die, for we have seen God." (Judg 13:17-22 RSV)

This is the story of the Angel of the Lord that appeared to Samson's mother and father to announce his birth. We can see that the Angel of the Lord is more than just an angel when we observe Him in this encounter. When they asked His name, He says it is wonderful. The NIV® says beyond understanding. Who in the Scripture is named wonderful other than Jesus in Isaiah 9:6? Another thing is that when they gave the reason for asking His name, it was to honor Him. He didn't rebuke them and tell them to honor God even though He told them to sacrifice to the Lord (verse 16). He also ascended with the flames of the offering demonstrating that the sacrifice was acceptable to the Lord. Manoah believed that they had seen the face of God when they realized it was the Angel of the Lord. Clearly the Angel of the Lord and God were the same in their mind.

In Revelation 8, this angel could be Jesus, except that everywhere else in the entire book, Jesus is not hidden but revealed. Revelation speaks of the Lamb, the Lion, and a few other things, but when He is shown it is clearly evident that it is Jesus.

> How does this angel remind us of the Trinity?

Since he has been given much incense to offer with the prayers of the saints, he reminds us that Jesus stands in intercession for us. The angel takes our prayers, mixes them with incense, and passes them along to the Father. In this way he also reminds us of the Holy Spirit.

> And in the same way the Spirit also helps our weakness; for we do not know how to pray as we should, but the Spirit Himself intercedes for us with groanings too deep for words; and He who searches the hearts knows what the mind of the Spirit is, because He intercedes for the saints according to the will of God. (Rom 8:26-27 NASB)

Even when we think we know the will of God, we can be wrong. The Holy Spirit cleans up our prayers. This is a great relief to many of us who struggle with knowing how to pray about different situations. We know that even if we pray amiss, the Holy Spirit cleans them up according to God's will.

The angel took fire from the altar and flung it on the earth. It is as if the beginning of the destruction comes straight from the hand of God the Father. We also have the familiar thunder, lightning, and earthquakes associated with the presence of God. Whether this is Jesus or not, he certainly reminds us of the Trinity, which is exactly what a ministering spirit or messenger is supposed to do.

> Compare the use of fire from the altar by this angel with the use of fire in Isaiah 6:6-7.

There is a contrast between the uses of the fire from the altar in this case, i.e. to cause destruction on the earth, as opposed to the fire in the altar in Isaiah 6:6-7 (ESV).

> Then one of the seraphim flew to me, having in his hand a burning coal that he had taken with tongs from the altar. And he touched my mouth and said: "Behold, this has touched your lips; your guilt is taken away, and your sin atoned for."

The fire of the Lord can be used to cleanse or punish. The coals of Isaiah must be the type of fire we as believers see in 1 Corinthians 3:12-15 (NIV®).

> If any man builds on this foundation using gold, silver, costly stones, wood, hay or straw, his work will be shown for what it is, because the Day will bring it to light. It will be revealed with fire, and the fire will test the quality of each man's work. If what he has built survives, he will receive his reward. If it is burned up, he will suffer loss; he himself will be saved, but only as one escaping through the flames.

All the impurities of our work and motivation will be burned away. In the case of the earth, there is so much impurity that we will see a third of almost everything being destroyed at the sound of the first four trumpets.

Thirds

Ezekiel 5:11-16 describes a time when God pours out His wrath in thirds.

> "So as I live," declares the Lord God, "surely, because you have defiled My sanctuary with all your detestable idols and with all your abominations, therefore I will also withdraw, and My eye will have no pity and I will not spare. "One third of you will die by plague or be consumed by famine among you, one third will fall by the sword around you, and one third I will scatter to every wind, and I will unsheathe a sword behind them.
>
> "Thus My anger will be spent and I will satisfy My wrath on them, and I will be appeased; then they will know that I, the LORD, have spoken in My zeal when I have spent My wrath upon them. Moreover, I will make you a desolation and a reproach among the nations which surround you, in the sight of all who pass by. So it will be a reproach, a reviling, a warning and an object of horror to the nations who surround you when I execute judgments against you in anger, wrath and raging rebukes. I, the LORD, have spoken. When I send against them the deadly arrows of famine which were for the destruction of those whom I will send to destroy you, then I will also intensify the famine upon you and break the staff of bread." (NASU)

> Why does the Lord destroy these people by thirds? What does this tell us about the destruction of the earth by thirds in Revelation?

The Lord describes how He will kill two thirds of the people of Israel, a third at a time. He also makes it abundantly clear why. It is because of their vile images and detestable practices. Even the third that doesn't die will be scattered. The result is that they will become an object of horror to the nations. He did this in a very specific manner and had His prophets announce it so that all nations would know exactly why it occurred and it would horrify them. The same is true in the book of Revelation. The Lord starts with a description of the thirds of the earth that He will destroy. He has given mankind all of history to come to Him though grace. The majority of mankind has rejected this offer and as a result, the things that will happen will bring horror on mankind. The judgments in thirds remind me that He has always provided for a remnant that remains true to Him.

> What is God's ultimate purpose when He brings disasters like this?

> "And it shall come to pass in all the land," Says the LORD, "*That* two-thirds in it shall be cut off *and* die, But *one*-third shall be left in it: I will bring the *one*-third through the fire, Will refine them as silver is refined, And test them as gold is tested. They will call on My name, And I will answer them. I will say, 'This *is* My people'; And each one will say, 'The LORD *is* my God.'" (Zech 13:8-9 NKJV)

Again, the Lord's purpose is clear. Just as in the days of Noah, He is seeking a people to call His own. He continually has to purge the wicked from among those He has chosen. It is sad to think that only a third of the people at this point in history turned to Him, and even then, it is only after they suffered. It is very hard for us to imagine a God who would do something like this.

> When people complain about God destroying so many, what must we remember?

We must not forget several things. One of them is the vile and detestable practices that lead up to these things.

> And now they sin more and more, and make for themselves metal images, idols skillfully made of their silver, all of them the work of craftsmen. It is said of them, "Those who offer human sacrifice kiss calves!" (Hos 13:2 ESV)

They actually had human sacrifices at that time. As we get further into Revelation we will see that the end times will also bring some very ugly and horrifying things. We must not forget His holiness. We must not forget His sovereignty. We must not forget His patience and the gift that He has offered in Jesus Christ and how often it has been rejected and even cursed.

I was reading about how the Jews respected the name of God so much that they were afraid it would become commonplace. They made restrictions so that it would only be used in special places and then finally, it could not be pronounced aloud at all. Now the opposite has occurred. The phrase, "Oh my God" (OMG if texting) has become so common that you see it in the comic strips, on TV, and in movies. Even Christians use it without any sense of reverence to our Lord. The name of Jesus has become so common that people use it as a swear word.

> Neither is there salvation in any other: for there is none other name under heaven given among men, whereby we must be saved. (Acts 4:12)

How sad that the name by which we must be saved has been brought down this way. No wonder these horrors will occur.

Bitter Water

> What does Wormwood and bitter water represent? What is the cure for bitterness?

> When they came to the oasis of Marah, the water was too bitter to drink. So they called the place Marah (which means "bitter"). Then the people complained and turned against Moses. "What are we going to drink?" they demanded. So Moses cried out to the LORD for help, and the LORD showed him a piece of wood. Moses threw it into the water, and this made the water good to drink. It was there at Marah that the LORD set before them the following decree as a standard to test their faithfulness to him. He said, "If you will listen carefully to the voice of the LORD your God and do what is right in his sight, obeying his commands and keeping all his decrees, then I will not make you suffer any of the diseases I sent on the Egyptians; for I am the LORD who heals you." (Ex 15:23-26 NLT)

When the Israelites came upon the bitter water, wood was thrown in and the water became drinkable. This was their first time of grumbling, complaining, and bitterness. In Revelation, a star named "Wormwood" will be thrown into the water and it becomes undrinkable (Rev 8:11). Wormwood's Greek definition is:

> *Apsinthos* (ap'-sin-thos); of uncertain derivation; wormwood (as a type of bitterness, i.e. [figuratively] calamity).[32]

Figuratively, bitterness is thrown into the water.

> What happens to us when we drink from the waters of bitterness? What is the cure?

The symbolism here is very potent; people destroy themselves with bitterness. He made the Old Testament an example for us and this is what the Lord can do for our bitterness and problems if we turn to Him. He has given us a wooden cross that produces fresh water when it is thrown into our lives. He will heal us from our bitterness. If we listen to His voice and pay attention to His Word, we will avoid the diseases brought by bitterness. This is in contrast to the rest of the world who reject Jesus and His living water. He will turn fresh water bitter with "wormwood" and destroy many people.

---

[32] *Strong's*, s.v. "NT:894".

As far as the actual event is concerned, we can speculate on how the Lord is going to do it. Many think it is because we are polluting our ground water with chemical dumps; others think that the great star called Wormwood is actually a nuclear explosion that contaminates the water with fallout. Others think that it could be the result of bio-chemical bombs. Some think it is some kind of asteroid filled with arsenic that collides with the earth. It really doesn't matter how. It is the result of God's will.

Global War

Many people think that what is happening with the first four trumpets is a global war. They look to Ezekiel 38 and say that this is the result. Looking back to the preview in chapter 6, we saw a time of peace created by the strong ruler that is followed by a war that could be the one described in Ezekiel.

<u>When</u>

> Looking at Ezekiel 38 and 39, what are the important things to know about this war in these verses?
> 39:8
> 38:4
> 38:8
> 38:11
> 39:9, 12

I don't have enough room to get into too much detail, but there are some things that stand out in these two chapters.

> Behold, it is come, and it is done, saith the LORD GOD; this is the day whereof I have spoken. (Ezek 39:8)

It will surely take place because our Sovereign Lord has said it will. That doesn't leave any room to wonder if, only when and how.

> And I will turn you about, and put hooks into your jaws, and I will bring you forth, and all your army, horses and horsemen, all of them clothed in full armor, a great company, all of them with buckler and shield, wielding swords. (Ezek 38:4 RSV)

Many people speculate on who these countries were in Ezekiel's time and who they will be in our time or the future. When it comes right down to it, it doesn't matter. The Lord is the one who brings about this war. He has set a time and will use the covetousness and greed of nations to start this war. The Lord declares from the beginning that it is because of His sovereign will that this is taking place.

> After many days you will be summoned; in the latter years you will come into the land that is restored from the sword, whose inhabitants have been gathered from many nations to the mountains of Israel which had been a continual waste; but its people were brought out from the nations, and they are living securely, all of them. (Ezek 38:8 NASB)

The time in history, or more accurately, the future is established. This is far in the future for Ezekiel. The people have been brought back from many nations, they have gone through many wars, and now they are living in safety. This cannot refer to the return from Babylon because it says that they will come from many nations, not just one. Nehemiah demonstrates that when they came back from Babylon they didn't live securely.

> And say, "I will go up against the land of unwalled villages. I will fall upon the quiet people who dwell securely, all of them dwelling without walls, and having no bars or gates," (Ezek 38:11 ESV)

Another very important item is the fact that they will live in safety and unwalled villages. This describes the attitude of the people in Israel, not just their physical security. They are unsuspecting. This cannot even come close to the situation in Israel today. Israel is very suspecting, highly fortified, and certainly not living in safety. This hasn't described any time in their short modern history or any time in history since this prophecy was made.

This sheds light on Revelation 6:1-2. It has to be at a time when a strong ruler has provided a guarantee of peace in the land that is so believable that Israel would actually disarm. This would place the war before the tribulation or at the end of the first half.

> And they that dwell in the cities of Israel shall go forth, and shall set on fire and burn the weapons, both the shields and the bucklers, the bows and the arrows, and the handstaves, and the spears, and they shall burn them with fire seven years: (Ezek 39:9)

> And seven months shall the house of Israel be burying of them, that they may cleanse the land. (Ezek 39:12)

These verses help pin down when this will occur by describing what will happen afterwards. If this were the battle of Armageddon when all ends and Jesus restores the earth for the 1,000-year reign, then there wouldn't be any need to pick up the weapons to use for fuel. (I will leave the explanation of the renewal of the earth to our study of Revelation 20.) There would also be no need to cleanse the land because Jesus would do it.

Who

> What nations will be involved in this war?

> You [Gog] will come from your place in the far north, you and many nations with you, all of them riding on horses, a great horde, a mighty army. (Ezek 38:15 NIV®)

This verse lets us know these attackers come from Gog. Historians can link the people of Gog (vs. 2) and Magog to the current Russians.[33] While this fits with the direction they are coming from (the north), some try to tie the fulfillment of this prophesy to current events rather on the fact that God can lift up a nation from these people at any time He wants. Also note that many nations join in. They will have many allies who actually join in on the battle. Verses 38:19-23 describe the events of the war and make it clear that God is in control of the outcome.

> And I will send fire upon Magog and those who inhabit the coastlands in safety; and they will know that I am the LORD. (Ezek 39:6 NASU)

God does some amazing things. Nothing happens to people that is not used by God to bring them to Himself or at least make us aware of Him and His glory. This battle will affect many besides those in the battle. The word "coastlands" is thought to describe any who live along the Mediterranean Sea. In a broader sense, it could be any overseas area separated from Palestine by water.[34] This could mean the United States is also affected.

We are sitting back in what we think is safety, all the while flirting with abortion, homosexuality as well as many other grievous sins. The plague of AIDS has hit, but the destruction of war has not. We are proud and think we can build a missile defense system to protect ourselves. In reality, we don't think that anyone would start a war with us. However, if this war were started against Israel by allies of Russia, it is not hard to imagine a scenario where we are all suddenly involved. It could very well be His judgment on our nation.

Two Battles

> I will set My glory among the nations; all the nations shall see My judgment which I have executed, and My hand which I have laid on them. So the house of Israel shall know that I *am* the LORD their God from that day forward. (Ezek 39:21-22 NKJV)

> Therefore thus says the LORD GOD: "Now I will bring back the captives of Jacob, and have mercy on the whole house of Israel; and I will be jealous for My holy name — after they have borne their shame, and all their unfaithfulness in which they were unfaithful to Me, when they dwelt safely in their own land and no one made *them* afraid." (Ezek 39:25-26 NKJV)

> "And I will not hide My face from them anymore; for I shall have poured out My Spirit on the house of Israel," says the LORD GOD. (Ezek 39:29 NKJV)

> How do these verses in Ezekiel 39 indicate that the prophecies of Ezekiel 38 and 39 describe two battles?

---

[33] Unger, s.v. "Gog," "Magog."
[34] Ibid., s.v. "Coastland."

This is a difficulty that many have with this prophecy. The Lord often tells what He is going to do because of a disobedient people and then slips right into things that can only occur much later, such as after His return. This one is no different. In Ezekiel 39:21-22, He slips past this battle, and goes right on to something that happens just before the 1,000-year reign. Verse 21 is ambiguous enough to apply to this battle before or at the midpoint of the tribulation or to the last battle of the tribulation at Armageddon. Verse 22 can only apply to a time when all of Israel will know that the Lord is God.

Ezekiel 39:26 can occur only if all in Israel are indeed Christians, which I think can only happen after He returns and the true gathering of the whole house of Israel will take place, not the partial that we see today.

Ezekiel 39:28-29 clinches the argument because only in the perfect reign of Jesus could all the Jews be assured of coming back to Israel and having His Spirit poured out on them in this way. It becomes apparent that these verses describe the aftermath of a different battle than the one described earlier. The logical explanation is that they apply to the battle of Armageddon, which will be similar to the earlier one.

Our God is awesome! Even in the prelude to His judgment, we are reminded of the Trinity. We have seen how He has provided salvation and provision for those who walk in His ways. While we rejoice that He will come back again to set all things straight, we also need to be solemn because of the destruction that will come because it will end forever the opportunity of many to turn to Him for salvation.

Revelation 8:7-13

> And the seven angels which had the seven trumpets prepared themselves to sound. The first angel sounded, and there followed hail and fire mingled with blood, and they were cast upon the earth: and the third part of trees was burnt up, and all green grass was burnt up. And the second angel sounded, and as it were a great mountain burning with fire was cast into the sea: and the third part of the sea became blood; And the third part of the creatures which were in the sea, and had life, died; and the third part of the ships were destroyed. And the third angel sounded, and there fell a great star from heaven, burning as it were a lamp, and it fell upon the third part of the rivers, and upon the fountains of waters; And the name of the star is called Wormwood: and the third part of the waters became wormwood; and many men died of the waters, because they were made bitter. And the fourth angel sounded, and the third part of the sun was smitten, and the third part of the moon, and the third part of the stars; so as the third part of them was darkened, and the day shone not for a third part of it, and the night likewise. And I beheld, and heard an angel flying through the midst of heaven, saying with a loud voice, Woe, woe, woe, to the inhabiters of the earth by reason of the other voices of the trumpet of the three angels, which are yet to sound! (KJV)

Hail, Fire and Blood

How do you account for this phenomenon of hail, fire, and blood mixed together being thrown upon the earth?

What are some problems with looking for natural causes or completely spiritualizing these events?

So tomorrow at this time I will send a hailstorm more devastating than any in all the history of Egypt. Quick! Order your livestock and servants to come in from the fields to find shelter. Any person or animal left outside will die when the hail falls. (Ex 9:18-19 NLT)

This is a fairly graphic description of the hail that the Lord poured on Egypt. If this hail is large enough to kill people, then it doesn't take any special imagination to see what John was talking about in Revelation when he describes the hail mixed with blood. The only problem is that the verse says that it is mixed before it is hurled down. That means that the blood is not a result of the hail. The same thing can be said for the fire.

When we think in the natural realm, the fire could easily be the result of lightning, but again the Word says it is mixed, and then hurled down. Our natural tendency is to look at these things and try to put them into a human perspective and remove the power of God, robbing Him of His glory. The other extreme is to spiritualize the events so that they become too remote and lose any practical meaning.

This is what happens when people try to explain how Jesus walked on water. The naturalists have flat out denied it for centuries. At best, they would say that the water was shallow and it appeared He was walking on water. The result is a faith that has no supernatural component. God becomes the embodiment of good thoughts and actions in every person but has no power to save.

On the other extreme, spiritualists would say that Jesus walked on water because He was here in spirit but not physically. In this case, God becomes a high and lofty being who has maintained His separate state from mankind. He can't save because He hasn't physically paid the price for our sins.

How is this hail different from that described in Exodus 9:18-23? What other events are you reminded of in the Old Testament?

There is one interesting thing about this hailstorm; apparently no one dies as a result. Unlike the plague on Egypt, all the damage appears to be done to vegetation. While it says that a third of the earth was burned up, it goes on to explain that it was a third of the trees and all the grass. Hail, as we know it, would not result in this kind of fire because all the ice on the ground would prevent it.

Then the LORD rained on Sodom and Gomor'rah brimstone and fire from the LORD out of heaven; (Gen 19:24 RSV)

The fire that is brought down appears to be more like the fire that was brought on Sodom and Gomorrah.

When we see events like this, what should we remember about God and ourselves? See Psalm 18:12-15 and Isaiah 28:2.

From the brightness before Him passed His thick clouds, Hailstones and coals of fire. The Lord also thundered in the heavens, And the Most High uttered His voice, Hailstones and coals of fire. And He sent out His arrows, and scattered them, And lightning flashes in abundance, and routed them. Then the channels of water appeared, And the foundations of the world were laid bare At Thy rebuke, O Lord, At the blast of the breath of Thy nostrils. (Ps 18:12-15 NASB)

Behold, the Lord has a strong and mighty *agent*; As a storm of hail, a tempest of destruction, Like a storm of mighty overflowing waters, He has cast *it* down to the earth with *His* hand. (Isa 28:2 NASB)

When I read these verses, I am struck with an awe of the might of God. We are fragile beings but think that we are indestructible. When forces of nature catch us up, we snap like twigs and are no more. In contrast, the earth is laid bare simply from the breath of His nostrils. It is completely evident that the Lord could accomplish the destruction of the earth with conventional hail, however He has chosen a special hail that is hurled upon the earth. It is forceful, deliberate and there can be no mistake that it has come from Him.

Huge Mountain

Disaster movies abound, and many involve approaching asteroids as big as mountains. Sometimes heroes are able to divert the asteroid and other times the story is more about people surviving the cataclysm that results when it crashes into the earth. The authors of these stories often show panic, looting, and mayhem when people find out what is about to happen.

How do you think you would react if scientists predicted a huge asteroid were about to crash into the sea?

God is our refuge and strength, a very present help in trouble. Therefore we will not fear though the earth gives way, though the mountains be moved into the heart of the sea, though its waters roar and foam, though the mountains tremble at its swelling. Selah

There is a river whose streams make glad the city of God, the holy habitation of the Most High. God is in the midst of her; she shall not be moved; God will help her when morning dawns. The nations rage, the kingdoms totter; he utters his voice, the earth melts. (Ps 46:1-6 ESV)

As we approach the destruction of the earth, several things come to mind. The terrible time of suffering that comes on people is one. The physical destruction of things of beauty is another. We become so focused on what is going on that we forget Who is in charge. I may sound like a broken record, but then God Himself reminds us many times. Therefore, we constantly need to look at these reminders. Many times, Christians are ridiculed for turning to God in times of trouble. If that is the only time we turn to Him, then we are the poorer for missing Him in the other times. Psalm 46:1 starts by reminding us that He is our refuge in times of trouble and affirms that He is also an ever-present help. This must be firmly entrenched in our minds. If we do not constantly turn to Him for everything, then how will we not fear when we see a blazing mountain hit the sea and a third of the sea turn to blood? Will we be able to say with the psalmist, we will not fear? We are the city of God and the river is the Holy Spirit. He makes us glad, able to enjoy Him as He dwells in us. Unlike the nations, He will never fall. He may bring an end to the temporal things of life, but what counts is that His people will live forever.

Third of Light

> How will shutting off a third of light coming from the heavens affect people? How should Christians react to this or other disasters?

Reducing the light of the sun by a third will have disastrous effects on the earth as temperatures drop dramatically. We recently had a solar eclipse. I watched as 90% of it was obscured. The temperature dropped significantly in those few minutes. It will also be a significant psychological blow to people when they realize that what they trusted will be suddenly removed. With the spread of evolutionary theory and the concept of a very old earth, people think that it will continue the same way very much as it has (2 Peter 3:5-6). Those who preach global warming as the end of the earth will be shaken to the core as they see just the opposite happen in a matter of hours.

I lift up my eyes to the hills — where does my help come from? My help comes from the LORD, the Maker of heaven and earth. (Ps 121:1-2 NIV®)

As long as the earth endures, seedtime and harvest, cold and heat, summer and winter, day and night will never cease. (Gen 8:22 NIV®)

The LORD watches over you — the LORD is your shade at your right hand; the sun will not harm you by day, nor the moon by night. (Ps 121:5-6 NIV®)

Just as with the mountains, the sun, stars, and moon can seem unchanging to men. We depend on them and in a sense trust that they will always be there. Indeed, they will, for God promised that we would always have our seasons as long as the earth exists. But the Lord wants us to trust in Him, not His creation. He wants us to look past the hills to the Maker. We have this promise that He watches over us and that the harm He is bringing on the sun, stars, and moon will bring no permanent harm to us. We may have to refocus our attention on Him if we see these disasters arrive, but we will know that it is near the end because of His promise that the seasons will be there as long as the earth remains. As Christians, we can look past the temporal things of this life and look forward to the eternal things because He watches over us now and forever.

> How might we find spiritual significance in the reduction of light?

Give thanks to the LORD, for He is good, For His lovingkindness is everlasting. (Ps 136: 1 NASU)

To Him who made the great lights, For His lovingkindness is everlasting: The sun to rule by day, For His lovingkindness is everlasting, The moon and stars to rule by night, For His lovingkindness is everlasting. (Ps 136:7-9 NASU)

These verses reaffirm that it is the Lord who has created all things. He has made the sun, stars, and moon to "rule" – to be shown prominently as a reminder to all that He is God. This does not mean that they in any way control us. If a third of the light is missing it certainly suggests that there is the possibility that people will be a third less likely to gaze upon His creation and give honor and glory to Him. I think that the light diminishing by a third is also symbolic of the spiritual trend in mankind. We already know that there are more people born every year than are "born again." Every year, the Light of the world is being reduced. This disaster is a reflection that humanity is losing its sensitivity to God.

> How could diminishing the light by a third actually help people turn to Jesus or grow in their faith?

Violence shall no longer be heard in your land, Neither wasting nor destruction within your borders; But you shall call your walls Salvation, And your gates Praise.

The sun shall no longer be your light by day, Nor for brightness shall the moon give light to you; But the LORD will be to you an everlasting light, And your God your glory. Your sun shall no longer go down, Nor shall your moon withdraw itself; For the LORD will be your everlasting light, And the days of your mourning shall be ended. (Isa 60:18-20 NKJV)

Very often, the Lord removes physical blessings from us so that spiritual blessings may increase. As the physical light in the earth diminishes, it reminds me of the promises for the future when the only light will come from the Lord. Whenever any kinds of affliction overcome us, we must focus on His promise. If the rapture doesn't come when we expect and we actually see part of the tribulation, we must focus on the eternal aspect that He will be our total light. At some point the sun and moon will be gone forever, but we won't care. Jesus is our sun. When we see all things by His light the shadows disappear as we evaluate everything by eternal perspectives.

We often ask, "Why, God?" when we are inundated with problems and we can't understand. Why do some people behave the way they do? Why can't we seem to help them? Why do they even reject help? And it just isn't them, but us as well! Why did this happen to me? At these times instead of becoming frustrated, we need to turn to Jesus, who, in His time will give us light and understanding. In the meantime, He enables us to endure patiently with the light we now have. We know He wants us to endure and we do it as we study His Word and abide in Him. As we abide in Him, His light illuminates our way and the reasons for what we consider obstacles become clearer and clearer. As we grow in Christ, our lives will reflect the opposite of the last times when the darkness increases as more and more people reject Jesus.

Three Woes to Come

> What is the primary reason these three woes come upon the earth?

Now I will sing for the one I love a song about his vineyard: My beloved had a vineyard on a rich and fertile hill. (Isa 5:1 NLT)

This chapter in Isaiah is a nutshell description of God's dealing with Judah and Jerusalem specifically and all of mankind in general. Our Lord has given us everything we need. He has provided us with salvation and His Holy Spirit to enable us to live a life and produce fruit like a vineyard. People in many churches are doing this while in others it would be amazing if anyone is actually saved. However, the world in general is (1) ignoring God, (2) rejecting Jesus and (3) has no concept of the Holy Spirit.

> What are some of the things that cause us to ignore or reject Jesus? See Isaiah 5:8-15.

Woe to those who join house to house, who add field to field, until there is no more room, and you are made to dwell alone in the midst of the land. (Isa 5:8 RSV)

Prosperity has distracted both Christian and unbeliever alike. The Lord promises that the once desired houses will become desolate and famine will be the eventual outcome.

Woe unto them that rise up early in the morning, that they may follow strong drink; that continue until night, till wine inflame them! (Isa 5:11)

Hedonism (pursuing drink) reaches into every rank of our nation and even our churches. Christian leaders may not be pursuing drink, but many are definitely looking out for their own comfort. God promises that there is no limit to this appetite for pleasure and comfort. It will end in the grave and He will humble us.

Woe to those who drag iniquity with the cords of falsehood, And sin as if with cart ropes; Who say, "Let Him make speed, let Him hasten His work, that we may see it; And let the purpose of the Holy One of Israel draw near And come to pass, that we may know *it*." (Isa 5:18-19 NASB)

There is even a woe for those who want Jesus to come again, but for the wrong reasons, not so that sin may be destroyed, not because they hunger after righteousness, but because they simply want to see a perfect life established. These are the ones that followed Jesus only because He fed them.

Woe to those who call evil good and good evil, who put darkness for light and light for darkness, who put bitter for sweet and sweet for bitter! Woe to those who are wise in their own eyes, and shrewd in their own sight! Woe to those who are heroes at drinking wine, and valiant men in mixing strong drink, who acquit the guilty for a bribe, and deprive the innocent of his right! (Isa 5:20-23 ESV)

The woes go on and on. It is a condemnation not only for then but also for today.

What is the result of these woes that God has pronounced?

Therefore the LORD's anger burns against his people; his hand is raised and he strikes them down. The mountains shake, and the dead bodies are like refuse in the streets. Yet for all this, his anger is not turned away, his hand is still upraised. (Isa 5:25 NIV®)

Think about it. The Lord's anger burns against His people! How many people will go through the tribulation as unbelievers because people who should have known better (Christians) let themselves become so polluted by the world system that the church is rendered ineffective? The rest of this chapter in Isaiah describes Him using other nations to purify His people. It is only through adversity that His Church will be cleansed. When the cost of discipleship is expensive, only the sincere will follow. We need to prepare ourselves for the costliest decisions we will ever make.

Jesus also pronounced some woes in Matthew 11:21-24. What surprising concept about eternal judgment do you find in His woes?

Woe to you, Chorazin! Woe to you, Bethsaida! For if the miracles had occurred in Tyre and Sidon which occurred in you, they would have repented long ago in sackcloth and ashes. Nevertheless I say to you, it will be more tolerable for Tyre and Sidon in *the* day of judgment than for you. And you, Capernaum, will not be exalted to heaven, will you? You will descend to Hades; for if the miracles had occurred in Sodom which

occurred in you, it would have remained to this day. Nevertheless I say to you that it
will be more tolerable for the land of Sodom in *the* day of judgment, than for you.
(Matt 11:21-24 NASU)

Judgment is something other than we might first expect. Looking at the fiery lake
at the end of Revelation, it looks equally bad for all. But this indicates that it will be
far worse for some than other. This isn't saying that some will escape the flames, but it
appears that some will not suffer as much as others. Depending upon the knowledge
people have received, they will be judged.

For since the creation of the world His invisible *attributes* are clearly seen, being
understood by the things that are made, *even* His eternal power and Godhead, so
that they are without excuse. (Rom 1:20 NKJV)

Lest people try to claim that they had no knowledge of God, He has told us that
observing creation should make it evident that God exists. Many evolutionists freely
admit that they cling to a faulty theory simply because they don't want to admit the
existence of God. I wonder if it will be even worse for those who have deliberately
suppressed the truth. If you are interested in the answer, read Romans 1:18.

> Do you think eternal judgment will be worse for people who cause others to
> sin? Explain why or why not?

Woe to the world for temptations to sin! For it is necessary that temptations come, but
woe to the man by whom the temptation comes! (Matt 18:7 RSV)

This is a very brief woe, but packed with much meaning. The world, the system
that tempts us and tries to get us off the track, will be judged. But think of the people
who cause others to sin, the ones that go out of their way to bring sin into other's lives.
I think of those who develop false religions to divert people from the right path.
Others peddle drugs, alcohol, and pornography so that their minds and souls are so
clouded that they never even think of getting on the right path.

I was told that during the depression, Al Capone had set up many soup kitchens
and fed many people. My daughter met one of these people. His admiration was
evident in that he spoke well of Capone. He obviously wasn't thinking about all the
people that Capone assisted in going to hell. Jesus makes it clear that there is only woe
for these.

Several years ago, T.V. programs like Donahue started becoming open forums for
deviants to express and propagate their evil. (I would think that today Donahue would
be considered conservative.) They do it under the guise of exploring controversial
issues. What will their judgment be?

> How will those who practice outward morality but don't have inward
> holiness fare?

118

> But woe to you, scribes and Pharisees, hypocrites, because you shut off the kingdom of heaven from men; for you do not enter in yourselves, nor do you allow those who are entering to go in. (Matt 23:13 NASB)

Matthew 23:13-39 is a series of woes that are all directed to the teachers of the law and Pharisees. These are different. They are not directed to those who are wicked outwardly but inwardly. They follow all the external, observable conditions of being good people, but harbor sin in their hearts. They are self-righteous and should know better. At this point Jesus closes the circle on all who would come by any other means than Himself. In verses 33 and 34 He asks how they can escape being condemned to hell unless they respond to His message. Instead, they crucify Him.

> O Jerusalem, Jerusalem, the city that kills the prophets and stones God's messengers! How often I have wanted to gather your children together as a hen protects her chicks beneath her wings, but you wouldn't let me. And now, look, your house is abandoned and desolate. For I tell you this, you will never see me again until you say, 'Blessings on the one who comes in the name of the LORD! (Matt 23:37-39 NLT)

Jesus was speaking to the religious leaders of His day, the future of Jerusalem, and the Jewish system of worship. The Jewish system of worship has been left desolate because it rejected Jesus as the Messiah.

The woes in Revelation are three, God's number again. Even as we get into the woes in the next chapter, we need to remember that the inhabitants of the earth can include believers. Some of these woes will be directly executed against the lost, but persecution will be woeful for Christians as well. An example is the persecution the Egyptians inflicted on Israelites when they saw them spared in the land of Goshen at the time of the plagues.

> What has impressed you most about the study of Revelation, Chapter 8? What do you need to remember and do as a result?

Let's remember the awe and wonder of all our Lord has provided. Let this help us fix our minds and souls on Him as our ever-present help. Let His light guide us as we avoid the woes and help others avoid them as well.

Lesson 8 – Revelation 9:1-21

Revelation 9:1-12

And the fifth angel blew his trumpet, and I saw a star fallen from heaven to earth, and he was given the key of the shaft of the bottomless pit; he opened the shaft of the bottomless pit, and from the shaft rose smoke like the smoke of a great furnace, and the sun and the air were darkened with the smoke from the shaft. Then from the smoke came locusts on the earth, and they were given power like the power of scorpions of the earth; they were told not to harm the grass of the earth or any green growth or any tree, but only those of mankind who have not the seal of God upon their foreheads; they were allowed to torture them for five months, but not to kill them, and their torture was like the torture of a scorpion, when it stings a man. And in those days men will seek death and will not find it; they will long to die, and death will fly from them.

In appearance the locusts were like horses arrayed for battle; on their heads were what looked like crowns of gold; their faces were like human faces, their hair like women's hair, and their teeth like lions' teeth; they had scales like iron breastplates, and the noise of their wings was like the noise of many chariots with horses rushing into battle. They have tails like scorpions, and stings, and their power of hurting men for five months lies in their tails. They have as king over them the angel of the bottomless pit; his name in Hebrew is Abad'don, and in Greek he is called Apol'lyon.

The first woe has passed; behold, two woes are still to come. (RSV)

Star Fallen from Heaven

The book of Revelation is full of symbols and stars are one of them. The context usually gives us clues that reveal the meaning.

> What things can you see here and elsewhere in the Bible that will identify this star that had fallen from heaven?

It is obvious that the star that had fallen from heaven is something different from a physical star that fell in chapter eight. This star is immediately personified when *he* is giving a key. Since he came from heaven, it is possible that he is an angel of some kind. It isn't clear from the text whether this star is the angel who is king over the Abyss or he releases the king of the Abyss when he opens the shaft. Assuming that the star is an angel, it is doubtful that he is a good angel since it says that he fell from heaven sometime in the past. He didn't just come forth at God's bidding, which has been the case of other angels we have seen.

Where in the Bible are we provided with some possible identities for this fallen angel and how do they fit with this angel?

How you are fallen from heaven, O Lucifer, son of the morning! *How* you are cut down to the ground, You who weakened the nations! For you have said in your heart: "I will ascend into heaven, I will exalt my throne above the stars of God; I will also sit on the mount of the congregation On the farthest sides of the north; I will ascend above the heights of the clouds, I will be like the Most High." Yet you shall be brought down to Sheol, To the lowest depths of the Pit. (Isa 14:12-15 NKJV)

Son of man, take up a lamentation for the king of Tyre, and say to him, Thus says the Lord GOD:

"You *were* the seal of perfection, Full of wisdom and perfect in beauty. You were in Eden, the garden of God; Every precious stone was your covering: …

"You *were* the anointed cherub who covers; I established you; You were on the holy mountain of God; You walked back and forth in the midst of fiery stones. You *were* perfect in your ways from the day you were created, Till iniquity was found in you.

"… And you sinned; Therefore I cast you as a profane thing Out of the mountain of God; And I destroyed you, O covering cherub, From the midst of the fiery stones.

"Your heart was lifted up because of your beauty; You corrupted your wisdom for the sake of your splendor; I cast you to the ground, I laid you before kings, That they might gaze at you." (Ezek 28:12-17 NKJV)

These verses were directed to the king of Babylon and the king of Tyre. At the same time God condemned these men, He moved on to explain how Satan had sinned and lost his position in heaven. As he brings these kings to destruction, He also shows how He cast Satan out of heaven. These verses refer to bringing Satan to the depths of the pit. Could this be the angel in the abyss? Probably not, because we know that Satan is still active in the world. Luke 22:3 says that Satan entered into Judas Iscariot. Acts 5:3 says that Satan filled the heart of Ananias (a believer) to lie to the Holy Spirit. If he were locked in the Abyss He wouldn't have been able to tempt Jesus or control Judas. This star could very well be Satan who is given permission to release the angel of the abyss at this time. The angel of the abyss is probably one of the other demons that Satan dragged down with him. Revelation 12:4 gives a description of Satan taking others with him. Revelation 9:11 says that the king over the locusts is named Abaddon or Apollyon, both of which mean a destroying angel.

In the description of Satan, what was his biggest problem? How do we face the same temptation?

As we look at this fallen star and Satan, it is interesting to note that Satan's biggest problem is a lust for power driven by pride. He had more than any of us could imagine. He was beautiful, wise, and perfect in all ways. But he wasn't satisfied with this and wanted more. He was most likely the highest-ranking angel in heaven so the only thing more he could get was to be God. With all his power, he must have forgotten that he was a created being; otherwise, he would have understood how ludicrous it is to think he could become more powerful than his Creator. I don't think that we have a very good concept of how insidious pride is until we see what it did to Satan. It should be a warning to us all. Contrast Satan's desires as well as most of ours with Paul's.

> Not that I speak from want; for I have learned to be content in whatever circumstances I am. I know how to get along with humble means, and I also know how to live in prosperity; in any and every circumstance I have learned the secret of being filled and going hungry, both of having abundance and suffering need. (Phil 4:11-12 NASB)

Can we say that we are content regardless of the circumstances? We should; we have more than Satan ever dreamed because we are co-heirs of God's kingdom because of what Jesus has done for us. If we aren't content, then we have a big hole in our spiritual armor that Satan can use to cause us no end of problems. After all, he is the expert in discontentment.

How much power does Satan have to tempt us and cause problems for us?

What are some things we need to remember when we are tempted?

> The LORD said to Satan, "Very well, then, everything he has is in your hands, but on the man himself do not lay a finger." Then Satan went out from the presence of the LORD. (Job 1:12)

> The LORD said to Satan, "Very well, then, he is in your hands; but you must spare his life." (Job 2:6)

Satan still has much spiritual power as evidenced by Ananias in Acts 5:3. He also has physical power to harm as demonstrated by what he did to Job. However, his power is limited to what God allows. Knowing this helps us when we undergo time of trials whether they are in health, wealth, relationships, spiritual battles, or anything else. Job suffered in all these areas more than most of us will ever face. He struggled with the question of why God would allow this to happen to him since he had been faithful to the Lord. When God revealed Himself to Job, he finally understood that it wasn't really about him, but it was to bring glory to God. When we trust that our loving heavenly Father is in control of all things, even the hurtful circumstances of our lives, we will not succumb to Satan's schemes to destroy our faith or our witness.

> Therefore let anyone who thinks that he stands take heed lest he fall. No temptation has overtaken you that is not common to man. God is faithful, and he will not let you be tempted beyond your ability, but with the temptation he will also provide the way of escape, that you may be able to endure it. (1 Cor 10:12-13 ESV)

We have God's promised limit on our temptations, but we must be willing to take the way out that He has provided. Most people don't quote verse 12, but it needs to be remembered because pride in our spiritual strength gets in the road of taking His way out and we end up falling under the temptation instead.

> How has Satan's power been reduced and what will be his future?

> Now is the time for judgment on this world; now the prince of this world will be driven out. But I, when I am lifted up from the earth, will draw all men to myself. (John 12:31-32 NIV®)
>
> … the prince of this world now stands condemned. (John 16:11 NIV®)
>
> He threw him into the Abyss, and locked and sealed it over him, to keep him from deceiving the nations anymore until the thousand years were ended. After that, he must be set free for a short time. (Rev 20:3 NIV®)

Satan had power over death until Jesus was crucified and resurrected. His power has been limited even more now that Jesus lives in us and we know that we have Jesus' resurrection power living in us (1 John 4:4). We also have the promise that Satan will be bound for 1,000 years when he will be totally incapable of harm to anyone. He will be released, and then forever incarcerated in the lake of fire. The point is that God is in control, not Satan. The verdict over Satan has been given. It is only a matter of time before it is executed. Do as the saying suggests, "If Satan is threatening you about your past, remind him of his future."

> If we successfully resist Satan in one temptation, can we be assured we won't have to deal with that temptation again? Explain your answer.

> And when the devil had ended all the temptation, he departed from him for a season. (Luke 4:13)

This indicates that even Jesus had another contest coming after He successfully triumphed over Satan's temptations in the wilderness. It was in the Garden of Gethsemane when Jesus was tempted to avoid the cross.

... for the prince of this world cometh, and hath nothing in me ... (John 14:30)

Jesus was able to win that contest because Satan had no hold on Him and now Jesus is living in us. We need to remember that when Satan starts bugging us. I have written a more comprehensive study of Satan's power and our victory in *Battling Satan with the Armor of God*, a short booklet.[35]

The Abyss

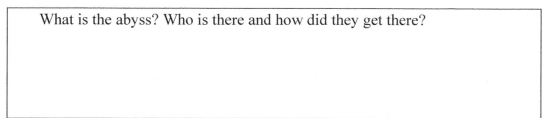

What is the abyss? Who is there and how did they get there?

And they cried out, saying, "What business do we have with each other, Son of God? Have You come here to torment us before the time?" (Matt 8:29 NASU)

They were imploring Him not to command them to go away into the abyss. (Luke 8:31 NASU)

These two verses have to be taken together to get the full picture of what is happening. The first point is that there will be an appointed time of torture for all demons. That includes a time when they will be sent into the abyss and locked up with Satan for a thousand years. From this account, it appear that Jesus usually sent demons into the abyss ahead of time, when He casts them out of someone. In this case, He didn't. My conclusion is that the abyss is a place where demons are kept from people. It is populated with some demons at this time while some are still free to roam.

For if God did not spare the angels who sinned, but cast *them* down to hell and delivered *them* into chains of darkness, to be reserved for judgment; (2 Peter 2:4 NKJV)

And the angels who did not keep their proper domain, but left their own abode, He has reserved in everlasting chains under darkness for the judgment of the great day; (Jude 6 NKJV)

The population includes demons that Jesus cast out of people as well as some that have been locked up since they rebelled. These latter ones were angels that sided with Satan and were so bad that they were sent directly to hell and some to dungeons – perhaps to the Abyss. Some may have been of high position and deemed too dangerous to allow them to be free.

The fallen star (most likely Satan) is given the opportunity to release the demons from the Abyss. As they are released, the sun and sky are darkened. This may be symbolic of extreme demonic activity of the last days. These will be days when the

---

[35] *Battling Satan with the Armor of God* is available as a book or eBook. Visit http://www.rayruppert.com/battling-satan.html.

light of Jesus is hard to see because it will be blocked by much satanic deception. We can thank God that He has restricted the demonic activity in the world at this time.

Locusts

> What is the first abnormality that you see in these locusts?

The first strange thing about these locusts is that they don't do what normal locusts do. They don't devour all of the grass and trees in sight. Look at Joel 2:1-11 for a description of what an army of natural locusts does. The Lord leads them to bring His people to repentance. He does it by having the insects devour everything in sight. But other than crawling all over people, they don't actually harm them. These in Revelation are different. They don't touch the vegetation, but only sting unbelievers.

> What could the locusts' ability to harm only unbelievers signify?

This could symbolize divine protection that keeps believers from falling into the trap of the enemy as indicated in Matthew 24:24:

> For false messiahs and false prophets will rise up and perform great signs and wonders so as to deceive, if possible, even God's chosen ones. (NLT)

> The locusts have the ability to harm so that people seek death but can't find it. What could this signify, or could it be literal?

It is possible that these five months of torment is spiritual when people who are "stung" become demon possessed. That could explain why people seek death, but it eludes them. They could be in such spiritual and emotional turmoil that they want to commit suicide, but the demons themselves ensure that it can't be done. Demons are not interested in quickly destroying their host unless they think they may lose the person to Christ. There are examples of this in the following verses.

> And when he had come out of the boat, there met him out of the tombs a man with an unclean spirit … Night and day among the tombs and on the mountains he was always crying out, and bruising himself with stones. (Mark 5:2, 5 RSV)

> "Lord, have mercy on my son, for he is an epileptic and he suffers terribly; for often he falls into the fire, and often into the water." And Jesus rebuked him, and the demon came out of him, and the boy was cured instantly. (Matt 17:15, 18 RSV)

You would think that the man living in the tombs would have long since killed himself, yet he was kept alive. The boy in Matthew appears to have epilepsy causing him to fall into the fire or water but it is actually a demon. This demon would also seem to kill the boy, yet he continues to live. If what the locust hoard is describing is actually demon possession, then it supports the belief that a believer cannot be possessed by a demon for it says they can only harm those who do not have the seal of God. Praise God for that!

On the other hand, is the possibility that this is as it is described, physical torture inflicted by some kind of mutant ninja locust? Some have speculated that these locusts are mutants, perhaps caused by nuclear radiation. (This isn't very scientific as mutations from radiation usually kill the recipient rather than produce Spider Man or the Incredible Hulk.) Since they are nothing seen on earth, they would have to be supernaturally created – not mutants. They inflict a sting that causes a person such pain that they simply wished they were dead. The source is supernatural since it is only a fallen angel who releases them. Naturally occurring locusts are usually indiscriminate unless God has prevented them from harming Christians.

> You increased your merchants more than the stars of the heavens. The locust spreads its wings and flies away. Your princes are like grasshoppers, your scribes like clouds of locusts settling on the fences in a day of cold—when the sun rises, they fly away; no one knows where they are. (Nah 3:16-17 ESV)

How did Nahum use locust and grasshoppers as symbols and how would this fit with Revelation?

What warnings can we derive from this?

Nahum did an interesting turn on locust symbolism. He used locusts to describe the bureaucracy of government and the greed of merchants who only desire riches for themselves. They only see the immediate gain that can be made. They are a torment to the rest of people because they are willing to take what is needed at the expense of the poor. The poor can be left with malnutrition, tormented but very much alive. When the time of accounting comes, they are not to be found.

In our business dealings, we need to be conscious of our impact on others. There may be many things that are legal and proper, but in the long run may have bad effects on others. Waste disposal is an example. For a long time, it was perfectly legal to put chemicals in the garbage or down the sewer. This has left people disfigured, tormented, and killed by cancer. Today we know better, but laws had to be made to prevent it.

> Do nothing from selfishness or empty conceit, but with humility of mind let each of you regard one another as more important than himself; do not *merely* look out for your own personal interests, but also for the interests of others. (Phil 2:3-4 NASB)

127

We need to have an attitude in which we are looking out for the interests of others and these problems will diminish.

While this merchant and government symbolism is interesting and provides a good warning, I don't think this is a good explanation for the locusts because Christians aren't harmed. It is obvious from the rest of the book of Revelation that Christians will be greatly harmed by merchants in the last days.

> Do you have any other explanations for the bizarre description of the locusts?

I have not drawn anything else from the description of the locusts except they are not in any sense like normal locusts. The hair, teeth, breastplates, etc. all may have symbolic meaning, but they don't relate to anything I've found in the Bible. Author Hal Lindsey says that a friend of his was in the Green Berets and after reading the description he immediately thought of Cobra helicopters.[36] The description fits very well with the breastplates and sound that they make. I've seen pictures with teeth painted on them and hair painted on them, so the image is very realistic. Lindsey's friend speculates that the sting could be some kind of nerve gas sprayed from the tails. However, this is also a stretch to explain what these locusts are. Yet the Lord may indeed have shown something like this to John, who had a hard time explaining what he saw. However, the bottom line is that they don't harm Christians, so this would not support this military explanation. It is also poor exegesis since they come from the abyss, this explanation would require a mixing of literal and spiritual interpretation that is inconsistent.

> Why do the locusts only harm people for five months?

I've read claims that these five months are symbolic and each could represent a decade (50 years being the length of time helicopters have been existence[37]). Since this is part of the tribulation, it makes sense to consider that the five months are exactly that, five months. There is nothing in the context or even other biblical passages to suggest otherwise.

The fact that these creatures, demons, or armed forces have the ability to torture for only five months is puzzling. It is possible that the Lord, even in displaying His wrath upon the lost, stops and gives them a rest to repent before the next woe comes.

The fact that the locusts have a king, and that his name is destroyer, leads me to believe that the locusts are most likely demons. Other explanations simply don't fit.

---

[36] Lindsey, 138.

[37] The problem with this theory is that time marches on. The first practical helicopter was flown September of 1939. Now, it is more than 78 years. This is a clear example why reading current events to explain Revelation doesn't often work.

So What?

> Summarize what you have learned from this woe announced by the fifth trumpet that you can apply to your life.

At this point you may be asking this question. How does this really affect me? Again, it is a huge reminder that God is in control, even over the forces of evil. It is also a warning that pride can interfere with a Christian's spiritual armor, causing us problems. While Satan may cause any number of problems, especially by having his demons possess the unsaved, turning our lives over to Jesus is the only way to guarantee our victory over spiritual forces of evil.

May the Lord bless you as you focus on Jesus our Lord.

Revelation 9:13-21

> Then the sixth angel blew his trumpet, and I heard a voice from the four horns of the golden altar before God, saying to the sixth angel who had the trumpet, "Release the four angels who are bound at the great river Euphrates." So the four angels, who had been prepared for the hour, the day, the month, and the year, were released to kill a third of mankind. The number of mounted troops was twice ten thousand times ten thousand; I heard their number. And this is how I saw the horses in my vision and those who rode them: they wore breastplates the color of fire and of sapphire and of sulfur, and the heads of the horses were like lions' heads, and fire and smoke and sulfur came out of their mouths. By these three plagues a third of mankind was killed, by the fire and smoke and sulfur coming out of their mouths. For the power of the horses is in their mouths and in their tails, for their tails are like serpents with heads, and by means of them they wound.
>
> The rest of mankind, who were not killed by these plagues, did not repent of the works of their hands nor give up worshiping demons and idols of gold and silver and bronze and stone and wood, which cannot see or hear or walk, nor did they repent of their murders or their sorceries or their sexual immorality or their thefts. (ESV)

Sixth Trumpet – Second Woe

<u>Horns of the Alter</u>

> What is the golden altar, whose voice commands this woe, and how does this relate to the prayers of the saints?

They serve at a sanctuary that is a copy and shadow of what is in heaven. This is why Moses was warned when he was about to build the tabernacle: "See to it that you make everything according to the pattern shown you on the mountain." (Heb 8:5 NIV®)

We are reminded several times in Scripture that Moses built everything in the tabernacle after the pattern that he had been shown. Exodus 30:1-10 describes the altar of incense that was in the sanctuary on earth. It was small, only about 18 inches square and three feet high. It was overlaid with gold and represented the altar that is before the Lord described in Revelation. Twice a day, the high priest was to offer incense on it. It appears that the heavenly version of it is where the angel offered the incense and prayers of the saints. Previously, we saw that the souls of martyrs were under it. It is from the horns on the ends of the altar that the voice commands the next woe to come. It impresses me that the Lord is the only one who can authorize these disasters, yet in this case it appears to be in response to the prayers and death of His saints that the Lord lets the second woe loose on mankind.

Four Angels Loosed

> Explain why you would describe these angels as either willing servants of God or demons.

God bound these four angels for this very time. Because they are bound, I doubt that they were holy angels in willful obedience to God. Otherwise, like the angels in Revelation 7:3, they would have simply been told to restrain themselves.

> But the prince of the kingdom of Persia was withstanding me for twenty-one days; then behold, Michael, one of the chief princes, came to help me, for I had been left there with the kings of Persia. (Dan 10:13 NASU)
>
> Then he said, "Do you understand why I came to you? But I shall now return to fight against the prince of Persia; so I am going forth, and behold, the prince of Greece is about to come." (Dan 10:20 NASU)

In Daniel, God revealed that nations have spiritual princes that are not from God. They resist the efforts of the godly angels. Perhaps the angels that have been bound are powerful spiritual princes that will guide other nations into war. If this is true, can you imagine what kind of war will ensue when these four angels are released? The war involves 200 million troops and will wipe out a third of all mankind that is left on the earth.

> What is the significance that the angels have been prepared for an hour, day, month, and year?

Since all angels, even the demons, have been created by God, it is significant that their purpose was prepared even before the creation of the world. Just as Jesus' death was planned before the creation of the earth, these demons were created with the full knowledge of God that they would rebel and be bound for this exact time. When you think about this, it reveals God's sovereignty in ways that we can never imagine. Some may see this as a negative attribute of God asking why He would create beings that He knew would be so powerful and evil. Others of us recognize that the answer to this question is beyond our comprehension but trust in the goodness of our Holy and awesome God.

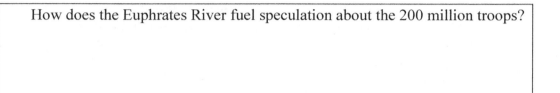

How does the Euphrates River fuel speculation about the 200 million troops?

Because these angels are bound at the river Euphrates, it is assumed by many that these troops will be coming from the East. In 1961, China reported that they had this many militiamen. If they were to mobilize at the direction of these demon princes, and come to the Euphrates though India, surely a third of the world's population would be killed either as they tried to resist or even as the troops simply plunder along the way. We think that their intent is simply to invade the Holy Land; however, we need to remember that they are led by demons and would therefore wreak havoc along the way. The area of the Euphrates has always been the center of spiritual problems. It is where the Garden of Eden was located and it is where the first sin occurred. Cane committed the first murder there. The tower of Babel was erected in this area, which was the forerunner of the city of Babylon with its spiritual decadence. Perhaps, even in their bound state, these angels have been able to influence mankind through the ages.

While this speculation seems to fit with modern possibilities, we need to remember that the forces that finally do enter the Holy Land will be from the north. This raises the possibility that these are not armies of men but armies of demons that are being unleashed upon the earth.

What can you learn from John's description of these troops to help identify them?

The description of the mounted troops, like the locusts, is very obscure, which leads to speculation that they are from China. At one time, I thought that it was clear they were people; however, there is nothing in the description that would preclude demonic troops much as those depicted in the *Left Behind* series of books. Because they are numbered, I thought that it seemed more likely to be human beings rather than demons. However, the Greek for the number is not specific, as some translations would imply. Rather, it is made up of two words, both of which could be translated as myriads.

> *Dismurias* or *dis murias* (dis-moor-ee-as'); an indefinite number of incalculable immensity; found only in Rev 9:16: a double myriad, twenty thousand.[38]

> *Murias* (moo-ree'-as); a ten-thousand; by extension, a "myriad" or indefinite number: [39]

This could have been translated, "The number of troops that I heard was so large that I have no way to express it other than it was a double myriad times a myriad." This significantly reduces the probability that these are human forces.

In addition, the horses aren't anything that we can identify with any certainty. When Native Americans saw the first trains, they called them iron horses. What John saw had about as much in common with a horse as a steam engine. The description of fire, smoke, and sulfur could be supernatural, or it could relate to almost any kind of tank, rocket launcher, or vehicle used to launch chemicals. This could explain John's reference to plagues of fire, smoke, and sulfur. If this is true, then God is using mankind to destroy mankind. We also need to remember that God doesn't need our help.

The breastplates of these troops are brilliant. They are decorated with fiery red, dark blue, and brilliant yellow. The last I saw, troops around the world are currently dressing in camouflage rather than drawing attention to themselves. Even the vehicles are designed to avoid detection. Of course this could change in the future as it has over the ages. These troops must be either demonic or symbolic of the troops of many nations.

Ezekiel 23 describes what the Lord did to Israel and Judah because she had gone after other gods and put her trust in the powers of other nations and their gods. Israel was overcome by Assyria and Judah by Chaldea (Babylon). The interesting thing is that the princes and warriors of these nations are described as wearing either blue or red.

> And they shall come against you With chariots, wagons, and war-horses, With a horde of people. They shall array against you Buckler, shield, and helmet all around. (Ezek 23:24 NKJV)

These who are dressed in red and blue came against Judah and there were hordes of them. It has already happened once when Babylon took over. In Revelation, the horsemen are wearing red, blue, and yellow. Perhaps what is happening is a combination of these nations coming against Israel once again rather than a Chinese invasion. Yellow isn't mentioned but it could possibly represent the alliance of another country that is not mentioned in association with a color. Perhaps it is Egypt because they were also mentioned in the passages in Ezekiel.

---

[38] *Strong's*, s.v. "NT:1364a."
[39] *Strong's*, s.v. "NT:3461."

The rest of mankind

> What comes to your mind about people and even how you raise children when you see that after a third of mankind is killed, the remaining people don't repent?

God has been saying it for a long time now; people who do not repent will be destroyed. It is sad, but true. When God first gave His covenant to His people, He warned them and followed with quick punishment as in the following example.

> And the LORD said unto Moses, The man shall be surely put to death: all the congregation shall stone him with stones without the camp. (Num 15:35)

Later, the Lord gave them longer and longer periods of time to repent before bringing disaster on the nation. It is similar to what we do with our children. When they are very young, quick discipline is needed to keep them from danger. As they grow older, we give them more and more latitude. Finally, when they are grown, we no longer punish them, but society takes over. The rules of society are basically the same as the moral instructions we give our children. When society stops punishing immorality, it is left to God.

> Whoever stubbornly refuses to accept criticism will suddenly be destroyed beyond recovery. (Prov 29:1 NLT)

We may have many rebukes, but there is never a promise that this is the last one before we will be punished. We really don't know when the last will come. Even though one third of mankind was killed, the remaining people don't take the warning and refuse to repent.

> Which of you will listen to this or pay close attention in time to come? Who handed Jacob over to become loot, and Israel to the plunderers? Was it not the LORD, against whom we have sinned? For they would not follow his ways; they did not obey his law. So he poured out on them his burning anger, the violence of war. It enveloped them in flames, yet they did not understand; it consumed them, but they did not take it to heart. (Isa 42:23-25 NIV®)

Who will listen? We all belong to God; we are His creation and as such, He has the absolute right to set the rules and declare what is the right way to live. He has the power to turn individuals or nations over to punishment when they don't follow His ways. People want sin so badly that they ignore and reject the very words that will save them, not just from physical punishment in this life, but eternal punishment.

> What keeps God from judging the earth right now? Does His delay imply individuals won't suffer His wrath?

Or do you presume upon the riches of his kindness and forbearance and patience?
Do you not know that God's kindness is meant to lead you to repentance? But by your
hard and impenitent heart you are storing up wrath for yourself on the day of wrath
when God's righteous judgment will be revealed. (Rom 2:4-5 RSV)

Do we sometimes get impatient with God, wanting Him to judge people because of their sin? It is a horrible thing that we are talking about, this idea of God's wrath. These verses make it clear that there is a day of punishment when His wrath will be revealed. It isn't just on the Day of Judgment, but also at other times in history. We may all face it the day we die, or in some other part of our life. It is only His kindness that keeps it from the whole earth right now. He wants everyone to repent, and is waiting. He will keep His promise.

When the final outpouring of His wrath comes, people will not repent as described in Revelation 9:20. Maybe He is waiting to bring final judgment until He knows that all who will repent have done so. Since the rest did not repent at this time, it is a solid indication that there will be very few who will believe and come to Him from this point on.

> What will the rest of mankind do to prepare for the end of the age? What should we do?

For as in those days which were before the flood they were eating and drinking, they
were marrying and giving in marriage, until the day that Noah entered the ark, and
they did not understand until the flood came and took them all away; so shall the
coming of the Son of Man be. Then there shall be two men in the field; one will be
taken, and one will be left. Two women will be grinding at the mill; one *will be* taken,
and one will be left. (Matt 24:38-41 NASB)

It is passages like Revelation 9:20-21 that bring out thoughts of the very end of the age. Jesus says that just like in the time of Noah, people will be carrying on doing what is normal with no regard for God, but more importantly, their sin will be increasing. God flooded the earth because of what they were doing in the time of Noah. Before the Roman Empire crashed, sexual sin was rampant and God judged them. Look at where we are today with unabashed homosexuality and open demon worship. Years ago, this would not have been tolerated. Either this is a sign that the very end is coming or that we are at the end of an age for our society. Our present society cannot exist much longer in the direction it is going. However, no matter how bad things get, some will never respond. Salvation is available for all but not all will take it. These refuse it, at least at this time.

The rest of mankind did not repent. This doesn't mean that there aren't any Christians on earth at this time or that no more will come to Jesus. Revelation 11 discusses two witnesses that are on the earth at the end. Revelation 13:7 and 10b lets us know that Christians will be on the earth when the Antichrist rules. Revelation 14:12-13 indicates that there will be Christians and even more people coming to Christ while other people take the mark of the beast. However, it will become harder and harder for Christians and even harder for those who do repent to make that decision.

But exhort one another every day, as long as it is called "today," that none of you may be hardened by the deceitfulness of sin … As it is said, "Today, if you hear his voice, do not harden your hearts as in the rebellion." (Heb 3:13, 15 ESV)

May you continue in your faith in Jesus and strive to bring others into this relationship before it is too late.

Lesson 9 – Revelation 10:1 – 11:3

Revelation 10:1-7

I saw another strong angel coming down out of heaven, clothed with a cloud; and the rainbow was upon his head, and his face was like the sun, and his feet like pillars of fire; and he had in his hand a little book which was open. He placed his right foot on the sea and his left on the land; and he cried out with a loud voice, as when a lion roars; and when he had cried out, the seven peals of thunder uttered their voices. When the seven peals of thunder had spoken, I was about to write; and I heard a voice from heaven saying, "Seal up the things which the seven peals of thunder have spoken and do not write them." Then the angel whom I saw standing on the sea and on the land lifted up his right hand to heaven, and swore by Him who lives forever and ever, WHO CREATED HEAVEN AND THE THINGS IN IT, AND THE EARTH AND THE THINGS IN IT, AND THE SEA AND THE THINGS IN IT, that there will be delay no longer, but in the days of the voice of the seventh angel, when he is about to sound, then the mystery of God is finished, as He preached to His servants the prophets. (NASU)

The Mighty Angel

> We can see God's characteristics by looking at those who are in close proximity Him. How does this angel's description remind you of God and what is the significance of this?

The description of this angel is very much like some of the descriptions of God Himself. Still John describes him as an angel. Because of this, I think the description is used to paint a scene that strikes awe in us. The robe of a cloud and the rainbow above his head provide an image of a huge figure, perhaps several thousand feet tall. His head is above the clouds and his midsection is in them. His face is shining like the sun. He comes from the presence of the Lord and the glow on his face reflects this, as did Moses' face (Ex 34:29). To those who love the Lord, this is a comfort. To those who don't, it will produce fear.

His feet are anchored. They are not going to move. This is a final decision that is going to be announced. It is not something fleeting. One foot on the sea and the other on the land lets us know that nothing is going to escape this pronouncement. All people everywhere will be affected. For us who know Jesus, it will be the promises described above. For those who don't, it will be the assurance of destruction. The roar of the lion is comforting to the cubs, but strikes fear into the heart of its prey.

> What characteristics of God do you see in this mighty angel's voice?

But this is what the LORD has told me: "When a strong young lion stands growling over a sheep it has killed, it is not frightened by the shouts and noise of a whole crowd of shepherds. In the same way, the LORD of Heaven's Armies will come down and fight on Mount Zion. the LORD of Heaven's Armies will hover over Jerusalem and protect it like a bird protecting its nest. He will defend and save the city; he will pass over it and rescue it." Though you are such wicked rebels, my people, come and return to the LORD. I know the glorious day will come when each of you will throw away the gold idols and silver images your sinful hands have made. "The Assyrians will be destroyed, but not by the swords of men. The sword of God will strike them, and they will panic and flee. The strong young Assyrians will be taken away as captives." (Isa 31:4-8 NLT)

One aspect of this angel in relation to God is that he shouts with a roar like a lion. Isaiah relates a last chance pronouncement for Jerusalem to repent. In it, the Lord gives both hope and judgment. To His enemies, He promises battle, but to His saints, He gives protection after they repent. We have a similar promise of protection once we come to Christ.

My sheep hear my voice, and I know them, and they follow me: And I give unto them eternal life; and they shall never perish, neither shall any man pluck them out of my hand. My Father, which gave them me, is greater than all; and no man is able to pluck them out of my Father's hand. I and my Father are one. (John 10:27-30)

No one can drag us away from Him. Not even when the evils of the world band together, as they will be doing in the end times, will they be able to take us away from our Lord. He growls over us, His prey. Have you ever tried to take the prey away from a lion? The noise and clamor of the world may distract us and even lead us off, but He is not bothered by it. His purpose will not change. Many may appear to fall away from the Lord, but this shows that there will be a great awakening in the end times, not in numbers but in purity and zeal for the Lord. Many who have wandered will be brought back. Israel will embrace Jesus. We also need to remember that the others will fall by the sword as Assyria did.

Seven Thunders

How does the voices of seven thunders relate to a description of God and the mighty angel?

This angel has a shout that inspires the voices of seven thunders to answer. We have previously recognized that the voice of the Lord is often associated with thunder. Seven thunders would naturally fit into a description of the voice of the Lord as well.

The voice of the LORD is upon the waters; The God of glory thunders, The LORD is over many waters.

The voice of the LORD is powerful, The voice of the LORD is majestic.

The voice of the LORD breaks the cedars; Yes, the LORD breaks in pieces the cedars of Lebanon. And He makes Lebanon skip like a calf, And Sirion like a young wild ox.

The voice of the LORD hews out flames of fire.

The voice of the LORD shakes the wilderness; The LORD shakes the wilderness of Kadesh.

The voice of the LORD makes the deer to calve, And strips the forests bare, And in His temple everything says, "Glory!" (Ps 29:3-9 NASB)

Here are seven descriptions of the voice of the Lord. His voice is over the water as this angel in Revelation is standing over the water. His voice is majestic, just as this angel has a voice that is like the roar of a lion. Even though the voice of the Lord shakes and rips apart the earth, He is enthroned in heaven. He is sovereign and just as important, He strengthens us and gives us peace. It is only by the peace of knowing His voice that we are able to get through tough times. When we work things out for ourselves, we may get the job done, but how much easier it is when we carry everything to Him in prayer and leave it there. Rather than the possibility of becoming a frightening figure, this angel becomes a symbol of our hope and trust in God.

God speaks to people out of thunder as we have seen several times before. Here it is described as the seven thunders, seven being the number of perfection. It is the same number as the Spirits of God in Revelation 4:5. The phrase "seven thunders" is repeated three times. This is important. It isn't a casual; "by the way," I heard this voice. It comes directly from God.

Seal it Up

Why would John be prevented from writing down what the seven thunders said? What other places in Scripture do we find a similar command?

And I knew such a man, (whether in the body, or out of the body, I cannot tell: God knoweth;) How that he was caught up into paradise, and heard unspeakable words, which it is not lawful for a man to utter. (2 Cor 12:3-4)

What is said by the thunders, just like the things Paul heard, is inexpressible and not permitted for man to tell. I am glad I don't have to keep a secret like that.

Revelation 10:4 is a short but significant verse in the book of Revelation. Up until this time, John was faithfully writing down everything he saw and heard. Suddenly, he is told not to include a bit of information. I believe this information is withheld because it would enable us to precisely piece together much of the timing of the end time scenario.

But thou, O Daniel, shut up the words, and seal the book, even to the time of the end: many shall run to and fro, and knowledge shall be increased. (Dan 12:4)

The words of the thunders are simply shut away. Daniel's are different in that there is an implication that at the end, the information will become understandable. Other things in Revelation will make more sense as they are fulfilled, but it will have to be done without the seven thunders' information.

The Lord wants us to look to Him for everything. If we knew His timing, we could easily think we could wait for the last minute before repenting or doing what He wants. We could map things out and therefore hedge our bet. I know that most dedicated Christians would not, but many would, especially unbelievers. With the information of the seven thunders, people may be able to know or figure out so clearly the events of the last days that they may think that they could wait for the last minute to accept Christ.

> Why would it be bad for people to be able to wait for the last minute to accept Christ?

This would be bad in at least two ways. Their motivation to come to Him would be insincere; He wouldn't really be Lord, otherwise they would come now. If they thought they could wait, then they overlook the fact that they could die at any minute for a multitude of reasons and they would be unprepared because they thought they would live long enough to see the events of Christ's return. Either way, Jesus would say He doesn't know them.

> Therefore, stay awake, for you do not know on what day your Lord is coming. But know this, that if the master of the house had known in what part of the night the thief was coming, he would have stayed awake and would not have let his house be broken into. Therefore you also must be ready, for the Son of Man is coming at an hour you do not expect.
>
> But if that wicked servant says to himself, "My master is delayed," and begins to beat his fellow servants and eats and drinks with drunkards, the master of that servant will come on a day when he does not expect him and at an hour he does not know and will cut him in pieces and put him with the hypocrites. In that place there will be weeping and gnashing of teeth. (Matt 24:42-44, 48-51 ESV)

Jesus knows that people will act differently if they know exactly when He will return. His delay and His secrecy about when He is coming are designed to separate the true believers from the false professors. The people who truly believe are waiting and doing His will at the same time. The false professors are only concerned with getting caught doing something wrong. They are not concerned with the fact that it is wrong. So, if they think the Lord is not returning, they don't plan on dying or think they have time to repent; they are mistaken. His patience has proven their true heart and He will come when they are not aware.

140

> If Satan could read what the seven thunders said, would it make a difference?

Another reason this is sealed is so Satan cannot know the information either. This is my speculation, but I don't think he was present in heaven to see this vision, he can only read about it as we do. He is limited, but knows God's Word. If he could figure it out, would things then change? God knows better than to even open up that possibility even though He is sovereign and could thwart Satan. If the seven thunders did tell something that Satan could use against God, then God would have to change it to stop him. This would give Satan justification in saying "no fair". God won't change His Word, even when it isn't written down. So it is best that we can't know what He said this time.

> Now the generation to come, your sons who rise up after you and the foreigner who comes from a distant land, when they see the plagues of the land and the diseases with which the LORD has afflicted it, will say ... "Why has the LORD done thus to this land? Why this great outburst of anger?" Then *men* will say, "Because they forsook the covenant of the LORD, the God of their fathers ... They went and served other gods and worshiped them ..."
>
> The secret things belong to the LORD our God, but the things revealed belong to us and to our sons forever, that we may observe all the words of this law. Deut 29:22-26, 29 NASU

> How does God's revelation in the Bible differ from other religions?
>
> What are some of the secret things that belong to the Lord?

Our God has revealed much to us over the centuries. We have example after example in the Old Testament of God's wrath. One point of these many examples is so that people will ask why. The answer is always the same. The people have turned away from God. These things are not secret but public knowledge. Unlike some religions that have secret rituals, or knowledge that only the higher echelon may know or understand, the Lord has written these things down so that all who want may benefit.

The secret things that God has held back are few. The exact time that Jesus will come back is one. The exact manner in which it will all end is another. The time of the rapture is also a secret. But He has provided all we need to know to be ready. Being ready is therefore more important than when He will come back. Being ready is really simple; follow His commands.

The Oath

> What is the significance of the angel swearing by Him Who lives forever?

For when God made a promise to Abraham, because He could swear by no one greater, He swore by Himself. (Heb 6:13 NKJV)

For men indeed swear by the greater, and an oath for confirmation *is* for them an end of all dispute. (Heb 6:16 NKJV)

This confirms this is an angel as he is swearing by one who is greater. It is a confirmation that there will be no more delay because it is God who has sent the message and it is God who will confirm and ensure that there will be no more delay. There will be no more delay because the promise is made by the Lord who lives forever. Because He lives forever, He is omniscient and can confidently say whether or not there will be a delay.

In Isaiah, God challenged the people to understand His eternal nature. He asked them which of their idols could declare what would happen in the future to prove that they were gods. To prove that He is God, the Lord, has declared what will happen in the future as well as what had already come true in His prophecies. His ultimate goal in this was salvation, not destruction, but when all of His warnings are not heeded, then His destruction will not be delayed (Isa 41:21-23, 43:9, 45:21, 46:9-10, 48:3, 48:14.)

> What is the significance of the angel swearing by the Creator?

Since God has created the heavens, the earth and all that is in them, He can do what He wants with it, when He wants. He has decided and will enforce what the angel says since this is His messenger.

In Numbers 5:11-31, the Law specified that a woman who was accused of unfaithfulness (simply because her husband was jealous) had to take an oath to prove her innocence. In the oath, she agrees that her thigh will waste away and stomach swell after drinking water that had dust from the tabernacle floor and the oath washed from a scroll into the water. It was once explained to me that the dust from the floor of the tabernacle was dirt from around the altar where the blood of the sacrifices flowed. The probability of the woman getting sick was almost a certainty. Therefore, it was in God's hands to keep her well if she was innocent.

On closer examination, the tabernacle was inside the tent or the building in later years. While the priests could track dirt into the temple, it isn't certain that contaminated dust would be in the water (don't trust things people tell you without some verification). Instead of God needing to protect an innocent woman from certain disease, I believe the oath would only bring a divine act of accusation upon the guilty. Either way, it is God's responsibility to show the guilt or innocence of the person.

> How does this oath relate to the angel's oath in Revelation and the scroll?

In both cases, an oath is given before God. The people of Israel were compared many times to an unfaithful wife. The woman was to drink bitter water (trials and tribulation) to prove her guilt or innocence in response to the oath. The charges were written on a scroll and washed into the water. If she were guilty, then her abdomen would swell. In Revelation, John is to take the scroll and eat it. After John ate, his stomach was sour. The oath of the angel is that there will be no delay, God will judge to demonstrate whether or not the world has been faithful to Him. Tribulation and trial have already come, but John eats the scroll and proves that the accusations of our jealous God are true by his stomach turning sour. The inhabitants of the earth have been unfaithful to the Creator. According to Jewish tradition, if the woman was guilty and didn't die, she could no longer have children.[40] In like manner, it is possible that after this, no more will come to Christ from out of the earth.

> When the angel says there will be no more delay, can we expect immediate punishment upon the earth for sin? Explain why your answer.

The man dressed in linen, who was standing above the river, raised both his hands toward heaven and took a solemn oath by the One who lives forever, saying, "It will go on for a time, times, and half a time. When the shattering of the holy people has finally come to an end, all these things will have happened." (Dan 12:7 NLT)

This is another instance of an angel swearing by God that things will occur as they have been told. When we see angels swearing it must be serious and not to be taken lightly. It is God's Word that it will happen and it is worthy of our study. However, God's timing isn't always what we think it will be. In the next chapter of Revelation, we will see a reference to 42 months, which is the same as time (year), times (two years) and half a time (six months). The angel swears that there will be no more delay even though it appears there will still be three and a half years before the end. It also implies that until this time, there has been a delay, which we know to be at nearly 2,000 years and counting.

> What is a reason for the delay to end?

And except those days should be shortened, there should no flesh be saved: but for the elect's sake those days shall be shortened. (Matt 24:22)

---

[40] Matthew Henry, *Matthew Henry's Commentary on the Whole Bible*, (Seattle: Biblesoft, 2006), Numbers 5:11-31, Electronic database.

Jesus told us why the delay of the end of all things will end. It is so that some of the remaining Christians on earth will be able to survive. Those that the Lord has chosen are precious in his sight. Some trials and tribulation are expected and we are all called to suffer. But God has His limits on what He will do. The angel says that in the days when the seventh angel is about to sound his trumpet, the mystery will be accomplished. It is not until Revelation 11:15 that the last trumpet is sounded. A lot is to occur before that time.

The Mystery of God

> I earlier stated that the elements of the Christian faith are not secret but public knowledge. So what is this mystery of God that will be revealed?

There are several mysteries mentioned in Scripture. A mystery is something God knows and reveals to us when He decides.

> My purpose is that they may be encouraged in heart and united in love, so that they may have the full riches of complete understanding, in order that they may know the mystery of God, namely, Christ, in whom are hidden all the treasures of wisdom and knowledge. (Col 2:2-3 NIV®)

One mystery is all the treasures of wisdom and knowledge are in Jesus. How could this be, except that Jesus is Himself God? Until Jesus came, it was a mystery that God is three in One.

> When you read this you can perceive my insight into the mystery of Christ, which was not made known to the sons of men in other generations as it has now been revealed to his holy apostles and prophets by the Spirit; that is, how the Gentiles are fellow heirs, members of the same body, and partakers of the promise in Christ Jesus through the Gospel. (Eph 3:4-6 RSV)

This mystery is that the Gentiles are to become part of Christ (saved) as well as Jews. While that may seem a no-brainer to us, it was pretty hard for many Jews to accept.

> Behold, I tell you a mystery; we shall not all sleep, but we shall all be changed, in a moment, in the twinkling of an eye, at the last trumpet; for the trumpet will sound, and the dead will be raised imperishable, and we shall be changed. (1 Cor 15:51-52 NASB)

In the Old Testament, life after death was not clearly defined. In the New Testament, not only is it defined, but goes even further, letting us know that there will be a day when both the dead and the living in Christ will take on immortal bodies. The Word gives us enough to hope but not enough detail for unnecessary speculation.

The rapture, as described in 1 Thessalonians 4:13-17, is still a mystery to many and is completely rejected by several denominations. It was unknown to the believers before Christ came.

Revelation 10:8-11

> Then the voice which I heard from heaven spoke to me again and said, "Go, take the little book which is open in the hand of the angel who stands on the sea and on the earth." So I went to the angel and said to him, "Give me the little book." And he said to me, "Take and eat it; and it will make your stomach bitter, but it will be as sweet as honey in your mouth." Then I took the little book out of the angel's hand and ate it, and it was as sweet as honey in my mouth. But when I had eaten it, my stomach became bitter. And he said to me, "You must prophesy again about many peoples, nations, tongues, and kings." (NKJV)

The little scroll

> Why do you think the scroll is little instead of huge like the one in Zechariah 5:1-4, which has curses written on it for those who swear falsely?

You would think that the scroll at the end times would be even larger than the one in Zechariah. We have many more sins piled up over the years as well as the evils of the end of the age. The scroll is little for two reasons. First, it demonstrates that there is not much time left. Secondly, it is little because God has already said everything before. This is the final warning to the people of the earth. There will be no more end time prophecies from God after this. John is told that one more time a prophecy must be given and he is the one to deliver it. The following verses and the symbolism of the small scroll really put the lid on any more information being given on the end times. We have plenty to learn from and study, but nothing more will be revealed beyond what is said in Revelation.

> I warn everyone who hears the words of the prophecy of this book: if anyone adds to them, God will add to him the plagues described in this book, and if anyone takes away from the words of the book of this prophecy, God will take away his share in the tree of life and in the holy city, which are described in this book. (Rev 22:18-19 ESV)

> Why does John have to eat the scroll?

> Your words were found and I ate them, And Your words became for me a joy and the delight of my heart; For I have been called by Your name, O LORD God of hosts. (Jer 15:16 NASU)

Why has my pain been perpetual And my wound incurable, refusing to be healed? Will
You indeed be to me like a deceptive *stream* With water that is unreliable? Therefore,
thus says the LORD, "If you return, then I will restore you — Before Me you will stand;
And if you extract the precious from the worthless, You will become My spokesman.
They for their part may turn to you, But as for you, you must not turn to them. … So
I will deliver you from the hand of the wicked, And I will redeem you from the grasp of
the violent." (Jer 15:18-19, 21 NASU)

Jeremiah had one of the toughest prophet jobs in the Old Testament. God's Word
brought Him joy, but also grief because he was persecuted for the prophecies. It got to
the point where he gave up. The Lord promised that he would be kept safe as long as
he repented and was obedient to relay the message to the people.

God's words are an immediate joy to us because they come from God Himself.
They are the words of our Father and because we are part of the family, we delight in
hearing from Him. As with Jeremiah, there will be times when His Word causes other
to ostracize or persecute us. However, He will always be with us and will support us
when we are obedient. John was already familiar with persecution; that is why he was
on Patmos in the first place. Because of his obedience, he is given the most
comprehensive book of end time prophecy in the Bible.

Ezekiel had a very similar position as John including a scroll that he was to eat
(Ezek 2:7-3:3). He was given a prophecy to give to the Israelites that had already been
carried off to captivity. It was not pleasant, and the people were not ready to listen.
Had they listened before, they would not have been taken into captivity. The words are
sweet in the mouth because they are God's Word. As Jeremiah above and David say
over and over again, they delight in God's Word, His law.

Psalm 119 is amazing in that it is the longest chapter in the Bible and in it David
expressed the goodness and delight of God's Word in almost every verse.
Unfortunately, there is the flip side for those who do not delight in his Word. They are
the ones who will suffer.

And you shall speak my words to them, whether they hear or refuse to hear; for they
are a rebellious house. (Ezek 2:7 RSV)

But the house of Israel will not listen to you; for they are not willing to listen to me;
because all the house of Israel are of a hard forehead and of a stubborn heart. (Ezek
3:7 RSV)

The sad part is that God's Word has been open to all, even those who reject it. It is
symbolized in the scroll that is lying open in the hand of the angel available for all to
read for centuries.

The word turns sour in John's stomach because he was called the Apostle of Love.
He had no desire to see people tortured and killed, even if they deserve it. John is told
he must be the one to bring this news to the world. It really isn't news. It is God
restating what He has always said. But He is faithful and makes sure that all may
know.

> How does the cup in the following verses in Jeremiah, the angel in Revelation, and Jesus' cup relate to each other?

> For thus says the LORD God of Israel to me: "Take this wine cup of fury from My hand, and cause all the nations, to whom I send you, to drink it. And they will drink and stagger and go mad because of the sword that I will send among them." (Jer 25:15-16 NKJV)

Instead of eating a scroll of prophecy, this prophecy is brought in a cup. It is the cup of God's wrath. Two things are very striking about it as I read on through verse 29. It is followed by a list of nations that is very specific. But make no mistake; all of the nations on the face of the earth are included across land and sea. This will happen to all. It relates back to the angel in Revelation because that prophecy will also encompass the land and the sea. The next thing is that all the nations are compelled to drink; there isn't any way to escape. God points to His own city, Jerusalem; if it does not escape His punishment, what makes others think they can? Unrepentant sin will be punished.

> And he took a cup of wine and gave thanks to God for it. He gave it to them and said, "Each of you drink from it, for this is my blood, which confirms the covenant between God and his people. It is poured out as a sacrifice to forgive the sins of many." (Matt 26:27-28 NLT)

Think for a few moments of the contrast that we are offered in Jesus. In Jeremiah and in Revelation, there is no choice, you will drink God's wrath if you have not already accepted Jesus' offer. He offers the cup of forgiveness, not taking and drinking of Him leaves only the unwilling consumption of His wrath. We escape the cup of God's wrath because Jesus drank all of it on the cross.

> What was there in this part of the lesson that may have caused you to take time and ponder?

Just as we had a pause at the opening of the seventh seal, so we have a pause at the seventh woe. This chapter is a pivotal point. Next, we will be looking at the time just before the last woe. It may even flash back a little to pick up events before the sixth woe, but we know that we have just received a grave pronouncement.

In these studies in Revelation, we have looked at many passages that express what will occur in the end times. Each is a little different and can be related to problems in Israel and Judea. The astounding message throughout history has been the same. God will come and judge the earth, nations, and people. It will be a time of terrible calamity for those who are not ready. The next woe will be the summation of many of these warnings to mankind.

This is a sobering chapter because it announces the end is near. It is also sobering if we realize that we have the same information as John to share with the world. Let's seek every opportunity to proclaim the forgiveness and love of Christ to a dying and sinful world.

Revelation 11:1-3

> Then I was given a measuring rod like a staff, and I was told: "Rise and measure the temple of God and the altar and those who worship there, but do not measure the court outside the temple; leave that out, for it is given over to the nations, and they will trample over the holy city for forty-two months. And I will grant my two witnesses power to prophesy for one thousand two hundred and sixty days, clothed in sackcloth." (RSV)

The Temple

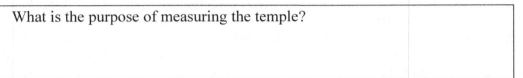

What is the purpose of measuring the temple?

> So he measured the length thereof, twenty cubits; and the breadth, twenty cubits, before the temple: and he said unto me, This is the most holy place. (Ezek 41:4)

> Thou son of man, shew the house to the house of Israel, that they may be ashamed of their iniquities: (Ezek 43:10a)

In Ezekiel chapters 41 and 42, Ezekiel watches in a vision as a "man" measures the temple that was supposed to have been built sometime after the Babylonian captivity. Ezekiel is finally told that the detailed description in his vision is to inspire the Israelites to be ashamed of their sins. The inner temple and the outer temple are carefully measured and a detailed description of the temple is provided. Only the priests could enter into the inner temple for it was holy. When they returned to the outer temple areas they even had to remove their holy clothes and put on common clothes. The holiness of the temple was in stark contrast to the sins of the people.

Why is there a distinction between the inner and outer courts of the temple and how does that relate to believers today?

What might this tell us about the existence of believers on earth during this part of the end times?

But you are a CHOSEN RACE, A ROYAL PRIESTHOOD, A HOLY NATION, A PEOPLE FOR *GOD'S* OWN POSSESSION, that you may proclaim the excellencies of Him who has called you out of darkness into His marvelous light; (1 Peter 2:9 NASB)

Do you not know that you are a temple of God, and *that* the Spirit of God dwells in you? (1 Cor 3:16 NASB)

The distinction was a reminder that access to God was only available to holy people. Holy people are separated or set apart. Today, all Christians are members of the priesthood. We are temples with God living in us and not in a physical building. This all leads me to believe that when John measures the temple and counts the worshipers, God is showing us that there are still true Christians left on earth at this time. They have separated themselves from the world and kept themselves holy.

Excluding the outer temple court and giving it to Gentiles to trample could then indicate that God has not yet intervened to bring about His kingdom on earth. He is still letting evil trample over all that is holy. Christian persecution will be increasing and if everything continues the way it is going, Christians will be eliminated from the earth. However, we need to remember our previous lesson that explained God will shorten the days so that His elect will survive. It also shows that the Antichrist hasn't yet been given permission to wage war against the saints and conquer them.

> Measuring the temple also confirms one thing that must happen before the end times start. What is that requirement?

There will also be a physical temple in Jerusalem during the end times and measuring it is an indication that God will protect it to accomplish His purposes and fulfill Scripture. The exclusion of the outer temple and trampling of the holy city means that Jews are not in control of Jerusalem. They may lose what they now have in that area or it may remain a divided city.

Forty-Two Months

> When the Bible uses measurements of time simply with the word "time" or "times," how do we know what it means?

... It is a decree of the Most High, which has come upon my lord the king, that you shall be driven from among men, and your dwelling shall be with the beasts of the field. You shall be made to eat grass like an ox, and you shall be wet with the dew of heaven, and seven periods of time shall pass over you, till you know that the Most High rules the kingdom of men and gives it to whom he will. (Dan 4:24-25 ESV)

The use of the word "time" was used to represent a year. The prophecy about King Nebuchadnezzar came to pass and substantiated this. How do we know that it was

149

seven years and not seven months, days, hours, or seconds? It isn't recorded in any history books that I can quote even though I've heard of some ancient references indicate a large gap in Nebuchadnezzar's reign. However, if we look at what happened in Daniel 4:33, we can see that his hair was long as eagle's feathers and fingernails grew long like bird's claws while he was in exile. This would have taken much longer than seven months.

> How does the three and a half years of Daniel 7 relate to the forty-two months of Revelation 11?

As I watched, this horn was waging war against the saints and defeating them, until the Ancient of Days came and pronounced judgment in favor of the saints of the Most High, and the time came when they possessed the kingdom. (Dan 7:21-22 NIV®)

He will speak against the Most High and oppress his saints and try to change the set times and the laws. The saints will be handed over to him for a time, times and half a time. But the court shall be seated, And they shall take away his dominion, To consume and destroy it forever. (Dan 7:25-26 NIV®)

The vision Daniel received clarifies that there will be a future time of three and a half years when the Antichrist will subject Christians to persecution. But the war ends when God steps in, takes the Antichrist's power away, and hands the kingdom over to the saints. Since this does not happen in Revelation 11, the 42 months described must be the first half of the tribulation.

Because Revelation now introduces a specific period of time, it is appropriate to dig further into the book of Daniel and try to get a better handle on the timeline of events of the tribulation and why it is seven years, or two sets of 42 months.

24 Seventy weeks are determined For your people and for your holy city, To finish the transgression, To make an end of sins, To make reconciliation for iniquity, To bring in everlasting righteousness, To seal up vision and prophecy, And to anoint the Most Holy.

24 Know therefore and understand, *That* from the going forth of the command To restore and build Jerusalem Until Messiah the Prince, *There shall be* seven weeks and sixty-two weeks; The street shall be built again, and the wall, Even in troublesome times.

26 And after the sixty-two weeks Messiah shall be cut off, but not for Himself; And the people of the prince who is to come Shall destroy the city and the sanctuary. The end of it *shall be* with a flood, And till the end of the war desolations are determined.

27 Then he shall confirm a covenant with many for one week; But in the middle of the week He shall bring an end to sacrifice and offering. And on the wing of abominations shall be one who makes desolate, Even until the consummation, which is determined, Is poured out on the desolate. (Dan 9:24-27 NKJV)

> What is the main concept presented in verse 24?
>
>
> What role do Jews have in this?

The main concept of verse 24 is that God has set a time limit on bringing salvation to the world. Salvation is from the Jews as Jesus told the woman at the well. This was not something new.

Some think that because Jesus has atoned for wickedness, that there is nothing more for Jews to do. These verses would indicate otherwise. Transgression must be finished and all sin ended. This will only be accomplished when Jesus comes back again. However, in accomplishing this, there are many promises to the Jews that still need to be fulfilled.

> How are these seventy weeks to be interpreted?

By looking at history, we can discern that these weeks are groups of seven years. From the time of the issuing of the decree to rebuild Jerusalem to its accomplishment was 49 years. These were years of 360 days (Jewish calendar of the time), not our year of 365 days. In 455 BC the decree was given. From then until AD 32 was 447 years as we count. Converting to 360-day years, it comes out to 483 of our years. This is exactly seven "weeks" plus 62 "weeks." This is the very year that Jesus, the Anointed One, was crucified. The title "Anointed One" is the Hebrew word from which we get the word Messiah. The Greek word used in the New Testament is Christ.

> *Mashiyach* (maw-shee'-akh); anointed; usually a consecrated person (as a king, priest, or saint); specifically, the Messiah:[41]
>
> *Christos* (khris-tos'); from NT:5548; anointed, i.e. the Messiah, an epithet of Jesus:[42]

Is there any question that Daniel's vision was referring to Jesus? Sixty-nine "sevens" passed by from that decree to rebuild Jerusalem until Jesus was crucified. There has been many more than one "seven" since then.

> What happened to the 70th "seven" and the promise to put an end to sin?

---

[41] *Strong's*, s.v. "OT:4899".
[42] Ibid., s.v. "NT:5547.

Even though Jesus died to pay the penalty for sin, sin still exists. For some reason God has interrupted this timetable for the Jews.

> I want you to understand this mystery, dear brothers and sisters, so that you will not feel proud about yourselves. Some of the people of Israel have hard hearts, but this will last only until the full number of Gentiles comes to Christ. (Rom 11:25 NLT)

That reason is so that the full number of Gentiles (all those who are not of Jewish heritage) will have an opportunity to be saved and come to Jesus. At some point, God will determine that it is no longer the time of the Gentiles and will again focus His attention on the salvation of the Jews. When that happens, the timetable will start again. This leads many to believe that the rapture must take place before the last seven years as a mark that the time of the Gentiles is finished.[43] While that sounds very attractive and makes sense, it is not a reason that the rapture would have to mark the end of the time of the Gentiles.

Consider these verses in Daniel along with previous ones we've examined in this lesson.

> Out of one of them came another horn, which started small but grew in power to the south and to the east and toward the Beautiful Land. It grew until it reached the host of the heavens, and it threw some of the starry host down to the earth and trampled on them. It set itself up to be as great as the Prince of the host; it took away the daily sacrifice from him, and the place of his sanctuary was brought low. Because of rebellion, the host [of the saints] and the daily sacrifice were given over to it. It prospered in everything it did, and truth was thrown to the ground. (Dan 8:9-12 NIV®)

> He said to me, "It will take 2,300 evenings and mornings; then the sanctuary will be reconsecrated." (Dan 8:14 NIV®)

> As he came near the place where I was standing, I was terrified and fell prostrate. "Son of man," he said to me, "understand that the vision concerns the time of the end." (Dan 8:17 NIV®)

What are some distinct prerequisites that must occur before the seven years of tribulation and after Jesus is crucified as we've seen in Daniel?

---

1. Jerusalem and the temple must be destroyed. The people of the ruler who is to come will destroy it. This ruler can be identified in the verses above as the Antichrist. History has already recorded this destruction was done by

---

[43] Arnold G. Fruchtenbaum, "Israelology," *Chafer Theological Seminary Journal* 60, no. 1 (January 2000): 57, accessed March 12, 2016, http://www.galaxie.com.ezproxy.liberty.edu:2048/article/ctsj06-1-03.

Rome in 70 AD. This first requirement has already been fulfilled and also identifies that the Antichrist has to be of Roman descent. However, according to Andrew Steinmann, a professor of theology and Hebrew, some interpret Daniel 11:37 to show that the Antichrist will be Jewish.[44] Steinman and I both agree this is not a good interpretation.

2. There must be a time of unprecedented peace. This would be the covenant that the Antichrist establishes with "the many" (see Daniel 9:27 and the white horse in Lesson 5). It is possible that part of this peace is what enables Israel to rebuild the temple.

3. Also, the temple must be rebuilt. It could be rebuilt after the last "seven" starts or any time before. We know the temple is rebuilt because the Antichrist will stop the sacrifice and offering, which can only be done in the temple. He also sets up an abomination in the temple. By implication, Israel must be restored as a nation. The only way to build a temple in Jerusalem would be for Jews to be in control of the nation and the city.

> How do the 2,300 morning and evening sacrifices in Dan 8:14 fit in the end time scenario?

In the vision recorded in Daniel 7, Daniel was also given information about the end times. The additional information in chapter eight can either clarify or confuse the time line, but they are part of the puzzle. From his vision in chapter seven, we are first introduced to a three-and-a-half-year period that ends with the Antichrist losing his power forever. These verses specifically indicate that 2,300 mornings and evening sacrifices will be made to the Antichrist rather than to the "Prince of the host." After these stolen sacrifices, the sanctuary will be reconsecrated which can only happen after Jesus comes back and the Antichrist is defeated.

One explanation is that the removal of the sacrifices mentioned in Daniel 8 is what happened when Antiochus Epiphanes invaded and took away the elements in the temple. The confusion occurs because this prophecy is very much like the prophecies against the king of Babylon in Isaiah 14 and the king of Tyre in Ezekiel 28. There is a near term fulfillment and as well as an explanation of what happened to Satan in the past.

When we look back at history, we can see that, in accordance with the interpretation of the vision, Alexander the Great conquered Persia and one of the four generals that succeeded him, Antiochus Epiphanes, fulfilled some of it – removing the sacrifices for 1,150 days. However, the prophecy also speaks of reaching the host of heaven and throwing them down to the earth. This is clearly not Antiochus.

The prophecy also says that the sacrifices were given over to him. This appears to be a reference to a future instance, not what happened with Antiochus, which is why I've included this reference in the time line of the tribulation.

Another explanation and to find a logical time when the sacrifice is taken away requires that we count backward from the end of the tribulation by 2,300 sacrifices,

---

[44] Andrew E. Steinmann, "Is the Antichrist in Daniel 11?," *Bibliotheca Sacra* 162, no. 646 (April 2005): 206, www.galaxie.com.ezproxy.liberty.edu:2048/article/bsac162-646-05.

one in the morning and one in the evening. To confuse the issue, some Bible versions translate this as 2,300 days, which is incorrect. Since the reference is to both morning and evenings it would be 1,150 days. This is roughly the "middle" of the seven when the sacrifices are stopped and would be about 38 months. The word used for middle is also used to mean divide into more than two parts or even in the midst. So, it doesn't necessarily mean that it has to be exactly in the middle of the "seven" or at 42 months.

This means that from the time the Antichrist breaks the covenant, it will be 110 days before he sets himself up in the temple as god.

Now look at these verses in Daniel 12 that also refer to the end.

> The man clothed in linen, who was above the waters of the stream, raised his right hand and his left hand toward heaven; and I heard him swear by him who lives for ever that it would be for a time, two times, and half a time; and that when the shattering of the power of the holy people comes to an end all these things would be accomplished. (Dan 12:7 RSV)

> And from the time that the continual burnt offering is taken away, and the abomination that makes desolate is set up, there shall be a thousand two hundred and ninety days. Blessed is he who waits and comes to the thousand three hundred and thirty-five days. (Dan 12:11-12 RSV)

How do these references to 42, 43, and 43.5 months fit in the time line?

When the power of the holy people has been finally broken, then it will be three and a half years. Looking back at the other descriptions of the end times ties together these events so that we can only know that they start somewhere around the middle of the tribulation or the last "seven."

Time Line for the Last "Seven" Or the Great Tribulation.

- The Start of the Seven Years
  - Covenant with Many (Dan 9:27)
  - Gentiles Trample Outer Court for 42 Months (Rev 11:2)
  - Two Witnesses for 1,260 Days (Rev 11:3)
- The Second Half of the Seven Years
  - Saints Handed Over to Antichrist For 3 1/2 Years (Dan 7: 25-26)
  - Daily Sacrifice and Saints Handed Over to Antichrist for 2,300 sacrifices (Dan 8:12,14)
  - Sacrifice Stopped and Abomination Set Up for 1,290 Days (Dan 12:11)
  - Woman Flees to Desert For 1,260 Days (Rev 12:6, 14)
  - Beast Given Authority for 42 Months and Wages War Against Saints and Conquers (Rev 13:5, 7)
  - Start Abomination That Causes Desolation Continues Until His End (Dan 9:27)
  - Power of Saints Broken After 3 1/2 Years (Dan 12:7)
- After Second Half
  - Temple Reconsecrated (Dan 8:14)

- o 1,290 Days After Sacrifice Stopped and Abomination Set Up (Dan 12:11)
- o Blessing for Those Who Reach the End of 1,335 Days (Dan 12:12)

> How do you explain the 1,290 days and 1,335 days that extend past the end of the tribulation (Dan 12:11)?

The sacrifices aren't restarted immediately after Jesus comes back at the end of the tribulation. Daniel 12:11 clearly says that they are stopped for 1,290 days implying that they are restarted. Many believe that there will be sacrifices offered during the millennial reign of Christ as described in the book of Ezekiel. This would support that. It is possible that cleaning and restoring the temple will take 30 days.

These sacrifices will obviously not be to remove sin, since Jesus has already done that once for all time. They will be ceremonial feasts that will proclaim all that Jesus has done. Some think that during the millennial reign, we will all be vegetarians and not kill animals for food. However, it looks like we will be enjoying meat and that will be part of the festivals as they were also enjoyed in the Old Testament.

The second part of the question is the introduction of 1,335 days, which is a real mystery. Does something happen 75 days after the end of the tribulation, 45 days after the sacrifices are reinstated? The answer to this seems to be the things that have been sealed up.

> Where does the rapture fit into this picture?

Now concerning the coming of our Lord Jesus Christ and our being gathered together to him, we ask you, brothers, not to be quickly shaken in mind or alarmed, either by a spirit or a spoken word, or a letter seeming to be from us, to the effect that the day of the Lord has come. Let no one deceive you in any way. For that day will not come, unless the rebellion comes first, and the man of lawlessness is revealed, the son of destruction, who opposes and exalts himself against every so-called god or object of worship, so that he takes his seat in the temple of God, proclaiming himself to be God. (2 Thess 2:1-4 ESV)

For God has not destined us for wrath, but to obtain salvation through our Lord Jesus Christ, who died for us so that whether we are awake or asleep we might live with him. Therefore encourage one another and build one another up, just as you are doing. (1 Thess 5:9-11 ESV)

These are probably the most compelling verses to suggest that the rapture occurs at the middle of the tribulation. The timing says that it will not occur until the rebellion happens. Daniel 8:12 ties the rebellion and the persecution of the saints to the last half of the tribulation. The man of lawlessness or the Antichrist isn't completely revealed until he establishes his worship in the temple.

I believe the reason for the rapture is to remove all believers so that they won't suffer God's wrath. If I'm right, then I would expect that God's wrath would begin at the same time. The power that the Antichrist has over the saints will be over those who come to Jesus after the rapture. However, I'll be hasty to add that I could be wrong. I have gone over these verses many times and there is enough ambiguity to say that no one can be 100% sure. I could even change my mind next week after more study.

> This lesson has been a bit cerebral, so what is the point? How does it help you in your Christian walk?

Hopefully, this lesson points out that God has known exactly what will happen long before it occurs. He is the One who knows because He is the One that ensures it will happen. If He can ensure that Jesus came at exactly the right time, He will also be able to bring all the rest of these events at the right time. The Antichrist will try to change the set times, but he will fail. If you have put your trust in Jesus, then you can also know that you will be with Christ forever. If you haven't, then you can know that you will be with the Antichrist for eternity – in hell. If you are waiting for the right time to turn your life over to Christ, then, think about the fact that we can't determine the exact time of the events at the middle of the tribulation much less the time the tribulation will start. In the same way, you can't be certain you will have an opportunity in the future to trust Christ. You must do it now while you have the chance!

May we be comforted by His control and may we be even more urgent in sharing the good news so that as many as possible will join us in the rapture and escape God's wrath.

Lesson 10 – Revelation 11:4-19

Revelation 11:4-13

These are the two olive trees and the two lampstands that stand before the Lord of the earth. And if anyone wants to harm them, fire flows out of their mouth and devours their enemies; so if anyone wants to harm them, he must be killed in this way. These have the power to shut up the sky, so that rain will not fall during the days of their prophesying; and they have power over the waters to turn them into blood, and to strike the earth with every plague, as often as they desire. (4-6)

When they have finished their testimony, the beast that comes up out of the abyss will make war with them, and overcome them and kill them. And their dead bodies *will lie* in the street of the great city which mystically is called Sodom and Egypt, where also their Lord was crucified. Those from the peoples and tribes and tongues and nations *will* look at their dead bodies for three and a half days, and will not permit their dead bodies to be laid in a tomb. And those who dwell on the earth *will* rejoice over them and celebrate; and they will send gifts to one another, because these two prophets tormented those who dwell on the earth. (7-10)

But after the three and a half days, the breath of life from God came into them, and they stood on their feet; and great fear fell upon those who were watching them. And they heard a loud voice from heaven saying to them, "Come up here." Then they went up into heaven in the cloud, and their enemies watched them. And in that hour there was a great earthquake, and a tenth of the city fell; seven thousand people were killed in the earthquake, and the rest were terrified and gave glory to the God of heaven. (11-13 NASU)

Two Witnesses

Who do you think these two witnesses are or represent?

As the tribulation starts, God calls two men into a unique ministry that has parallels to some of the prophets in the Old Testament. They are called to proclaim God's Word openly and in such a manner that evil people will try to silence them by killing them. Because of the parallels to the past, many believe that these men are reincarnations of the actual prophets.

Some believe that these two have the same spirit as two Old Testament prophets.

Others, who need to symbolize everything in Revelation, say they represent the Church because the Church is persecuted, but can't be killed. They argue that when they are killed and resurrected the rapture occurs. I'm going to dismiss this theory because there isn't any parallel in the Christian faith for us to pray for droughts, plagues, or for us to kill our enemies with fire.

> Why do some people believe the two witnesses are Elijah and Enoch?

> And as it is appointed for men to die once, but after this the judgment, so Christ was offered once to bear the sins of many. To those who eagerly wait for Him He will appear a second time, apart from sin, for salvation. (Heb 9:27-28 NKJV)

The Bible says that Enoch and Elijah didn't die but were taken up to heaven. It also says that man is destined to die once and then face judgment. Many people therefore say that these two people are Enoch and Elijah coming back so that they also physically die. In these theories, Enoch and Elijah must come back because they have not yet tasted death. They were spared and now must come back to fulfill this Scripture. Does this really make sense? If everyone must die once, then it negates the whole concept of the rapture. Using this logic, everyone who is raptured must also return to earth at some time to die physically.

Possibly Elijah

> What are some other things about Elijah that would make him appear to be one of the witnesses?

> Look, I am sending you the prophet Elijah before the great and dreadful day of the Lord arrives. His preaching will turn the hearts of fathers to their children, and the hearts of children to their fathers. Otherwise I will come and strike the land with a curse. (Mal 4:5-6 NLT)

The last recorded words in the Old Testament are a promise that God will send Elijah before the end. Malachi was the last of the Old Testament prophets. Elijah's purpose is to restore family structure. If it doesn't happen, God says He will come and curse the land. The scene in Revelation certainly fits this. Paul has described the scene much better than I could.

> But understand this, that in the last days there will come times of stress. For men will be lovers of self, lovers of money, proud, arrogant, abusive, **disobedient to their parents**, ungrateful, unholy, inhuman, implacable, slanderers, profligates, fierce, haters of good, treacherous, reckless, swollen with conceit, lovers of pleasure rather than lovers of God, holding the form of religion but denying the power of it. Avoid such people. (2 Tim 3:1-5 RSV emphasis mine)

Right in the middle is the key that Elijah is to try to start the process of repentance. Destruction of the family is at the center of the other sins. However, people are not listening to these witnesses and God is withholding the rain. Not only that, but the end is coming soon.

And he will turn back many of the sons of Israel to the Lord their God. And it is he who will go *as a forerunner* before Him in the spirit and power of Elijah, TO TURN THE HEARTS OF THE FATHERS BACK TO THE CHILDREN, and the disobedient to the attitude of the righteous; so as to make ready a people prepared for the Lord. NASB (Luke 1:16-17)

> This passage was a prophecy of John the Baptists' ministry. How can Elijah be John and also one of the two witnesses?

The angel of the Lord announced that John the Baptist would come in the spirit and power of Elijah. Now the question is, if Jesus came first to bear sin, and will appear a second time to bring physical salvation (Heb 9:28), can we expect Elijah to appear first to spiritually prepare people, and then appear a second time to usher in the physical kingdom of Jesus? If so, then this is a very compelling argument that one of the two witnesses is indeed Elijah or someone with his power and spirit.

He answered, "Elijah does come, and he will restore all things. But I tell you that Elijah has already come, and they did not recognize him, but did to him whatever they pleased. So also the Son of Man will certainly suffer at their hands." Then the disciples understood that he was speaking to them of John the Baptist. (Matt 17:11-13 ESV)

Jesus affirms that Elijah will come again, yet He said that he has already come as John the Baptist. He must come again because there is something still unfulfilled in the prophecies about Elijah. The whole story hasn't been told yet. What Jesus said of Elijah and John the Baptist doesn't mean that Elijah must appear physically any more than He meant that John the Baptist was a reincarnation of Elijah.

Elijah was a man just like us. He prayed earnestly that it would not rain, and it did not rain on the land for three and a half years. (James 5:17 NIV®)

The two witnesses' ability to withhold rain is one of the things that Elijah did. This is also used to support the theory that one of the two is indeed Elijah or rather has the same spirit and power. Is it only a coincidence that it didn't rain for three and a half years and this is also how long the two witnesses are to preach? I don't think so.

Elijah replied to them, "If I am a man of God, let fire come down from heaven and consume you and your fifty." Then the fire of God came down from heaven and consumed him and his fifty. (2 Kings 1:12 NASU)

Elijah was also able to call down fire from heaven to destroy his enemies. While the two witnesses have the ability to kill their enemies with fire, it comes from their mouths, not from heaven. The similarity is sufficient, however, to add even more credibility to one of the men's identity as Elijah.

> How is the fire that comes from the witnesses' mouths like the witness of all Christians?

> Therefore thus says the LORD God of hosts: "Because you speak this word, Behold, I will make My words in your mouth fire, And this people wood, And it shall devour them." (Jer 5:14 NKJV)

As prophets spoke the word of God, it burned within those who heard. That is why Christians have such a strong effect on the unsaved. That is why some people cannot stand to be around Christians. The Lord is going to use these men to deliver His final decree to the people of the earth. They will know it is the Word of God just as all will know about their death. Unfortunately, those who gloat over their death have rejected the message.

Identity of the Other Witness

> What biblical events would indicate that the second witness is Moses?

> Six days later Jesus took Peter and the two brothers, James and John, and led them up a high mountain to be alone. As the men watched, Jesus' appearance was transformed so that his face shone like the sun, and his clothes became as white as light. Suddenly, Moses and Elijah appeared and began talking with Jesus. (Matt 17:1-3 NLT)

Since Moses appeared in glory on the mountain with Jesus and Elijah, people have argued that the second witness is Moses. The witnesses have the ability to turn water into blood and bring plagues just as Moses did. The case for the second witness being Moses is much less compelling than for one being Elijah. The only case for the second to be Enoch has already been stated. It isn't very compelling either.

> Why was the impact of Moses' first signs before Pharaoh diminished and how does that relate to the same thing happening with the two witnesses and even today?

When Moses confronted Pharaoh, it was a time when Pharaoh was in strong control, and people thought he was a god. Magic was rampant as demonstrated by the magicians' ability to produce some of the miracles that Moses did (Ex 7:11-13).

The coming of the lawless one by the activity of Satan will be with all power and with pretended signs and wonders, and with all wicked deception for those who are to perish, because they refused to love the truth and so be saved. (2 Thess 2:9-10 RSV)

Some of the impact of the witnesses will be weakened because Satan is able to duplicate turning water into blood as well as other so-called miracles. We see the preparation of this through movies, TV, and even Saturday morning cartoons. Because of the futuristic, spiritualistic movies, and TV programs being produced, kids today are being raised in an environment where their imaginations are not limited by physical realities. We have always had this in the realm of fairytales, but the intensity and believability is mounting. Only by becoming a Christian can anyone hope to be able to tell the source of these powers. In the time of Elijah, it was a time of cruelty and open idol worship. Even though he should have known better, Ahab worshiped Baal. Nobody today would be surprised if the head of a modern nation were to announce that he was a follower of one of the new spirit guides.

Who They Really Are

There is nothing in Revelation 11:3-12 that says they are returned prophets or that they have the spirit of Old Testament prophets in the same way that John the Baptist was identified. We also need to look more closely at the concept of having a spirit of a previous prophet.

What does it mean when we say that someone has the same spirit as Elisha?

Now it came about when they had crossed over, that Elijah said to Elisha, "Ask what I shall do for you before I am taken from you." And Elisha said, "Please, let a double portion of your spirit be upon me." (2 Kings 2:9 NASB)

Now when the sons of the prophets who were at Jericho opposite *him* saw him, they said, "The spirit of Elijah rests on Elisha. ..." (2 Kings 2:15 NASB)

Elisha was given a double portion of the spirit of Elijah. Now it doesn't say that Elisha received double of the Holy Spirit but of Elijah's spirit. It is also interesting to note that the other prophets recognized that the spirit of Elijah was resting on Elisha. This is a strong argument, along with Jesus' statements, that the spirit of a person can be given to another person. I don't think that this means that Elijah came and took control of Elisha, because they were very different men. Elisha didn't show any of the fear that Elijah exhibited when he ran from Jezebel. John the Baptist was not Elijah physically nor did he show the fear that Elijah did. We know when he was born and who his parents were. So it is probable that these witnesses are not actually Elijah and Moses, but because of the types of miracles performed, they have been gifted by God to perform the same types of work in the spirit or character of these prophets.

What would be some problems if these two witnesses were actually O.T. prophets raised from the dead?

Now some people still argue that these two are physically returned prophets. They say that just as they returned on the mount when Jesus was transfigured, they will return for 1,260 days to witness. This appears to be the theory in the *Left Behind* series. The problem with this theory is that both will die. This isn't a problem for Elijah because he never died and conceivably, he could still have an opportunity to die. But for Moses, it would mean a second death, which contradicts Hebrews 9:27. So instead of Moses, some people argue that Enoch is the second witness.

> And Enoch walked with God: and he was not; for God took him. (Gen 5:24)

In a long list of people, each is said to have died except Enoch. The difference stands out so much that most people believe that he was essentially raptured. Enoch would make a better choice as the other witness than Moses because he apparently never died. While it makes sense that Moses shouldn't die twice, we have other cases where people died and were brought to life again (Mark 5:41, Luke 7:14, John 11:44, Acts 9:40). Lazarus was raised and died a second time, therefore there is no problem with Moses being brought back to life and dying again – except for one thing; Moses was in another realm, physically as well as spiritually for thousands of years before he appeared on the mountain. All the other examples were temporary deaths with their mortal bodies, which had not yet decayed to dust, being made alive again. With Moses and Elijah appearing on the mount of transfiguration, and then disappearing, it is clear that neither had their old physical bodies.

> Then we which are alive and remain shall be caught up together with them in the clouds, to meet the Lord in the air: and so shall we ever be with the Lord. (1 Thess 4:17)

Another argument against the need for Elijah or Enoch to come back and die is the hope that we all have in being here when Jesus returns. Since we will not all die there is no scriptural requirement for Elijah or Enoch to come back physically just to die. This, however, opens up the whole question of just what does Hebrews 9:27 mean. It means just what it says. The normal course for most people is to die then face judgment. God has His exceptions in the rapture as well as those whom He brought back to life for a period of time before they died a second time.

How might the timing of the rapture (before the tribulation or at the midpoint) affect our concept of who the two witnesses are?

The rapture does bring up another difficulty. If it occurs before the two witnesses appear and they are indeed Elijah and Moses, then I think they should have transformed bodies. If they have transformed bodies, how or why would they die again? If the rapture occurs three and a half days after their witnessing period is over, then it would make sense that they too, would come back to life. However, everyone sees them ascend in a cloud, but Paul implies that the rapture will be more instantaneous (1 Cor 15:52).

Tom, Dick, or Harry

> And he said to me, "What do you see?" I said, "I see, and behold, a lampstand all of gold, with a bowl on the top of it, and seven lamps on it, with seven lips on each of the lamps that are on the top of it. And there are two olive trees by it, one on the right of the bowl and the other on its left." (Zech 4:2-3 ESV)
>
> Then he said to me, "This is the word of the Lord to Zerubbabel: Not by might, nor by power, but by my Spirit, says the LORD of hosts." (Zech 4:6 ESV)
>
> Then he said, "These are the two anointed ones who stand by the Lord of the whole earth." (Zech 4:14 ESV)

> How do these verses in Zechariah help identify the two witnesses?

These verses apply to the Spirit of God who is supplying the power and ability for His two servants, Zerubbabel and Jeshua, who rebuilt the temple after the Babylonian captivity. Just as these two were anointed to do the work and were the servants of the Lord of the earth, the two witnesses are doing the work of the Lord of the earth to rebuild the spiritual temple of the Church. This may be very necessary because the rapture has already occurred and there are no spiritually mature people left on earth to take this role of leadership for those who believe and accept Christ during the post rapture period.

The two witnesses could be any Tom, Dick, or Harry. They will be two very ordinary people whom God calls and anoints with power to minister with the same strength and power that Elijah and Moses had. They will be like John the Baptist, who was a unique individual, yet Jesus called him Elijah.

Their Death

> Who kills the two witnesses?

The beast that comes out of the abyss is the only one who can overcome the witnesses. This is a spiritual battle unlike any we have ever seen. There are several references to beasts in the book of Revelation. It's pretty hard to figure them out and determine who is who. However, chapter 17 finally identifies this beast as the Antichrist. Since there are many references to the beasts and they start in chapter 13, we'll try to tie them all together then.

> Where do the witness minister and where do they die?

The two witnesses are brought to Jerusalem where they will die together. There isn't anything in these verses that limit their ministry to Jerusalem until they are killed. Jerusalem is identified because it is where Jesus was crucified. Since it is the birthplace of Christianity, is seems very strange to refer to the city as Sodom and Egypt. This probably indicates that the opposing powers Moses had to deal with in Egypt are now centered in Jerusalem along with the source of all sexual perversions that was centered in Sodom. We are informed by these two figurative names that the capital of sin is now in Jerusalem, which is what one would expect with the Antichrist in control.

> Why will the world gloat over the death of the witnesses?

O God, the nations have invaded your inheritance; they have defiled your holy temple, they have reduced Jerusalem to rubble.

They have given the dead bodies of your servants as food to the birds of the air, the flesh of your saints to the beasts of the earth.

They have poured out blood like water all around Jerusalem, and there is no one to bury the dead.

We are objects of reproach to our neighbors, of scorn and derision to those around us. (Ps 79:1-4 NIV®)

This psalm gives an indication of the disgust that accompanies the unburied. It is the ultimate disgrace for someone, after they are dead, to have their body left for animals to devour. To make it even worse, these evil people will make sure that their bodies are displayed to the whole world. This disgrace demonstrates that the world will then think that their troubles are over because the last thing to prick their conscience has been removed. It is possible that there are no more Christians, the two witnesses are dead, now is the time for sin to reign supreme. All semblance of God's righteousness has been removed from the earth and the wicked are going to party for three and half days.

> How might their death and resurrection relate to the rapture of the Church?

They stand before God and He gives them special protection and power for 1,260 days. They use the power so dramatically to point to God and bring punishment on the earth that the beast can no longer put up with it. He is the only one who is given permission to kill them. He does this at the end of the 1,260 days of their ministry. I believe that along with them, there will be a wholesale slaughter of Christians if the rapture doesn't occur at that time or hasn't already occurred. It will probably happen much as Haman planned for the Jews to be slaughtered in the book of Esther. The celebration by inhabitants of the earth will be unprecedented.

Some believe that unbelievers will be so joyful that they will publicly broadcast the scene of the bodies in the street on worldwide television and also on the internet. But then God raises them to life and catches them up in the clouds while the world is watching. It sounds a lot like the rapture and could add to the arguments that the rapture occurs at the middle of the tribulation. In opposition to this argument, the precision that has been provided for us about the events would allow us to pinpoint the date of the rapture if this were true. We would be able to date the rapture by finding out when these two start their ministry. When we see them killed, we would know there would only be three and half days until the rapture. This is a good argument that the rapture isn't coincidental with the resurrection of these witnesses. However, another possibility is that the rapture has already come and this will be an announcement to the world of what the rapture really was.

How will the witnesses' resurrection be different from the rapture?

The raising of the witnesses is timed to ensure that the whole world knows what is going on. First, it takes three and a half days. By this time, a body would probably start to bloat and smell badly. There will be no doubt that they are absolutely dead before they are raised. Everyone will also be able to hear the voice from heaven. Unlike the rapture, they first stand up on their feet. It won't be in the twinkling of an eye (1 Cor 15:52). Everyone will have time to see it and know exactly what has happened. The earthquake is there to ensure that people know what has happened is from God and God alone. The fear of unbelievers will be very great.

> Wherefore God also hath highly exalted him, and given him a name which is above every name: That at the name of Jesus every knee should bow, of things in heaven, and things in earth, and things under the earth; And that every tongue should confess that Jesus Christ is Lord, to the glory of God the Father. (Phil 2:9-11)

We will see a fulfillment of this verse as everyone who survives the earthquake gives glory to God. The only problem is that it will still not be a saving knowledge of God.

Summary

What have you learned from this part of the lesson about God and what is your response to what you have learned?

God calls these two guys to minister in a unique way and we get all tied up in knots trying to figure out who they are. We try to fit them into a scriptural box of our own understanding. The thing that I have learned from this is that God has always provided miraculous exceptions in His Word. These two witnesses are good examples. They could be any or all of the people listed above. God is not limited. In His Word, He has described some things that we will never fully understand until we see Him face to face.

> So then neither the one who plants nor the one who waters is anything, but God who causes the growth. Now he who plants and he who waters are one; but each will receive his own reward according to his own labor. For we are God's fellow workers; you are God's field, God's building. (1 Cor 3:7-9 NASU)

This is more important than knowing who the workers are or when the rapture occurs. Just as these two witnesses are faithful to their calling, even knowing they will die at the hands of the Antichrist, let us be faithful to the work to which He has called us.

Revelation 11:14-19

> The second woe is past. Behold, the third woe is coming quickly. Then the seventh angel sounded: And there were loud voices in heaven, saying, "The kingdoms of this world have become *the kingdoms* of our Lord and of His Christ, and He shall reign forever and ever!" And the twenty-four elders who sat before God on their thrones fell on their faces and worshiped God, saying:
>
> "We give You thanks, O Lord God Almighty,
>
> The One who is and who was and who is to come,
>
> Because You have taken Your great power and reigned.
>
> The nations were angry, and Your wrath has come,
>
> And the time of the dead, that they should be judged,
>
> And that You should reward Your servants the prophets and the saints,
>
> And those who fear Your name, small and great,
>
> And should destroy those who destroy the earth."
>
> Then the temple of God was opened in heaven, and the ark of His covenant was seen in His temple. And there were lightnings, noises, thunderings, an earthquake, and great hail. (NKJV)

The Seventh Trumpet

> Recount the number of woes, trumpets, and seals up to this point.

We are now about to see the third of three woes, which is part of the seventh of seven trumpets, which is part of the seventh of seven seals. The last woe will contain seven bowls of God's wrath, which are plagues. This is the beginning of the end. If there has been any doubt about when God's wrath is poured on the world, it should be removed now. Heaven has said that His wrath has come but more important is that Christ will begin His reign. Unfortunately, the nations don't like it and the beginning of His reign will be with anger and judgment.

> What will be the beginning of Christ's rule over the earth be like?

For unto us a Child is born, Unto us a Son is given; And the government will be upon His shoulder. And His name will be called Wonderful, Counselor, Mighty God, Everlasting Father, Prince of Peace. Of the increase of *His* government and peace *There will be* no end, Upon the throne of David and over His kingdom, To order it and establish it with judgment and justice From that time forward, even forever. The zeal of the Lord of hosts will perform this. (Isa 9:6-7 NKJV)

We are very familiar with verse six since it is quoted many times at Christmas to celebrate Jesus' first coming. However, I doubt that many people know verse seven, which promises judgment or justice as some translations say. At the sounding of the trumpet, the prophecy of Isaiah 9:7 is about to be accomplished. Jesus is Prince of Peace, but we also have the reality of Revelation 11:18 that says the nations are angry. The beginning of His reign isn't going to be peaceful.

The LORD said to my Lord, "Sit in the place of honor at my right hand until I humble your enemies, making them a footstool under your feet." (Ps 110:1 NLT)

But our High Priest offered himself to God as a single sacrifice for sins, good for all time. Then he sat down in the place of honor at God's right hand. There he waits until his enemies are humbled and made a footstool under his feet. For by that one offering he forever made perfect those who are being made holy. (Heb 10:12-14 NLT)

It is clear that David was speaking of the Messiah, Jesus, when he wrote this psalm. Hebrews not only reiterates that Jesus is waiting for His enemies to be made a footstool for His feet, but it adds some insight. Jesus first had to provide a sacrifice for sins that would be once for all. That sacrifice has made all believers prefect in Him and so He is also waiting for all who will accept Him to place their faith in Him to be made holy.

How are Jesus' enemies made a footstool under His feet?

Many people believe that it is the job of the Church to make His enemies His footstool. They believe that the only way He will return is for us to preach the Gospel to the entire world and subdue it. While I believe we are to preach to the whole world, I don't think that the Church is God's instrument to subdue the world. From long ago, God has announced that this was to be His work.

> "I have trodden the wine press alone, and from the peoples no one was with me; I trod them in my anger and trampled them in my wrath; their lifeblood is sprinkled upon my garments, and I have stained all my raiment. For the day of vengeance was in my heart, and my year of redemption has come. I looked, but there was no one to help; I was appalled, but there was no one to uphold; so my own arm brought me victory, and my wrath upheld me. I trod down the peoples in my anger, I made them drunk in my wrath, and I poured out their lifeblood on the earth." (Isa 63:3-6 RSV)

When Jesus begins His reign on earth, He will subdue the nations that are His foes. Just as there will be no one who can help Jesus pour His wrath on the nations, there isn't anything anyone can do to save himself or anyone else for that matter. Jesus has paid the price and has provided our salvation. Only when we accept that it is entirely by His merit and not our own we can be saved.

> The LORD will stretch forth Thy strong scepter from Zion, *saying,* "Rule in the midst of Thine enemies." Thy people will volunteer freely in the day of Thy power; In holy array, from the womb of the dawn, Thy youth are to Thee *as* the dew. (Ps 110:2-3 NASB)

> The Lord is at Thy right hand; He will shatter kings in the day of His wrath. He will judge among the nations, He will fill *them* with corpses, He will shatter the chief men over a broad country. (Ps 110:5-6 NASB)

These verses also clear up who it is that will establish the kingdom, and how. The Lord Jesus will do it. Note the use of small caps in the word LORD. It designates *Yahweh* in the Hebrew but Lord without the small caps designates *Adoni* the reference Jesus made to himself in verse 1. It is at this point in the book of Revelation that He extends the scepter to Jesus and causes Him to rule in the midst of His enemies. We can see that it will take a battle. A description of the troops sounds like glorified saints or angels, but certainly not missionaries. We are now concerned for souls and spreading the word, not physically conquering our enemies. Yet the Lord makes it clear that He will crush and overcome the kings of the earth.

Who is currently the rule of this world, Jesus or Satan?

Now is the judgment of this world: now shall the prince of this world be cast out. (John 12:31)

Hereafter I will not talk much with you: for the prince of this world cometh, and hath nothing in me. (John 14:30)

Of judgment, because the prince of this world is judged. (John 16:11)

Satan is currently in charge of the world. This doesn't mean that he is sovereign or that he can do anything he wants. The trumpet announces that it is now given to Jesus. In John, Jesus reiterates that Satan is in charge of the world. However, He also marks Satan's time as short. His influence is weakened as the death, burial, and resurrection of Jesus breaks his power and the power of sin over believers – but not the world. Just as he has no control over Jesus, he has no hold on us as long as we abide in Jesus.

Satan has been condemned for almost 2,000 years; however, the sentence has not yet been carried out. The trumpet is announcing that Jesus is now going to carry out the judgment that He announced to the apostles. However, Satan knows the end is near and is coming to do his worst even though he is condemned.

The god of this age has blinded the minds of unbelievers, so that they cannot see the light of the Gospel of the glory of Christ, who is the image of God. (2 Cor 4:4 NIV®)

Satan is the god of this age and he has blinded people. This is why they did not repent in the first part of Revelation 11.

Judging and Rewards

How are those who are to be judged described and why are they described in this way?

How are those who are to be rewarded described and why are they described in this way?

The time has come for judging the dead and rewarding His servants. Isn't it interesting that the Lord has divided people into two categories – the dead and His servants?

And you were dead in your trespasses and sins, (Eph 2:1 NASU)

When you were dead in your transgressions and the uncircumcision of your flesh, He made you alive together with Him, having forgiven us all our transgressions, (Col 2:13 NASU)

Over and over, the New Testament makes it clear that all who do not believe in Jesus are already dead, even though they are physically alive. This concept is necessary for unbelievers to grasp so that they will know that they need a Savior, someone to make them alive.

> Jesus said to her, "I am the resurrection and the life. He who believes in Me, though he may die, he shall live. And whoever lives and believes in Me shall never die. Do you believe this?" (John 11:25-26 NKJV)

The opposite is true for those who believe in Jesus. We are alive and even though we may physically die, we will still live. Jesus' question of Martha is one that every person needs to answer in the affirmative at some time before they die physically or they will stay spiritually dead forever.

Those who believe are called servants. This is something that must be emphasized over and over again. In a world where people are told that they can believe anything they want, it is easy for us to tell someone that all they need to do is believe in Jesus. While this is correct, the Bible also informs us that belief is shown by obedience (Luke 6:46-49). The Greek word for servant is *doulos*. A more accurate translation is slave.[45] When we understand that we have transition from being slaves of Satan to slaves of God (Rom 6:22), we are better equipped to obey because we have a better perspective of our position.

> So you see, faith by itself isn't enough. Unless it produces good deeds, it is dead and useless. (James 2:17 NLT)

How is it that these judgments and rewards are announced at what we thought was the midpoint of the tribulation? Shouldn't they come at the end of the tribulation?

Judgments and rewards sound like something that should be coming at the very end, not at the middle of the tribulation. This announcement could be similar to those we see many times in the Bible when God slips from near time prophecies right to the end. This occurs often when pronouncing judgment on a specific generation. Or, it could mean that it will take three and a half years to pour out His wrath on the earth while His raptured saints are being prepared to take over the kingdom.

We will have plenty of time to talk about the judgment, however it would make sense to stop and review the parables that Jesus told after a long discourse about end times (Matt 24). The first was told to emphasize staying ready for His return (Matt 25:1-13), the second to demonstrate and emphasize that His saints will be rewarded and that those who disobey will be punished (Matt 25:14-27). The third is a description of the final judgment providing rewards and punishment (Matt 25:31-46).

---

[45] S. Grimm and S. Wilke, *New Testament Lexicon*, Joseph Henry Thayer, ed., (Seattle: Biblesoft 2006), s.v. "NT:1401."

> What are the rewards and punishments Jesus described in Matthew 25?

> You have been faithful over a little, I will set you over much; enter into the joy of your master. (Matt 25:23 RSV) ... inherit the kingdom prepared for you from the foundation of the world; (Matt 25:34 RSV)

Jesus is teaching that there will be a time when the saints are in charge over much. This is something that has yet to come and it will be fulfilled on the earth as He has promised. It still boggles my mind to think that there will be a time when Jesus looks at what we have done and actually gives us charge over parts of His kingdom. We won't see any more details of rewards in the book of Revelation for several chapters. Before that occurs, there will much detail about the judgment to be carried out on the earth.

> And while they went to buy, the bridegroom came; and they that were ready went in with him to the marriage: and the door was shut. Afterward came also the other virgins, saying, Lord, Lord, open to us. But he answered and said, Verily I say unto you, I know you not. Watch therefore, for ye know neither the day nor the hour wherein the Son of man cometh. (Matt 25:10-13)

Those who are not ready will be barred from the festivities when the rewards are distributed. We will be enjoying the company of Jesus while the rest of the world will be knocking at the door wanting to get in, but it will be too late. I have a feeling that when this announcement is made at the seventh trumpet, there may not be any more opportunities for people to come to Jesus.

Environmentalism

> How should Christians regard and respect our world?

The term environmentalist unfortunately carries the connotation that the person who is concerned about protecting the environment has made it a political or philosophical issue so that it becomes a religion to him. Many put the environment above the needs of people and essentially worship creation instead of the creator.

This certainly isn't the attitude Christians should have toward the physical world. The last phrase in Revelation 11:18 points out that God is going to destroy those who destroy the earth. If we don't have the proper regard and respect for God's creation, then we will undergo His discipline. Those who disregard nature and do not know Jesus will suffer God's wrath.

> Then the LORD God took the man and put him into the garden of Eden to cultivate it and keep it. (Gen 2:15 NASB)

The first few verses in Genesis 2 describe the earth and the Garden of Eden when it was first created. Before the fall, man's job was to take care of the beautiful creation that God had provided. After the fall, it became more difficult, but man's responsibility to care for creation didn't change.

> For the creation was subjected to futility, not willingly, but because of him who subjected it, in hope that the creation itself will be set free from its bondage to decay and obtain the freedom of the glory of the children of God. (Rom 8:20-22 ESV)

Because of the fall, all creation started to decay. As Christians, we must understand that while we need to care for our environment, we know that it is in a state of decay. That means that some species will become extinct despite our best efforts. We cannot, therefore, put their preservation above the needs of mankind. We must have the proper perspective regarding man and creation.

That perspective is provided in Psalm 8 as it states that God's glory is manifested in His creation and mankind has been given dominion over it. But the psalm also put us at a higher level, just below the heavenly being. We don't want to mess over God's glory.

The Temple

> What is the biggest difference between the temple in heaven and the one that was on the earth?

When the door of the temple in heaven is opened, it is as if all on the earth could plainly see what it is that God expects. The Ark of the Covenant is on display. The Ark of the Covenant on earth contained the tablets of the Law, which must be completely obeyed in order for anyone to be declared righteous. It is impossible for any of us to keep every law for our entire lives. All it takes is one little white lie to fall into the category of sinners.

> For whosoever shall keep the whole law, and yet offend in one point, he is guilty of all. (James 2:10)

The temple on earth always reminded people of their sins and their separation from God. The temple in heaven reminds us that it is only by the blood of Jesus and His mercy that we can be saved. It reminds us that we now have access to God by the blood of Jesus and we are no longer separated from Him.

> But Christ being come an high priest of good things to come, by a greater and more perfect tabernacle, not made with hands, that is to say, not of this building; Neither by the blood of goats and calves, but by his own blood he entered in once into the holy place, having obtained eternal redemption for us. (Heb 9:11-12)
>
> Mercy triumphs over judgment! (James 2:13b NIV®)

Jesus has already been in the heavenly temple and has cleared the way for all believers to come to God because He has sprinkled His blood on the mercy seat that covers the Ark of the Covenant in heaven. God's mercy triumphs over the requirements of the Law as symbolized in the mercy seat covering the Ark of the Covenant.

When the heavenly tabernacle is revealed, it will condemn all who have decided to live without faith in Jesus and all those who have decided that they could live by the law, either the Mosaic Law or the law of their own consciences (Rom 2:12-24). Therefore, the law that is represented by the Ark of the Covenant in heaven will judge them. They will have no excuse since they have had the law within them.

> Some believe the Ark of the Covenant shown in heaven is the one that was lost on earth. How would you explain that this not correct?

The Ark of the Covenant in heaven is not the ark that was lost when the temple was destroyed as some claim. The one in heaven was there before the earthly Ark was made. The temple on earth and all the furnishings were made after the pattern that was shown to Moses. Therefore, the one in heaven had to exist before the one on earth. Hebrews 9:11-12 clarifies; the pattern wasn't simply drawings, but the perfect tabernacle that isn't man-made. While the earthly Ark was lost or destroyed, the one in heaven has always been there.

> How does revealing the Ark in heaven with lightning, thunder, an earthquake, and hail relate to the earthly temple?

Then a cloud covered the tent of the congregation, and the glory of the Lord filled the tabernacle. And Moses was not able to enter into the tent of the congregation, because the cloud abode thereon, and the glory of the Lord filled the tabernacle. (Ex 40:34-35)

And the Lord said unto Moses, Speak unto Aaron thy brother, that he come not at all times into the holy place within the vail before the mercy seat, which is upon the ark; that he die not: for I will appear in the cloud upon the mercy seat. (Lev 16:2)

When the Lord filled the earthly tabernacle, even Moses, God's friend could not enter it. When Solomon brought the Ark into the temple in Jerusalem, the priests couldn't minister because of the cloud of God's glory filling it (2 Chron 5:14). Now His glory is being exposed to all of mankind. The result is the storm of His wrath.

Only the high priest was to enter the holy of holies where the Ark of the Covenant was kept. If anyone entered at any other time or in any other way, he was to die. If the whole world is now able to see the Ark of the Covenant, then they are about to die.

These are strong arguments that there will not be any more people coming to a saving knowledge of Jesus from this time through the end of the tribulation.

Summary – Preview

God has given us every chance to come to Him. The message has been made plain to all by these last two witnesses. The announcement that the last woe is about to come indicates that there is still some time before the end. In fact, He will send three angels to make sure everyone on earth hears the message. His judgment has come upon the world. The next three chapters go into more detail of the last of the seven years as well as providing a historical summary of the battle between good and evil that has led up to this time.

> What will be the fate of those who haven't sworn allegiance to Jesus before this time? How are they like many people today?

Those who haven't sworn their allegiance to the Lord Jesus by the time the seventh trumpet has sounded may be so hardened that they will never do so. The rest of the book indicates over and over that people don't repent.

It is also the same with people today who don't know Jesus and continue to reject Him. These are people who have heard the message many times and have never responded to the Holy Spirit. There comes a point in their life that they will not repent either. They have scoffed too many times at the claims of Jesus. They may have simply said. "Tomorrow," too many times thinking they can accept Jesus at their leisure. Like pharaoh of Egypt, their hearts have become hardened.

> For anyone who refused to obey the law of Moses was put to death without mercy on the testimony of two or three witnesses. Just think how much worse the punishment will be for those who have trampled on the Son of God, and have treated the blood of the covenant, which made us holy, as if it were common and unholy, and have insulted and disdained the Holy Spirit who brings God's mercy to us. For we know the one who said, "I will take revenge. I will pay them back." He also said, "The Lord will judge his own people." It is a terrible thing to fall into the hands of the living God. (Heb 10:28-31 NLT)

Those who reject the testimony of the two witnesses in Revelation will have trampled the Son of God under foot, treated His sacrifice as unholy, and insulted the Spirit of grace. Anyone who has repeatedly rejected the message of Jesus Christ is doing the same thing now! The seventh trumpet may sound for them at any time. While they will always have the opportunity to repent, they will refuse to do so.

If you haven't turned to Jesus in faith, I urge you to place your faith in Him, now!

Let those of us who know Jesus continue to do all we can to repeat the message.

Lesson 11 – Revelation 12:1-17

Revelation 12:1-5

> Now a great sign appeared in heaven: a woman clothed with the sun, with the moon under her feet, and on her head a garland of twelve stars. Then being with child, she cried out in labor and in pain to give birth. And another sign appeared in heaven: behold, a great, fiery red dragon having seven heads and ten horns, and seven diadems on his heads. His tail drew a third of the stars of heaven and threw them to the earth. And the dragon stood before the woman who was ready to give birth, to devour her Child as soon as it was born. She bore a male Child who was to rule all nations with a rod of iron. And her Child was caught up to God and His throne. (NKJV)

What is the first clue that we have to help us properly interpret this chapter?

We are immediately told that most of this chapter is dealing with symbols since John says he saw a great sign in heaven. What follows is used to explain the truth of history from a heavenly perspective. If the Bible tells us that the passage is a parable or that signs appear, then we must not try to take them literally. The *Left Behind* series was so intent at making things literal that they had to take these signs and present them in a vision to one of the characters. In effect, they were saying that these signs literally had to appear to someone at this time in the future. However, it is obvious that these signs were given to John. They don't have to reappear to anyone any more than Daniel's visions have to reappear.

How are these signs both similar and different from Daniel's?

We've seen a few glimpses of signs in Daniel's visions that fit into this category. They appear very real to the person that is receiving the vision but they can't make sense of them. In Daniel, an angel must tell him what these things mean because they are so obscure and deal with the future. Daniel's visions deal with a long time span covering many centuries. The vision of the woman and the dragon is the same in that it refers to things that have taken place as well as the future. Because we should be able to figure out what these symbols mean, they aren't explained in the context as were Daniel's.

The Woman

> What are some of the things that the woman could represent? Explain how you determine this.

The most evident answer is that this woman is a symbol for the nation of Israel. This is based on the similarities between this vision and Joseph's dream.

> Now he had still another dream, and related it to his brothers, and said, "Lo, I have had still another dream; and behold, the sun and the moon and eleven stars were bowing down to me." He related *it* to his father and to his brothers; and his father rebuked him and said to him, "What is this dream that you have had? Shall I and your mother and your brothers actually come to bow ourselves down before you to the ground?" (Gen 37:9-10 NASU)

When Joseph told his dream to his father, Jacob immediately related the sun to the father of the family and the moon to the mother and the stars to the children. God later renamed Jacob Israel from whom came the nation of Israel and eventually, Jesus. The child is obviously Jesus, as we'll discuss later.

> Why would or wouldn't Jesus' mother, Mary, be a good fit for the woman in the vision?

Some say that the woman is a symbol of Mary because she gave birth to Jesus. But we need to remember that this is symbolic and the description of the child being caught up to heaven is not the way it happened but is symbolic of the whole life of Jesus on earth. Likewise, we wouldn't therefore expect the woman to be the actual person who gave birth to Jesus.

> And the woman fled into the wilderness, where she hath a place prepared of God, that they should feed her there a thousand two hundred and threescore days [1260]. (Rev 12:6)

The woman is taken to a desert area to be protected for three and a half years. Mary went to Egypt but it was an unspecified time and it was before Jesus was "caught up to heaven."

> Then the dragon was angry with the woman, and went off to make war on the rest of her offspring, on those who keep the commandments of God and bear testimony to Jesus. And he stood on the sand of the sea. (Rev 12:17 RSV)

> That is why it depends on faith, in order that the promise may rest on grace and be
> guaranteed to all his descendants — not only to the adherents of the law but also to
> those who share the faith of Abraham, for he is the father of us all, (Rom 4:16 RSV)

Revelation 12:17 enlightens us that the Savior is not her only child but all who are obedient to God. In the same way that all people who have faith are considered Abraham's children, all people who hold to the testimony of Jesus (Christians) are the children of the woman.

There are more biblical references that eliminate the consideration of Mary as the woman than there are to consideration that she is Mary.

Why would or wouldn't the Church be a good fit for the woman in the vision?

Some would say that she is a symbol of the Church because of the persecution in verse 17. This is most likely the view of some that hold that all the promises of Israel are fulfilled in the Church. The reasoning is that the Church was Israel before Jesus was born. Therefore, all the discussion about the woman being Israel would apply to the Church before Christ.

This approach would mean that the Church gave birth to Jesus rather than Jesus giving birth to the Church. It would also mean that many of the physical promises given to Israel would have to be spiritualized to be fulfilled by the Church. This theory presents more problems than it solves when we try to understand the book of Revelation. It is too much to discuss here and could be a topic for another book.

The symbol of the pregnancy is a vivid description of the painful and violent events that led up to the time of Jesus. Israel's history from the writing of the last book of the Old Testament is one of turmoil. They were conquered by Greece, then Rome. During the time of the Maccabees, there was constant war and persecution in which hundreds of thousands were killed. Israel was not exactly considered to be any Roman's first choice for overseas duty and the soldiers took it out on the inhabitants of the land. Spiritually, they had been almost totally taken over by a religious system that kept the people in bondage to performance and their position in society.

The Dragon

Who is the dragon and how do you know?

> And the great dragon was thrown down, the serpent of old who is called the devil and
> Satan, who deceives the whole world; he was thrown down to the earth, and his
> angels were thrown down with him. (Rev 12:9 NASB)

Fortunately, there isn't any argument over the identity of the dragon. He is clearly identified as Satan. He is identified with the serpent in the Garden of Eden and the generic name of devil. The Bible states that the devil tempted Jesus and Jesus responded by calling him Satan. It also says that the devil put it into Judas' heart to betray Jesus and later it says that Satan entered into Judas. If you missed the correlation between the devil and Satan because they weren't in the same verse, there is now no doubt that all three are one and the same. This verse and Revelation 20:2 are the only two verses in the Bible that tie together the serpent, the devil, and his name Satan.

His Horns

> After that, in my vision at night I looked, and there before me was a fourth beast — terrifying and frightening and very powerful. It had large iron teeth; it crushed and devoured its victims and trampled underfoot whatever was left. It was different from all the former beasts, and it had ten horns. While I was thinking about the horns, there before me was another horn, a little one, which came up among them; and three of the first horns were uprooted before it. This horn had eyes like the eyes of a man and a mouth that spoke boastfully. (Dan 7:7-8 NIV®)

> He gave me this explanation: "The fourth beast is a fourth kingdom that will appear on earth. It will be different from all the other kingdoms and will devour the whole earth, trampling it down and crushing it. The ten horns are ten kings who will come from this kingdom. After them another king will arise, different from the earlier ones; he will subdue three kings. He will speak against the Most High and oppress his saints and try to change the set times and the laws. The saints will be handed over to him for a time, times and half a time." (Dan 7:24-25 NIV®)

The dragon is described using some of the same language that describes the fourth beast in Daniel. The final king will also oppress the saints for three and half years. The parallel is significant enough to presume that we can expect to see a unified nation that takes over the whole earth and then collapses into ten nations. Or, it could be a confederacy made up of ten kingdoms under the influence and power of Satan.

When the European common market was formed, many thought that this prophecy was fulfilled. History has proved this speculation wrong as more and more nations have been added.

Some have thought that the beast was the Roman Empire because it conquered what many believed to be the whole earth. These believe that from the time of the collapse of the Roman Empire until the fulfillment of the prophecy with the ten kings, many centuries will have elapsed. Since the Roman Empire excluded a significant portion of the earth, it doesn't seem to fit the vision. In addition, the elapsed time for the ten kings to become visible is not a good argument to support the fourth beast being the Roman Empire.

Since this dragon exists from before Christ's birth and until the end described in the vision, it would be hard to say that the fourth beast represent any specific nation in history. It is most likely a nation that is in our future as well as John's.

> The ten horns which you saw are ten kings who have not yet received a kingdom, but they receive authority as kings with the beast for one hour. (Rev 17:12 NASU)

Since John is looking into the future, the horns are ten future kingdoms that will form an alliance and support the Antichrist. Since they receive authority for only an hour, it appears that their reign will be very short in comparison with the rest of

178

history and most likely at the very end. It gets confusing, but the heads and horns represent different kingdoms, not different views of the same kingdoms.

His Heads

> What do the dragon's seven heads represent and where do find the answer?

This calls for a mind with wisdom: the seven heads are seven mountains on which the woman is seated; they are also seven kings, five of whom have fallen, one is, the other has not yet come, and when he does come he must remain only a little while. As for the beast that was and is not, it is an eighth but it belongs to the seven, and it goes to destruction. (Rev 17:9-11 ESV)

Again, the Bible gives us some more information about the symbols we see. The first description is seven hills. This is not a big help! Speculation runs wild about the meaning of the hills. Some have said that they represent the city of Rome, which was built on seven hills. From this, they have deduced that the woman in chapter 17 is the Catholic Church since it is headquartered in Rome. I'll go into that in more detail when we get to chapter 17, but I don't agree with this simply because there are other cities that have been built on seven hills. The hills could easily represent individual cities or nations; however, we'll see a better argument for this in later lessons.

The description of seven kings is much clearer. At the time John wrote this, five had already passed and one was currently reigning. One will appear in John's future and then an eighth is introduced as being from the same line of kings. This eighth is the dragon. Above, we looked at Daniel 7:20, which identified the horns as ten kingdoms. The description is similar to the seven heads; however, John is looking at his history and his future, but from Daniel's perspective, it was all in the future. It is possible that the seventh head is the fourth beast from Daniel's vision. Revelation 17:12 would appear to confirm this.

His Mission

> What is the dragon's ultimate mission?

The desire of Satan has always been to subvert the authority of God and establish himself in His place. Daniel 7:7, quoted above, says that he will try to change the set times.

For thou hast said in thine heart, I will ascend into heaven, I will exalt my throne
above the stars of God: I will sit also upon the mount of the congregation, in the sides
of the north: (Isa 14:13)

How did Satan first attempt to do this?

And it grew up to the host of heaven; and it cast down *some* of the host and *some* of
the stars to the ground, and trampled them. (Dan 8:10 NKJV)

Satan had so much greed in himself that he used his power to reach heaven, throw
some of the starry host to the earth, and trampled on them. This is similar to the
description in Revelation 12:4. It is very possible that this is a description of a
rebellion of a third of the angels who have followed Satan. While Jude 6 says that
these have been securely bound until judgment, it appears that not all have been
bound, but some have been allowed to operate on earth as demons. Whatever the
situation may be; they have lost their position in heaven as a result.

How does Satan standing in front of the woman to devour her child reveal
his mission?

Satan continued to try to thwart God's authority in the Garden of Eden when he
led Adam and Eve astray. Since that time, he has been trying to annihilate the Jews
because he knew that the Savior would come from the Jews. By eliminating the Jews,
he would therefore also prevent the birth of Jesus before He came. He turned Israel to
idol worship and because of that, they were scattered. I'm sure Satan though he had
accomplished his purpose at that time. To make sure, he even tried to eliminate them
while in captivity (see the book of Esther). However, God brought the nation back
afterwards.

Since this failed, he turns his attention to trying to change any of God's
prophecies. I believe his hope is to prove God wrong at some point and to thereby
justify himself and escape his eternal punishment. If he can somehow show that there
is any flaw in God, then he will be able to stand before God and say, "You aren't
perfect so what right do You have to judge me?"

How do we demonstrate the same attitude as Satan?

In a way, we are doing the same thing as Satan when we try to make God out to be
the same as us. One way we do that is to say that we would never believe God would
send people to hell because that is not love. In other ways, we also try to find fault
with God in the hope that somehow that will keep Him from judging us.

I can of mine own self do nothing: as I hear, I judge: and my judgment is just; because I seek not mine own will, but the will of the Father which hath sent me. (John 5:30)

The bad news for anyone who uses this kind of logic to keep from surrendering himself to Christ is that Jesus is going to be the Judge and He will judge based on the facts and not what we think they are. He will be pleasing God and not us or our desires. Since God is perfect and no flaw can or ever will be found in Him, any who don't submit to Jesus will end up the same as Satan.

> How can Satan use us to further his mission, with or without our knowledge?

When Herod the king had heard these things, he was troubled, and all Jerusalem with him. And when he had gathered all the chief priests and scribes of the people together, he demanded of them where Christ should be born. And they said unto him, In Bethlehem of Judaea: for thus it is written by the prophet, (Matt 2:3-5)

The Magi unwittingly helped Herod find out that Jesus had been born. We aren't told why they went to Herod instead of following the star to Bethlehem. It is as if they stopped looking to the Lord for guidance (the star) and started using worldly wisdom when they went to Jerusalem. The king is where we would logically find the next king to be born. We do the same when we look to our own wisdom to solve our problems instead of letting the Word guide us. When we do that, we can inadvertently fall into Satan's traps and aid the enemy.

The Child

> We have already decided that the child is Jesus. How should His mission to rule the nations with a rod of iron to be interpreted?

There are many who would deny that Jesus would physically conquer nations. They quote verses like Matthew 11:28-29 where He says that we can come to Him with our burdens because He is humble and gentle. They quote 1 John 4:16 and say that God is love. He would never do the things described in Revelation. When they come to the book of Revelation, they must spiritualize the interpretation of these verses because it doesn't fit with their theology.

The problem with this is that it doesn't look at the whole picture of who God is. They ignore the passages where Jesus revealed that there will be physical punishment for those who reject Him as Savior. Matthew 25:41-46 speaks of the eternal punishment that will come upon those who thought they were doing His will but failed. Jesus' teaching in the parable of tenants who refused to acknowledge the king's son but killed him (Jesus) revealed that the king (God) would put the tenants to a miserable death (Matt 21:33-44).

There are also some who believe that the 1,000-year reign of Christ described in Revelation 20:1-6 is the symbolic time that Christ will reign with a symbolic rod of iron. They believe that through the Church's influence in the world, sin and Satan will be subdued. The rod of iron is then a symbol of the power of the Holy Spirit working and eventually bringing about Christ's righteous rule. At that time, He will physically return. I'm sure there are variations of this but this is just a quick overview of this theory.

The problem with this theory is that for nearly 2,000 years, the Church has not been able to subdue the nations. There are many verses that indicate that evil will prevail in the world until Christ returns (2 Thess 2:1-3 and 2 Tim 3:1-5).

> The king proclaims the LORD's decree: "The LORD said to me, 'You are my son. Today I have become your Father. Only ask, and I will give you the nations as your inheritance, the whole earth as your possession. You will break them with an iron rod and smash them like clay pots.'" (Ps 2:7-9 NLT)

> To all who are victorious, who obey me to the very end, To them I will give authority over all the nations. They will rule the nations with an iron rod and smash them like clay pots. (Rev 2:26-28 RSV)

> Blessed and holy are those who share in the first resurrection. For them the second death holds no power, but they will be priests of God and of Christ and will reign with him a thousand years. (Rev 20:6 NLT)

The symbol of ruling with a rod of iron has been around since Psalm 2. It is first used to describe Jesus conquering the nations. As we look through the book of Revelation, we see that it is not a pretty sight. However, it goes beyond the physical subjection of the nations to describe Jesus' rule during the millennium. It means that Jesus will be in firm control of all the nations. He will use His people who have been victorious to the end, but it will be after the first resurrection. I'm looking forward to that world where righteousness will reign, subdue evil, and prevent the evils that we see in the world today. Even as good as this will be, it isn't the ultimate home of righteousness that will be eternity in heaven.

> Submit to God's royal son, or he will become angry, and you will be destroyed in the midst of all your activities—for his anger flares up in an instant. But what joy for all who take refuge in him! (Ps 2:12 NLT)

Psalm 2 also tells the only way that we will be able to enjoy that 1,000 years and beyond. We must submit to Jesus as our Lord and Savior.

Revelation 12:6-17

> And the woman fled into the wilderness where she had a place prepared by God, so that there she might be nourished for one thousand two hundred and sixty days.

> And there was war in heaven, Michael and his angels waging war with the dragon. And the dragon and his angels waged war, and they were not strong enough, and there was no longer a place found for them in heaven. And the great dragon was thrown down, the serpent of old who is called the devil and Satan, who deceives the whole

world; he was thrown down to the earth, and his angels were thrown down with him. And I heard a loud voice in heaven, saying, "Now the salvation, and the power, and the kingdom of our God and the authority of His Christ have come, for the accuser of our brethren has been thrown down, who accuses them before our God day and night. And they overcame him because of the blood of the Lamb and because of the word of their testimony, and they did not love their life even to death. For this reason, rejoice, O heavens and you who dwell in them. Woe to the earth and the sea, because the devil has come down to you, having great wrath, knowing that he has *only* a short time."

And when the dragon saw that he was thrown down to the earth, he persecuted the woman who gave birth to the male *child.* And the two wings of the great eagle were given to the woman, in order that she might fly into the wilderness to her place, where she was nourished for a time and times and half a time, from the presence of the serpent. And the serpent poured water like a river out of his mouth after the woman, so that he might cause her to be swept away with the flood. And the earth helped the woman, and the earth opened its mouth and drank up the river which the dragon poured out of his mouth. And the dragon was enraged with the woman, and went off to make war with the rest of her offspring, who keep the commandments of God and hold to the testimony of Jesus. (NASB)

Fled into the Desert

What does the woman's flight into the wilderness for 1,260 days mean and where in history does it fit?

We've already discussed the option that the woman is Mary and that the 1,260 days is the time that Mary and Joseph went to Egypt. However, this doesn't fit the context. The child has already been born and snatched up to God before the woman flees to the desert. Egypt isn't the wilderness either. This has to come after Jesus' ascension into heaven. Even though several thousand years have been condensed into a few verses and some parts appear to be flashbacks in history, each section still proceeds in a normal historical order.

Ruling out the application to Mary leaves the possibility that the time is symbolic of God protecting the remnant of Israel until His promises will be fulfilled to the nation. Those who believe that all mention of Israel pertains to the Church would mean that the Church is protected for a symbolic amount of time. They can't believe the 1,260 is the second half of the tribulation because everything is symbolic, besides giving credibility to the rapture.

Another option is that this occurs during the time of the tribulation and it is as simple as what is stated. We have provided argument that the woman is Israel; this means many Jews will flee to a place in the desert and are protected during the last half of the tribulation.

Hal Lindsey is one of many scholars who agree with the last premise and thinks that this is an actual time when the Jews will undergo exceptional persecution at the end. They will flee from Jerusalem to the natural fortress of Petra, the ancient "City of Rock."[46]

What verses can you find that would substantiate this theory?

He will confirm a covenant with many for one 'seven.' In the middle of the 'seven' he will put an end to sacrifice and offering. And on a wing [of the temple] he will set up an abomination that causes desolation, until the end that is decreed is poured out on him. (Dan 9:27 NIV®)

These are the angel Gabriel's words explaining Daniel's vision. We start with this verse because it contains references to the middle of the "seven" that we have identified as the tribulation. A key event takes place where the Antichrist sets up an abomination in the temple. This is a sign for the Jews to take flight.

So when you see the abomination of desolation spoken of by the prophet Daniel, standing in the holy place (let the reader understand), then let those who are in Judea flee to the mountains. (Matt 24:15-16 ESV)

Jesus speaks of the abomination that causes desolation that was described in Daniel. This is a clear milestone in the path of history. It marks the middle of the tribulation and the beginning of an unprecedented time of persecution for God's people. It appears to take people by surprise in the way Jesus describes it. They are about their normal business when the abomination is announced. Their response must be immediate if they are to be saved. They must flee, making absolutely no provision for worldly possessions. Those who have read Jesus' words and believe Him will know to flee into the mountains when they see it. This is one of the reasons that lend credibility to the physical fulfillment of this symbolic prophecy. That is also why the city of Petra seems to fit. This will be a time like the destruction of Sodom in that there will not be time to look back.

How can we apply this to our own lives even now?

Both physically and spiritually, anyone who wants to be saved must make a commitment and keep it without looking back. We can make a note for our own lives from this. If we were as conscientious about sin in our own lives, we would immediately reject it and flee from it. We shouldn't take a second glance at worldly possessions, fame, peer pressure, creature comfort, or anything else when ridding the sin from our lives. Instead, we must flee in order to be saved from the consequence of

---

[46] Lindsey, 179.

duplicity in our lives. If anyone doesn't know Jesus as Savior, he or she must make a commitment in order to be saved.

> See Daniel 11:31-35 below. Who will resist the Antichrist at this time and what will be the results?

Forces from him will arise, desecrate the sanctuary fortress, and do away with the regular sacrifice. And they will set up the abomination of desolation. By smooth *words* he will turn to godlessness those who act wickedly toward the covenant, but the people who know their God will display strength and take action. Those who have insight among the people will give understanding to the many; yet they will fall by sword and by flame, by captivity and by plunder for *many* days. Now when they fall they will be granted a little help, and many will join with them in hypocrisy. Some of those who have insight will fall, in order to refine, purge and make them pure until the end time; because *it is* still *to come* at the appointed time. (Dan 11:31-35 NASU)

The abomination will be established with force. This has occurred once before in history and many think that this prophecy has already been fulfilled. However, the prophecy continues and speaks of the end times. Before the end occurs, we can get an interesting insight into the last three and a half years. God's people will resist the Antichrist. They will instruct as many as possible but they will not be spared from the tribulation. Among those who resist will be unbelievers – those who are not sincere. They may not like the evil of the Antichrist, but they are not committed to Christ either. Even some Christians will stumble during that time, but God will use it for their purification. Some of the books in the *Left Behind* series demonstrated this very thing in the lives of the characters.

Those who flee to the mountains will most likely be Christian Jews since most Jews who do not know Jesus have not read Jesus' words and will not know to flee. Hopefully, many in Israel will have an opportunity to hear the truth of His prophecy and believe when they see the abomination. Many may flee when they see their Christian brothers fleeing.

> What are the wings of an eagle given to the woman so that she may fly to the wilderness?

Some have been very adamant about the wings of an eagle that are given to the woman. They assure us that this is the symbol for the United States (because a symbol for our nation is the eagle) and that we will provide the airlift for them to escape. This is delusional thinking. Those that purport this are trying to sensationalize the situation in order to sell books or get on talk shows. Let's look at the Bible to see how it uses eagles symbolically.

> And the word of the Lord came unto me, saying, Son of man, put forth a riddle, and speak a parable unto the house of Israel; And say, Thus saith the Lord God; A great eagle with great wings, longwinged, full of feathers, which had divers colours, came unto Lebanon, and took the highest branch of the cedar: He cropped off the top of his young twigs, and carried it into a land of traffick; he set it in a city of merchants. (Ezek 17:1-4)

This is an interesting chapter using symbolic eagles. Two eagles are mentioned. Both turn out to be kings. The first was directed by God to take captives from Israel to Babylon. The second is the Pharaoh of Egypt. Using this as an example to interpret the wings of an eagle in Revelation, there is no need to think that this is the United States. It could be any nation.

> You have seen what I did to the Egyptians, and *how* I bore you on eagles' wings and brought you to Myself. (Ex 19:4 NKJV)

It could simply mean that the escape was swift, as it was for Israel when they left Egypt. However if we relate this to Israel's exodus from Egypt, we really should conclude that it is God who will deliver them. As we'll see a bit later, the help that comes is supernatural.

War in Heaven

> When did this war in heaven start and how long has it been going on?

> And He said to them, "I was watching Satan fall from heaven like lightning. Behold, I have given you authority to tread upon serpents and scorpions, and over all the power of the enemy, and nothing shall injure you." (Luke 10:18-19 NASB)

Depending on what version you read, it would appear that the battle starts when the abomination is set up in the temple. However, when we read what Jesus said, this battle has been going on for quite some time. As the NASB indicates, Jesus was watching while seventy-two disciples were on an evangelistic road trip. While it is still in the past tense it conveys the idea of an ongoing action.

The fall and the battle described in Revelation 12:7 has been going on since Satan's rebellion and because of Jesus' eternal perspective, He could see Satan's fall even at that time. To Jesus, the fall is lightning fast, but to us it seems slow. What we see in Revelation 12 is when Satan and his demons finally lose the battle and are thrown down to the earth. It is when Satan finally hits the ground.

> Who partakes in this battle, what part do we play?

If you look only at Revelation 12:7 Michael and his angels do the actual fighting Revelation 12:11 speaks about our part in the battle. Jesus saw Satan's defeat as the disciples learned to use the power and authority that Jesus gave them.

> And the seventy returned again with joy, saying, Lord, even the devils are subject unto us through thy name. (Luke 10:17)

This part of the battle has been going on ever since. In Revelation, it is as though more saints enter the kingdom of heaven and more power is given to the angels to fight Satan. Of course, any time we overcome, it occurs not in our own strength but it is by the blood of the Lamb. The word of our testimony is also used, which is to give all glory to Jesus Christ because of the salvation that He has purchased for us.

Accuser of Our Brothers

It's now time to take another side trip to study Satan. You may wonder why; it's because we need to know our enemy and his tactics so that we can be ready when he tries to harm us. If it weren't so, this information wouldn't be provided for us. We have already seen that Jesus has victory over him. We have seen that Satan has authority over the world. Now we'll look at his role as accuser.

Where in the Old Testament does Satan show up as our accuser?

> Satan replied to the LORD, "Yes, but Job has good reason to fear God. You have always put a wall of protection around him and his home and his property. You have made him prosper in everything he does. Look how rich he is! But reach out and take away everything he has, and he will surely curse you to your face!" (Job 1:9-11 NLT)

> Then the angel showed me Jeshua the high priest standing before the angel of the LORD. The Accuser, Satan, was there at the angel's right hand, making accusations against Jeshua. (Zech 3:1 NLT)

Chronologically, Job is the first time in the Bible that the name of Satan is used. As Satan approaches God, he accuses Job of only being loyal to God because of His physical blessings in Job's life. That's a pretty good accusation. While it wasn't true in Job's life, there are many who only serve the Lord because of the blessings. When adversity comes, their faith is shown not to be genuine as they fall away. It should give us something to ponder.

We are a lot more like Jeshua who was dressed in filthy clothes, representing his sins. Satan was ready to let God know that he had no right to stand before a Holy God. And this is what we now learn in Revelation, that Satan has been accusing all of us before God.

> Since Satan is capable to accuse us before God, what do you think he is doing to us at the same time?

He is also accusing us every time we sin. He's not only trying to get God to whack us, but he is trying to mess with our minds telling us we are not saved; we don't have any right to be a child of God. When he does this, we take our eyes off Jesus and His power that is available to us. Instead, we focus on ourselves, how lousy and rotten we are.

> While Michael and his angels are fighting in the spiritual realm, where is our battle?

The battle starts even before we come to Christ. 2 Corinthians 4:4 says that Satan has blinded the minds of unbelievers, establishing the battleground of our minds. It appears to me that Satan can drop his accusations directly in our minds.

> For though we live in the world we are not carrying on a worldly war, for the weapons of our warfare are not worldly but have divine power to destroy strongholds. We destroy arguments and every proud obstacle to the knowledge of God, and take every thought captive to obey Christ. (2 Cor 10:3-5 RSV)

Much of the battle between good and evil is waged in our minds with words, knowledge, and arguments. Many think that the battles are in picket lines and elsewhere, but the first and foremost battle is for the minds of people. When we make up our minds to follow Jesus, we have shifted sides but the battle isn't over. We need to look at our whole belief structure to make sure it has been taken captive and made obedient to Jesus. If we don't, the accuser will be able to thwart our efforts for godly living.

> The field is the world; the good seed are the children of the kingdom; but the tares are the children of the wicked one; The enemy that sowed them is the devil; the harvest is the end of the world; and the reapers are the angels. (Matt 13:38-39)

At the same time the Lord is using His Word to enrich our lives, Satan is busy sowing seeds of discontent, jealousy, bitterness, fear, rejection, and whatever else you can name.

> But Peter said, Ananias, why hath Satan filled thine heart to lie to the Holy Ghost, and to keep back part of the price of the land?

Then Peter said unto her, How is it that ye have agreed together to tempt the Spirit of
the Lord? behold, the feet of them which have buried thy husband are at the door,
and shall carry thee out. (Acts 5:3, 9)

This clearly demonstrates that a believer is not immune to Satan's suggestions. It
was not as though Ananias and his wife had no choice in the matter. Peter clearly
shows that they were in agreement. They make a thoughtful decision to lie to the Holy
Spirit. Satan is the father of lies.

So if all this is true, and Satan accuses us, then we generally feel guilty and afraid,
especially when we know that there is truth in what he says. After all, we are all
sinners. Ever since the beginning, when he deceived Eve, he has used the truth and
twisted it. If we do not rely on the blood of the Lamb, we will not overcome.

What are some other battlefields where Satan can besiege us?

So went Satan forth from the presence of the Lord, and smote Job with sore boils
from the sole of his foot unto his crown. (Job 2:7)

Satan can also cause us physical trouble. He can afflict us with anything from
illness to constant suggestions that we should disobey. Not to mention that he piles on
guilt when we do fail and sin. Satan is waging a battle against people. Even though he
physically afflicts us, the battle is not in the physical realm as Ephesians 6:10-12 and 2
Corinthians 10:3-5 indicate. It bears repeating; the mind is a battleground, for it is our
contact with spiritual things. If Satan can keep our thoughts off Jesus and the
awareness that we can overcome by the blood of the Lamb and even take the offensive
with our testimony, he has a chance. But as Paul says:

O wretched man that I am! who shall deliver me from the body of this death? I thank
God through Jesus Christ our Lord. So then with the mind I myself serve the law of
God; but with the flesh the law of sin. (Rom 7:24-25)

The key to mental health is the blood of the Lamb and the power of the Holy Spirit
in our lives.

How does the blood of the Lamb overcome Satan in our lives?

Whoever loves his life loses it, and whoever hates his life in this world will keep it for
eternal life. (John 12:25 ESV)

Jesus says that we will overcome because we do not love our lives. He shed His
blood on the cross so that we don't have to love this life more than we do eternal life.
We should not shrink from death and fear it. If we are not concerned with death, then

we should not be concerned with anything else life has to offer. We go over and over this because we need to be constantly reminded of it.

> Then said Jesus unto his disciples, If any man will come after me, let him deny himself, and take up his cross, and follow me. For whosoever will save his life shall lose it: and whosoever will lose his life for my sake shall find it. For what is a man profited, if he shall gain the whole world, and lose his own soul? or what shall a man give in exchange for his soul? (Matt 16:24-26)

We apply the blood of the Lamb to our lives when we do just the opposite of what the world wants. We hear it all the time. Do what feels good. Plan your goals and objectives to become the most you can be by worldly standards. You will then gain the whole world.

Satan promises us the world and the pleasures of "now." Jesus promises us the pleasures of His rewards later. When the pleasures of "now" offered by Satan are denied, Jesus gives us His peace that provides a far better "now" than the temporal pleasures of sin.

How does the power of the Holy Spirit overcome Satan in our lives?

> I pray also that the eyes of your heart may be enlightened in order that you may know … his incomparably great power for us who believe. That power is like the working of his mighty strength, which he exerted in Christ when he raised him from the dead … Eph 1:18, 19-20 NIV®

These verses came alive for me when I was facing constant temptations from my previous life of sin. It seemed like my body was stronger than my will to do the right thing. I then realized that the Holy Spirit is the power of God who raised Jesus from the dead. His Holy Spirit is in everyone who is in Christ. The same power that raised Jesus from the dead is available to all of us to overcome whatever sin we have been trying to defeat by our own will power. I prayed and asked God for that same power to work in me. I acknowledged that I had been trying to do it on my own and failed. I could only do it because of the infinite power of the Holy Spirit.

What do we do if we yield to sin?

The battle starts in the mind but it doesn't stay there. When we lose the battle in our mind, it goes into our actions. That's when the Accuser really gets busy. He wants to rub our faces in our failure and keep us inactive as long as possible. But the battle is still in our minds. The Word of God and our testimony of faith in that Word will overcome.

> If we confess our sins, he is faithful and just to forgive us our sins, and to cleanse us
> from all unrighteousness. (1 John 1:9)

Sure, we sin; it happens every day and sometimes we even recognize it. As soon as we do, we need to confess our sin and get right with God – immediately. Once we've done that, Satan will still try to accuse us. Either that's when we re-enter the battle or we get into a pity party about how rotten we are and lose another round. It doesn't matter how many times we fail. We know that Jesus will never leave us or forsake us and we know we can go back and ask for forgiveness again. So – instead of taking on the guilt trip – admit our failure but remind Satan that the blood of Jesus has cleansed us from our sins. That guarantees our future in heaven forever. It also guarantees his future in hell.

We will rejoice when we see the day that Satan is cast out of the spiritual realm and is restricted to earth. Even if we are still here on earth when that occurs, we too, will rejoice because we will also know that the time is short. In this case, I am sure that the rapture will be very soon if it hasn't already occurred. When Satan is on the earth, we will see unprecedented demon power. He will be full of fury and will be taking that out on any Christians that are left. This is the meaning of verse 17.

Satan's Pursuit

> How does Satan pursuit of the woman show that God isn't finished with the
> nation of Israel, that He still has promises to them that He will fulfill?

The obvious answer is to read the text. We have already established that the woman is Israel and not the Church, but there are still some who are not convinced and believe that the promises to Israel are fulfilled in the Church.

In Luke 21:24, Jesus said that Jerusalem would be trampled by the Gentiles until the times of the Gentiles are fulfilled. In Revelation 11:2, we saw that the outer court of the temple would be given to the nations (Gentiles) for three and a half years. We have to deal with another three and a half years before the end times are over. However, I think that the time of the Gentiles is almost over when the symbol of the fleeing woman occurs.

> For I do not want you, brethren, to be uninformed of this mystery — so that you will
> not be wise in your own estimation — that a partial hardening has happened to Israel
> until the fullness of the Gentiles has come in; and so all Israel will be saved ... (Rom
> 11:25-26 NASU)

Paul said it was a mystery, but one that is now revealed. Once the fullness of the Gentiles has been finished, all Israel will be saved. We can't attribute this partial hardening to the Church. Neither can we attribute all Israel being saved to the Church, people who are already saved. It is obvious that God isn't finished with Israel.

The symbol of Satan pursuing the woman is a demonstration of his hatred for the Jews. As mentioned before, from before Christ even to this day, he hates them. God gave them specific promises that He will fulfill. Maybe Satan is jealous of these promises, maybe he thinks that by destroying the Jews before God fulfills the promises, he will be able to change the future and finally usurp God.

When he starts pursuing the woman the seven-year covenant he made with Israel is broken. The Antichrist under the power and leading of the devil turns on Israel.

> What is the meaning of the river of water that Satan sends from his mouth to destroy the woman?

As the woman tries to escape, Satan tries to prevent it with a torrent of water from his mouth. Some say that this is an army under the Antichrist's orders. That is a good possibility; however, it is very possible that the water is water. In Matthew 24:20, Jesus says to pray that it isn't in winter. This indicates that Satan may try to use nature to accomplish his purpose. Satan is powerful and the Lord has let him use that power during the end times to bring down fire from heaven. It is very possible that he uses a massive storm to create a great flash flood to wipe out the fleeing people. With all the climate changes going on and their increase as described in Revelation, this is a very real possibility.

Recent events in the world also show how words can stir up untold destruction against people. Muslims have rioted and killed people in many countries when individuals or groups have been accused of burning the Koran or maligning Muhammad. This isn't new and it isn't only Muslims. Hitler nearly wiped out all the Jews in Germany and surrounding nations by falsely accusing them. Perhaps the river from Satan's mouth is a river of words.

While the river being a symbol of words makes sense, it doesn't fit with God's intervention to save the woman. There isn't a correlation between the earth opening to swallow words as it is with swallowing the river.

People also believe that an earthquake or some disaster like it occurs and saves those who flee. Whether it is an army that is swallowed or a flash flood, the earthquake seems to be a good fit.

> What are some reason that people are so quick to hate Jews and Christians? See Esther 3:8-9 for a start.

Then Haman said to King Ahasuerus, "There is a certain people scattered and dispersed among the people in all the provinces of your kingdom; their laws *are* different from all *other* people's, and they do not keep the king's laws. Therefore it *is* not fitting for the king to let them remain. If it pleases the king, let *a decree* be written that they be destroyed, and I will pay ten thousand talents of silver into the hands of those who do the work, to bring *it* into the king's treasuries." (Est 3:8-9 NKJV)

These verses point out how those who hate Jews will deceive people and use governments to persecute them. The same reason that people hate Jews is also the reason they hate Christians. Their customs are different and they do not obey the king's laws when those laws are opposed to God's. One of the main cultural differences about Israel was their separation from the world. The example that they gave us as Christians is to keep ourselves separate from the immoral practices of unbelievers. This irritates people because it exposes their sins. Hitler used the same tactics as Haman. The only difference is that when the tactics of calling them different worked, he went on to the next step. He eased into it rather than taking one huge leap like Haman. Esther 3:15 says the city was bewildered because the decree to eliminate the Jews came so suddenly. After World War II, people were bewildered because it came so slowly that they didn't notice what was happening, even though it only took a few years for Hitler to turn his nation against Jews. The dragon will be much more effective, and he has had several thousand years to correct his mistakes and perfect his techniques. He will use that against the rest of the offspring of Israel – believers.

There are many today who believe that Christians are the most evil and vile people around. They believe that Christians are out to destroy their way of life and take over the world. When the time is right, they will be right there along with the dragon, ready to persecute Christians.[47]

We are fortunate to be living before the tribulation starts. Providing the rapture occurs before the tribulation or Jesus delays His return, we won't have to go through the time when Satan's fury is unleashed. However, we also know that he and his demons are already busy trying to thwart our testimony of Jesus.

Let's not wait until Satan's plan has become so obvious that he is kicked out of heaven. Let's become aware of his schemes now and become his biggest enemy by overcoming him by the blood of the Lamb and our testimony of how Jesus has saved us and is enabling us to live victorious lives in Him.

---

[47] Frank Schaeffer, "Glenn Beck and the 9/12 Marchers: Subversives from Within," Huffpost Politics, last modified May 25, 2011, accessed March 17, 2016, http://www.huffingtonpost.com/frank-schaeffer/glenn-beck-and-the-912-ma_b_284387.html.

Lesson 12 – Revelation 13:1-18

Revelation 13:1-10

And the dragon stood on the shore of the sea.

And I saw a beast coming out of the sea. He had ten horns and seven heads, with ten crowns on his horns, and on each head a blasphemous name. The beast I saw resembled a leopard, but had feet like those of a bear and a mouth like that of a lion. The dragon gave the beast his power and his throne and great authority. One of the heads of the beast seemed to have had a fatal wound, but the fatal wound had been healed. The whole world was astonished and followed the beast. Men worshiped the dragon because he had given authority to the beast, and they also worshiped the beast and asked, "Who is like the beast? Who can make war against him?"

The beast was given a mouth to utter proud words and blasphemies and to exercise his authority for forty-two months. He opened his mouth to blaspheme God, and to slander his name and his dwelling place and those who live in heaven. He was given power to make war against the saints and to conquer them. And he was given authority over every tribe, people, language and nation. All inhabitants of the earth will worship the beast — all whose names have not been written in the book of life belonging to the Lamb that was slain from the creation of the world.

He who has an ear, let him hear. If anyone is to go into captivity, into captivity he will go. If anyone is to be killed with the sword, with the sword he will be killed.

This calls for patient endurance and faithfulness on the part of the saints. (NIV®)

The First Beast

His Identity

To understand the identity of the beast, we must look at other visions, expressly, those recorded in Daniel. Daniel recorded Nebuchadnezzar's dream and its interpretation. It is needed to understand visions given to Daniel later in his life as well as those in Revelation. God doesn't fool around giving a person one vision and another person a conflicting vision. There is truth in each and one sheds light on another.

In your vision, Your Majesty, you saw standing before you a huge, shining statue of a man. It was a frightening sight. The head of the statue was made of fine gold. Its chest and arms were silver, its belly and thighs were bronze, its legs were iron, and its feet were a combination of iron and baked clay. (Dan 2:31-33NLT)

You are the head of gold. But after your kingdom comes to an end, another kingdom, inferior to yours, will rise to take your place. After that kingdom has fallen, yet a third kingdom, represented by bronze, will rise to rule the world. Following that kingdom, there will be a fourth one, as strong as iron. That kingdom will smash and crush all previous empires, just as iron smashes and crushes everything it strikes. The feet and toes you saw were a combination of iron and baked clay, showing that this kingdom will be divided. Like iron mixed with clay, it will have some of the strength of iron. But while some parts of it will be as strong as iron, other parts will be as weak as clay. This mixture of iron and clay also shows that these kingdoms will try to strengthen themselves by forming alliances with each other through intermarriage. But they will not hold together, just as iron and clay do not mix. (Dan 2:38b-43 NLT)

> What countries are represented by the beasts in this vision?

We see four kingdoms in this vision, with Babylon as the current one. We can look back at history and see that the second kingdom was the joined force of Media and Persia. The next forceful nation was Greece, followed by Rome. After Alexander the Great of Greece died, his empire was divided into four parts, one to each of his generals. After that, two major factions emerged which could be represented by two legs.

Then the Roman Empire came. It was unstable at all times as represented by the feet of iron and clay even though it exercised power over a vast area. The toes of the statue can be related to the ten kings in later visions. Based on these visions, many believe that the ten kings will represent countries that are part of a revived Roman Empire.

The first time I did this study, the European Common Market only had eight members, up from the original six formed in 1951. There was great speculation that when the tenth member was added, we would see the fulfillment of this prophecy and possibly usher in the tribulation. The name was changed to the European Union when it had fifteen members. Negotiations then added twelve more members for a total of 28 as of July 1, 2013.[48]

It has expanded beyond ten counties that have had Roman influence to include countries that were never under Roman rule. With this as an example, it is rather foolhardy to predict what countries will be represented by the ten kings. All we can do is wait and see where they come from.

Daniel spake and said, I saw in my vision by night, and, behold, the four winds of the heaven strove upon the great sea. And four great beasts came up from the sea, diverse one from another. The first was like a **lion**, and had eagle's wings: I beheld till the wings thereof were plucked, and it was lifted up from the earth, and made stand upon the feet as a man, and a man's heart was given to it. And behold another beast, a second, like to a **bear**, and it raised up itself on one side, and it had three ribs in the mouth of it between the teeth of it: and they said thus unto it, Arise, devour much flesh. After this I beheld, and lo another, like a **leopard**, which had upon the back of it four wings of a fowl; the beast had also four heads; and dominion was given to it. After this I saw in the night visions, and behold a fourth beast, dreadful and terrible,

---

[48] "Europa - Eu Member Countries," European Union, April 11, 2015, accessed March 17, 2016, http://europa.eu/about-eu/countries/member-countries/.

and strong exceedingly; and it had great iron teeth: it devoured and brake in pieces, and stamped the residue with the feet of it: and it was diverse from all the beasts that were before it; and it had **ten horns**. I considered the horns, and, behold, there came up among them another little horn, before whom there were three of the first horns plucked up by the roots: and, behold, in this horn were eyes like the eyes of man, and a mouth speaking great things. (Dan 7:2-8 emphasis mine)

These great beasts, which are four, are four kings, which shall arise out of the earth. But the saints of the most High shall take the kingdom, and possess the kingdom for ever, even for ever and ever. (Dan 7:17-18)

I beheld, and the same horn made war with the saints, and prevailed against them; Until the Ancient of days came, and judgment was given to the saints of the most High; and the time came that the saints possessed the kingdom. Thus he said, The fourth beast shall be the fourth kingdom upon earth, which shall be diverse from all kingdoms, and shall devour the whole earth, and shall tread it down, and break it in pieces. And the ten horns out of this kingdom are ten kings that shall arise: and another shall rise after them; and he shall be diverse from the first, and he shall subdue three kings. And he shall speak great words against the most High, and shall wear out the saints of the most High, and think to change times and laws: and they shall be given into his hand until a time and times and the dividing of time [3 1/2 years]. (Dan 7:21-25)

And the rough goat is the king of Grecia [Greece]: and the great horn that is between his eyes is the first king. Now that being broken, whereas four stood up for it, four kingdoms shall stand up out of the nation, but not in his power. (Dan 8:21-22)

How are the beasts or nations in Daniel related to the beast in Revelation?

    The beast that John saw is a remarkable composite of the four beasts that Daniel saw. With the interpretation of Daniel's vision, it becomes clear that the last beast is the same as the beast that John sees. They both slander God and both have power to war against the saints and conquer them. Fortunately, Daniel's vision also concludes the matter by assuring us that the saints will obtain the final victory. The beast has a limited time, three and a half years. An important thing to remember is that the fourth beast and the ten kingdoms are in Daniel's future as well as ours (at the time of this writing).

    The kingdom of Greece is clearly explained with the four generals taking over after its prominence. But out of the four nations comes another ruler that can only be the final beast that we have encountered in the earlier visions and in Revelation. As is done in other visions, time is compressed. It starts with the known kingdoms of Media and Persia, goes into Daniel's future with Greece, and finishes with a huge jump in time to the very end with a description of the Antichrist. He is taking his stand against the Prince of princes, Jesus. Also he will be destroyed, but not by human power. The Lord is clearly in charge and will deal with him.

His Origin

> What is the origin of this beast represented by the sea?

Many scholars have said that the sea represents mankind.[49] The churning sea would represent the constant unrest and changing nature of sinful man. This is in contrast to the calm sea in front of the throne of God that we saw in Revelation 4. In the presence of God, there is peace. Apart From Him, there is unrest.

> Is the beast a nation or a person?

Since these beasts come from the sea, they represent the human side of the nations, their leaders, and the conflicts. Sometimes the beast represents a nation and other times the beast represents a person. While the beasts in Daniel's visions were identified as nations, the beast in Revelation is personalized. Even though it starts out sounding just like Daniel's beasts, he later receives a throne and authority from the dragon. The beast or the Antichrist will be of human origin.

The heads and horns match the description of the dragon. This is probably because the dragon gives his power to the beast.

> And the king shall do according to his will; and he shall exalt himself, and magnify himself above every god, and shall speak marvellous things against the God of gods, and shall prosper till the indignation be accomplished: for that that is determined shall be done. (Dan 11:36)

The king in Daniel 11 at first is described as one of the four kings that came out of Greece. Eventually, he is identified as the Antichrist as well. This description relates to the heads of the beast in Revelation that have blasphemous names written on them. Up to this time, the Antichrist was simply a man who had incredible charisma to gain control of most of the world (with Satanic backing to be sure). But now, the Antichrist utters blasphemies in which he tries to exalt himself above God. This indicates that the Antichrist is now possessed by Satan or under his direct control. The gloves are off and the fight has begun. Satan's war is in the open and he attacks those who follow his archenemy, Jesus.

His Wound

> Does the beast actually die and come back to life? What are the implications if he did or did not die?

---

[49] Adam Clark, *Clark's Commentary*, (Seattle: Biblesoft, 2005), Revelation 13:1, and other commentaries.

In Daniel we saw a time when one horn is broken off and another takes its place. This always represented the replacement of a ruler of a kingdom. In Revelation, we see that heads also represent rulers. One of these rulers receives a wound that several translations say is fatal but is healed. It's interesting to note that most translations leave the possibility that the wound didn't actually result in death. Several versions use the word "seemed" and another "as if." Verse 14 doesn't help. The NASU has taken the stance that the wound caused his death and he came back to life. However the ESV makes no definitive statement about the beast dying.

> ... telling those who dwell on the earth to make an image to the beast who *had the wound of the sword and has come to life. (Rev 13:14 NASU)

> * NOTE: An * in the text marks verbs that are historical presents in the Greek which have been translated with an English past tense in order to conform to modern usage. (Rev 13:14 notes NASU)

> ... *telling them to make an image for the beast that was wounded by the sword and yet lived.* (Rev 13:14 ESV)

According to the NASU footnote, the wound happened in the past but continues in the present, perhaps like one that doesn't heal. This makes it sound like the walking dead. The Greek simply says he was wounded and did live. It is apparent from the reaction of people that he certainly appears to have died. However, we don't have the world's perspective we have God's. His Word leads us to understand that death doesn't occur but is only a deception.

> It works great signs, even making fire come down from heaven to earth in the sight of men; and by the signs which it is allowed to work in the presence of the beast, it deceives those who dwell on earth ... (Rev 13:23-14 RSV)

The second beast has the job of doing deceptive work. I don't think the wound actually kills this ruler. There are two additional reasons. The first is that Jesus is the resurrection and the life as He has stated.

> For just as the Father raises the dead and gives them life, even so the Son also gives life to whom He wishes. (John 5:21 NASB)

Life comes from the Father and Jesus, the Son. I don't think that God would give this power to Satan. Secondly, unless God raises a person, once he is dead, he stays dead.

> And as it is appointed unto men once to die, but after this the judgment: (Heb 9:27)

We all only have one chance at life. If this ruler did die, he would then face judgment. His judgment doesn't come until chapter 19.

If this were truly a death and resurrection, then it would prove that the person was indeed Christ. It would mean that Jesus was the fake and that we have been following an imposter for thousands of years.

The wound that doesn't heal happens right after the dragon gives him his power. It is possible that Satan is going to produce an actual resurrection so that the Antichrist can claim that he is the Christ. But it is only a counterfeit. Satan has been trying to convince people for two thousand years that Jesus' resurrection was a hoax and now he is going to pull off a fake to try to grab the glory for himself.

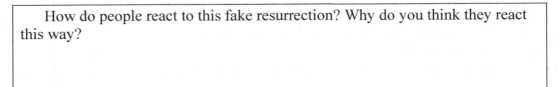

How do people react to this fake resurrection? Why do you think they react this way?

Look at what the people of the world do as a result. They are astonished, and follow the beast. They can't determine if the wound is fatal or not and are ready to believe the deception. They don't see a beast in the way John does. They see what appears to be a miraculous resurrection or healing of a world leader that they already respected and followed. As a result, they end up worshiping Satan.

They are also overwhelmed by his power. Make no mistake about it. Even though this is a fake, it has to be something special, dramatic, and public. If he simply went to the hospital and recovered, nobody would get this excited. When we take a look at the second beast, I think we will be able to see that it is the second beast that pulls off the healing or resurrection, which makes him a counterfeit of the Holy Spirit. The wound of the first beast is very important. As we look over the whole chapter, it is mentioned three times.

His Authority

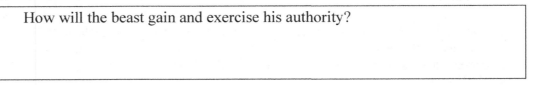

How will the beast gain and exercise his authority?

He will utter proud words and blasphemies. Much of his authority is going to be based upon his oral abilities, including his blasphemies. You don't think it can be done? We've already mentioned how Hitler took control. Some people thought he was the Antichrist because he was able to rise to power in such a short time based on his oratory skills. He was given the authority to rule in Germany. He didn't fight for it. His persecution of the Jews also helped fit the bill as the Antichrist.

Compare Jesus' demonstrations of authority to the beast's. How are they the same or different and what is the result?

The Antichrist will appear, as Jesus did, to have authority in his teaching. People could tell by the way that Jesus taught, He had authority.

> And it came to pass, when Jesus had ended these sayings, the people were astonished at his doctrine: For he taught them as one having authority, and not as the scribes. (Matt 7:28-29)
>
> And behold, some people brought to him a paralytic, lying on a bed. And when Jesus saw their faith, he said to the paralytic, "Take heart, my son; your sins are forgiven." And behold, some of the scribes said to themselves, "This man is blaspheming."
>
> "But that you may know that the Son of Man has authority on earth to forgive sins"— he then said to the paralytic—"Rise, pick up your bed and go home."
>
> When the crowds saw it, they were afraid, and they glorified God, who had given such authority to men. (Matt 9:2-3, 6, 8 ESV)

Jesus followed up His words with actions to show that He had authority. When He exercised His authority on earth, people were amazed, but the religious leaders accused Him of blaspheming. The Antichrist will blaspheme because he doesn't have the true authority to forgive sins, but he will demonstrate miracles to deceive the multitudes and the people will praise him. His blasphemies will not seem as such because of the signs and wonders he works. They will be blasphemies because he will try to impersonate Jesus in every way.

How will Christians be able to determine that the beast is not representing God?

The only way a believer could see this happening and know that it was not of God would be to be well versed in the Word, know these predictions, and know what Jesus told us in Matthew 24:23, "Then if any man shall say unto you, Lo, here is Christ, or there; believe it not" (KJV).

This is why many do not believe the gifts of tongues and prophecy are for today. They believe that these are manifestations of Satan to prepare us to welcome the Antichrist. They miss out on the fact that people of God heal or speak in tongues by the power of the Holy Spirit, in the name of Jesus, and therefore give glory to God.

We should look out for miracles, signs, and wonders that don't give glory to God. A good example is the amount of glory given angels today. Many people are ready to credit angels with saving their lives and other miracles, but they aren't ready to admit that Jesus is Lord and that angels only do His bidding. They won't give one bit of credit to Jesus. Like some TV preachers of today, the Antichrist will be taking the glory for himself.

Eventually, the beast will remove any pretense of being Christ and directly slander God.

Why will people put up with the beast's slandering God?

It isn't hard to imagine someone speaking directly against God. The Humanists and Atheists do that already. They say He is the one who keeps us shackled in myths. Marx called religion the "opium of the people."[50] Even some churches that call themselves Christian do the same thing by allowing any belief to be part of their system. Psychiatry has long blamed mental illness on Christianity. The Antichrist will only be voicing what millions of people have wanted to hear anyway. People want to get out from under the authority of God. They only want to answer to the authority they see standing before them in the mirror. The irony in this is that they end up worshiping both the dragon and the beast. Not only do they submit to a higher authority, but also one who doesn't have their best interests in mind.

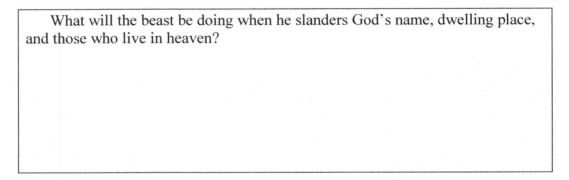

What will the beast be doing when he slanders God's name, dwelling place, and those who live in heaven?

Since the Antichrist is going to slander God's name, His dwelling place (Christians) and those who live in heaven, it could be that the Antichrist is going to spread a gospel in which the dragon is the father, the Antichrist is the son and the next beast is the spirit. He can only do that if he maligns and discredits the true Trinity. He may do this by maligning Christians once he gains power to fight us. It will be like the times of Nero. Rumors will spread about what the Christians do in their services such as drinking blood and eating flesh. Today, we are already called subversive and dangerous.[51]

By this time, the Church will have to meet in secret. That will also add to suspicions against Christians. The right of freedom of religion will be taken away even where it is now granted. The Antichrist will be as Saul was before his conversion. He will be legally enabled to jail and/or kill Christians.

> And I say also unto thee, That thou art Peter, and upon this rock I will build my church; and the gates of hell shall not prevail against it. (Matt 16:18)

We know that the gates of hell will never overcome the Church, but just as in the times of Nero and in many places in the world today, it will not be able to function openly.

To complete the counterfeiting of Jesus, the Antichrist will assume authority over every tribe, people, language, and nation. But only counterfeit Christians will worship him.

---

[50] Karl Marx, "Toward the Critique of Hegel's Philosophy of Law: Introduction," in *Writings of the Young Marx on Philosophy and Society,* trans. and ed. by Loyd D. Easton and Kurt H. Guddat, (New York: Doubleday Anchor, 1967).

[51] Schaeffer, "Glenn Beck …"

His Opposition

> Who will be able to oppose the beast, what will happen to them, and what is their hope?

From all outward appearances, there will be no opposition to the beast. In verse 7, he is allowed to wage war on Christians and even conquer them. We tend to miss this but as we continue reading, we see that he has authority over all peoples. Even worse, it says that all who live on the earth will worship the beast.

I've heard preachers ask what does the word "all" mean and then they say it means all, implying that there are no exceptions. However, the Bible often uses the word all and it isn't always completely inclusive. For instance in Exodus 9:6, it says that all the livestock of the Egyptians died. In Exodus 9:19 Moses tells the Egyptians to bring their livestock into shelter or they will be killed by hail. Obviously, not all the livestock died from the plague.

The same can be applied to these verses in Revelation because we know that one of the exceptions to those who worship the beast is those whose names have been written in the book of life. However, it will be a time of intense persecution signified by the fact that the beast will be able to conquer them.

> For there shall arise false Christs, and false prophets, and shall shew great signs and wonders; insomuch that, if it were possible, they shall deceive the very elect. (Matt 24:24)

> … I am with you alway, even unto the end of the world. Amen. (Matt 28:20)

Jesus warned us that the deception would be so great that it will almost deceive Christians. But we have His promise of spiritual protection. The only resistance to the beast will be Christians who have the protection of the real Christ, the Lamb that was slain from the beginning of the world. This points out that the true Christ and His plan of redemption outdates Satan. Jesus is the original. The only way to tell the counterfeit from the original is to become very familiar with the original. The counterfeit will then be obvious. Those who resist the beast have done that. They know that to live for Jesus is to suffer with Him.

Verse 10 could make those who have to go through this despair of all hope.

> And except those days should be shortened, there should no flesh be saved: but for the elect's sake those days shall be shortened. (Matt 24:22)

Fortunately, that time will be limited to 42 months. What they will need to remember, as well as anyone who is going through trials, is that we belong to the Lamb. He bought us with His blood; we do not belong to any other. If the Lamb bought us, and He is God, what makes anyone think that He is going to let somebody else take His possession? However, there is a certainty of persecution described in verse 10. This warning is for Christians and applies to us at any time, tribulation or not. We are to have patient endurance and faithfulness. We may moan and ask God why, but He is telling us that it is inevitable. There is not going to be an escape just because we are Christians. Some will die and some will be imprisoned.

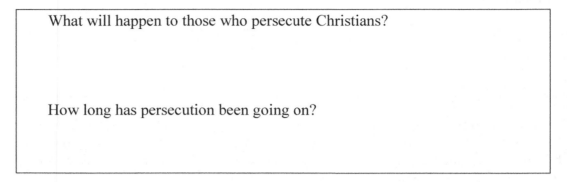

What will happen to those who persecute Christians?

How long has persecution been going on?

"You snakes! You brood of vipers! How will you escape being condemned to hell? Therefore I am sending you prophets and wise men and teachers. Some of them you will kill and crucify; others you will flog in your synagogues and pursue from town to town. And so upon you will come all the righteous blood that has been shed on earth, from the blood of righteous Abel to the blood of Zechariah son of Berekiah, whom you murdered between the temple and the altar. I tell you the truth, all this will come upon this generation." (Matt 23:33-36 NIV®)

Jesus warned the religious leaders of His time; however this warning is for any who mistreat His servants. Persecution of righteous people isn't something new but goes back even before His prophets. It goes back to Abel. There have always been godly people and the ungodly have shed their blood. Persecuting a Christian brings upon the persecutor the guilt of every persecution from the beginning of time. Thank God even they can be forgiven.

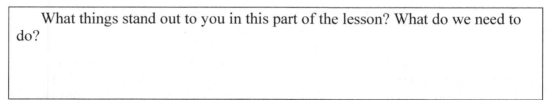

What things stand out to you in this part of the lesson? What do we need to do?

Two things stand out to me in this part of the chapter.

We need to be able to spot counterfeits. We could spend a lot of time examining other religions to see why they are wrong or we could spend our time getting to know Jesus. The most profitable time is spent knowing Jesus and the counterfeits will become obvious.

Persecution is a normal part of Christianity. Political situations can change in a few short years. Rights can be lost almost overnight. We should be prepared for persecuted and continue as an underground church. We should also pray that it doesn't happen.

Revelation 13:11-18

Then I saw another beast coming up out of the earth, and he had two horns like a lamb and spoke like a dragon. And he exercises all the authority of the first beast in his presence, and causes the earth and those who dwell in it to worship the first beast, whose deadly wound was healed. He performs great signs, so that he even makes fire come down from heaven on the earth in the sight of men. And he deceives those who dwell on the earth by those signs which he was granted to do in the sight of the beast, telling those who dwell on the earth to make an image to the beast who was wounded by the sword and lived. He was granted *power* to give breath to the image of the beast, that the image of the beast should both speak and cause as many as would not worship the image of the beast to be killed. He causes all, both small and great, rich and poor, free and slave, to receive a mark on their right hand or on their foreheads, and that no one may buy or sell except one who has the mark or the name of the beast, or the number of his name.

Here is wisdom. Let him who has understanding calculate the number of the beast, for it is the number of a man: His number *is* 666. (NKJV)

The Second Beast

> What is the significance, if any, that another beast comes out of the earth? What might be his nationality?

Scholars come up with some interesting thoughts regarding the statement that another beast comes out of the earth. First, some say that the word another could also be translated as one of the same kind. This would imply that the second beast is just as vile as the first and is empowered by Satan. This seems to be a logical conclusion, especially since he speaks as a dragon and exercises all the authority of the first beast. Scripture supports this conclusion.

The second thing that some scholars point out is that the word earth is translated as land in many verses (Matt 2:6, 20 and 21; 4:15). Since the ones listed refer to Israel or parts of Israel, some conclude the use of the word land is symbolic of Israel. Therefore (here comes a jump in logical) the second beast comes from the land of Israel and therefore must be Jewish.[52] What is not consistent is that the word is also used for the land of Sodom (Matt 10:15), Midian (Acts 7:29), and Egypt (Acts 7:36). Jesus said that the meek will inherit the earth (Matt 5:5) and used the same word to refer to the world.

These scholars further support their argument by pointing out that the first beast (of Roman origin) must have a confederate among the Jews in order to make a covenant with Israel. I think that's skating on thin logical ice. I haven't seen any other scriptural evidence to support this conclusion. Beside, I've quoted the verse many times that states that the covenant is with the many, not specifically Israel (Dan 9:27).

---

[52] Lindsey, 191-192.

Lambs Don't Have Horns

> Since lambs don't have horns, what is the significance of this reference to the beast having horns like a lamb?

When I read that the second beast had two horns like a lamb, I thought I'd better check out the word "lamb" to make sure we were talking about a young sheep. After all, lambs don't have horns, only grown sheep. The Greek checks out. The translation is lambkin.[53] So why would John choose these words to describe the second beast's horns? Are they so small that it appears he has no power? Are they references to two rulers who are weak and unable to have influence? Neither of these explanations seems to fit since the second beast is able to do great and miraculous signs.

This word for lamb is only used by John. He uses it once when he told of Jesus telling Peter to feed His lambs (John 21:15). Every other use of the word refers to Jesus in the book of Revelation other than this one verse. It then stands to reason (not a large logical jump) that the horns refer back to horns of the Lamb, Jesus, in Revelation 5:6. Jesus' horns and eyes represent the Spirits of God. From this and the fact that there are no references to the beast's horns as rulers, I conclude that this reference to horns like a lamb (like Jesus') refer to his spiritual power. In fact, this is why I think he represents a false holy spirit. Scholars, however, say that because they are horns of a lamb, he will proclaim himself to be the Jewish Messiah.[54]

> What other reasons can you give that would agree or disagree with the scholars?

The horns can be seen as counterfeit authority of Jesus. Using that authority, he makes people worship the first beast, which is what he does while exercising authority on behalf of the first beast. If the first beast sets himself up as god in the temple, and this beast exercises his power, then it appears that we have a parallel to God and Jesus. That seems to make sense. However, the problem with this is that the first beast is the one that is wounded and has an apparent resurrection. The first beast fits the bill of the false Messiah better than the second does. Since people at that time will not have spiritual discernment, it probably doesn't matter that it isn't consistent which beast claims to be the false messiah, holy spirit, or father. They will buy into this masquerade because he does exercise authority on behalf of the first beast and causes fire to come from heaven in front of men. It is possible that the second beast is the one who actually fakes the miracle of raising the first beast.

---

[53] *Strong's*, s.v. "NT:721."
[54] Lindsey, 192.

Miraculous Signs

> Are these miraculous signs actually signs or are they sleight of hand trickery? How do you know?

Then Pharaoh also called the wise men and the sorcerers: now the magicians of Egypt, they also did in like manner with their enchantments. (Ex 7:11)

And the magicians of Egypt did so with their enchantments: and Pharaoh's heart was hardened, neither did he hearken unto them; as the Lord had said. (Ex 7:22)

And the magicians did so with their enchantments, and brought up frogs upon the land of Egypt. (Ex 8:7)

It amazes me that the Egyptian magicians were able to do anything by their secret arts. We simply don't see this kind of magic anywhere in the world today (except on TV). All magic we see now is sleight of hand that provides an illusion. Yet the magicians of Pharaoh were able to do the same things as Moses. Clearly, Satan had empowered these miracles, yet only to a limited extent. For instance, he is able to imitate but not create. Neither could they reverse the signs that Moses performed by the power of God. (I should note that there are some extraordinary feats performed by witch doctors and such in some areas of the world. However, they usually involve injuring or healing people, but nothing like the things done by the Egyptian magicians.)

These signs are meant to deceive people into believing that the beast is god. Even in the times of Jesus, people who were not believers were casting out demons. In Matthew 12:26, Jesus said that if Satan cast out Satan, then he is divided against himself. He then asks how his kingdom can stand.

> How do Jesus' statement and the signs in Revelation demonstrate the unity of Satan's plan?

Not every one that saith unto me, Lord, Lord, shall enter into the kingdom of heaven; but he that doeth the will of my Father which is in heaven. Many will say to me in that day, Lord, Lord, have we not prophesied in thy name? And in thy name have we cast out devils? And in thy name done many wonderful works? And then will I profess unto them, I never knew you: depart from me, ye that work iniquity. (Matt 7:21-23)

I've used these verses to show that many people who think they are Christians simply because they claim Jesus as Lord are not saved. However, in light of the miracles performed by the second beast, it also shows that the demon world will obey and cooperate with each other to fake miracles if it furthers their interests. In the last times, the demonstrations will bring many into an everlasting bondage to sin.

For there shall arise false Christs, and false prophets, and shall shew great signs and wonders; insomuch that, if it were possible, they shall deceive the very elect. (Matt 24:24)

Jesus said they would do this so it should not be surprising to us. Yet I have heard Christians say that a sign must be from God if it does good. We cannot underestimate the power of these miracles. They will be so persuasive that even the elect (Christians) will almost believe them.

Even now, I get emails from Christians who have little or no discernment. They pass on obvious lies about political leaders because the email erroneously reports that is true and verified by snopes. Some stories are cute and inspirational but others have subtle (and sometimes blatant) theological errors that would encourage believers in the wrong direction or even convince a non-believer that they didn't need Jesus.

What is the purpose of these miracle performed by Satan?

Why will people believe them?

This man will come to do the work of Satan with counterfeit power and signs and miracles. He will use every kind of evil deception to fool those on their way to destruction, because they refuse to love and accept the truth that would save them. So God will cause them to be greatly deceived, and they will believe these lies. Then they will be condemned for enjoying evil rather than believing the truth. (2 Thess 2:9-12 NLT)

They are demonic spirits who work miracles and go out to all the rulers of the world to gather them for battle against the Lord on that great judgment day of God the Almighty. (Rev 16:14NLT)

Satan and his demons have had power to perform what appear to be miracles throughout the ages. Paul clearly labels them as counterfeit, which means they are a copy or imitation in order to defraud or deceive people. They have a specific purpose and that is to deceive those who are perishing, in contrast to God's miracles, which are aimed at glorifying God and bringing salvation. In the end times, deceptive miracles will be unprecedented in numbers and power. Satan's miracles will also increase in evil.

They occur only because God allows it to bring out the truth in people's hearts. People will no longer be riding the fence. They will have to choose, as they never have before. God already knows people's hearts. He acts in concert with what they want by sending them the things that will lead them that way. We must remember that God has already sent the truth in Jesus and people have rejected it. He is not tricking them, only letting the full force of what they have chosen become manifested. Note: the love of truth keeps us from being deceived along with the truth itself.

One thing that seems to impress people who dwell on the earth is fire from heaven. It could also be done specifically as a countermeasure to discredit the two witnesses since fire came from their mouths. John describes people who dwell on or inhabit the earth four times from Revelation 13:8-14.

What does this description of dwelling on or inhabiting the earth reveal about people?

How is or should this be different for Christians?

The objects of the deception are those who dwell in the earth. Since Christians aren't going to be deceived, that means that only people who have not yet accepted Christ as Lord and Savior will be deceived. The word for "inhabitants" in the Greek is *katoikeo* (kat-oy-keh'-o); to house permanently, i.e. reside (literally or figuratively).[55] Since those who inhabit the earth are the ones who are living there permanently, they can't be believers. This is a big difference between believers and the lost. The lost are tied to the things of this world and don't want to leave it. Believers are looking for another land and recognize that this world is only a temporary home.

> These all died in faith, not having received the promises, but having seen them afar off, and were persuaded of them, and embraced them, and confessed that they were strangers and pilgrims on the earth (Heb 11:13)

> But now they desire a better country, that is, an heavenly: wherefore God is not ashamed to be called their God: for he hath prepared for them a city. (Heb 11:16)

We are people of faith just like the people mentioned in these verses. We are aliens and strangers on earth longing and waiting for our new heavenly home (1 Peter 2:11a). We are strangers in the world. We are just passing through. While there may still be Christians on the earth at this time, it is clear that unbelievers will be deceived, not Christians.

The Image of the Beast

What kind of an image could be set up that will appear to be alive, speak, and kill all who don't worship it?

---

[55] *Strong's*, s.v. "NT:2730."

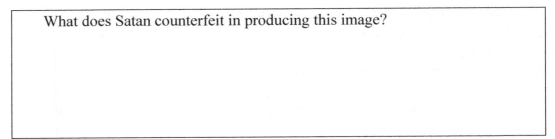

What does Satan counterfeit in producing this image?

It is ludicrous for anyone to attempt to speculate what this image is. Man's imagination has come up with so many things, like androids and transformers (those Sci-Fi robot-people that can change shapes) so I'm not surprised that Satan would come up with his own version of something that could do all this. Whatever it is, I'm sure it still falls into counterfeiting God's glory since it will be set up in the temple.

> Then a cloud covered the tent of the congregation, and the glory of the Lord filled the tabernacle. And Moses was not able to enter into the tent of the congregation, because the cloud abode thereon, and the glory of the Lord filled the tabernacle. (Ex 40:34-35)

This abomination will be set up in the temple to take the place of the Glory of God that appeared there in the Old Testament. Satan wants this kind of glory for himself. It reminds me of the Wizard of Oz and the man behind the curtains running the controls to produce a visual affect that frightened people. Unfortunately, the technology to do this will not be physical but spiritual, but the concept is the same – a pretender will be behind the scenes. The death that strikes people who do not worship will be a counterfeit of the death that struck people who entered the Holy of Holies without the proper sacrifice and in the proper manner. Satan doesn't care about holiness or sacrifice, he only cares that he is worshiped. This has been his way forever, which is any way but God's.

The image is given breath to speak. This is another one of Satan's counterfeits, the replication of the creation of man.

> And the Lord God formed man of the dust of the ground, and breathed into his nostrils the breath of life; and man became a living soul. (Gen 2:7)

God formed man from the dust and breathed into him the breath of life. Does the beast really have power to give breath? No, we saw before that life only comes from God the Father and Jesus the Son. However, Satan certainly wants people to think that he has power to do what only God can do.

It is interesting to see that the second beast ordered the people to set up an image. At this point, the people have so ensnared themselves in the evil that they are essentially slaves. Some may not want to set up the image, but now they have no choice. Next, he forces them to receive a mark.

The Mark 666

> How does the mark counterfeit God's Word?

These words, which I am commanding you today, shall be on your heart. You shall teach them diligently to your sons and shall talk of them when you sit in your house and when you walk by the way and when you lie down and when you rise up. You shall bind them as a sign on your hand and they shall be as frontals on your forehead. (Deut 6:6-8 NASU)

God's Word is so important that it should be a central point of our lives. It is so important that God told the Israelites to tie them to their hands and foreheads. I am sure that it is not just a coincidence that the beast wants people to put his mark on their hand or forehead. He wants to usurp God even in this way.

> How does the mark counterfeit God's provision for us?

The mark of the beast is essentially a mark of ownership. Just as slaves were branded with the mark of their owner, so will this be. The Beast owns the inhabitants of the earth.

A slave could go to the market and buy on behalf of his master because he had a mark that showed where the bill was sent. The mark is a means of economic control as well, as is clearly stated. They receive a physical mark that controls their life. It shows what is important to them.

> But seek ye first the kingdom of God, and his righteousness; and all these things shall be added unto you. Take therefore no thought for the morrow: for the morrow shall take thought for the things of itself. Sufficient unto the day is the evil thereof. (Matt 6:33-34)

Our Lord expects us to turn to Him for all our needs. In the same way, the beast wants everyone to turn to him for his or her needs. He has found a way to force people to turn to him by ensuring they can't buy or sell without the mark.

> How is the mark a counterfeit of God's seal by the Holy Spirit?

In him you also, who have heard the word of truth, the Gospel of your salvation, and have believed in him, were sealed with the promised Holy Spirit, which is the guarantee of our inheritance until we acquire possession of it, to the praise of his glory. (Eph 1:13-14 RSV)

Since Satan likes counterfeits, the mark also has the same effect as being a counterfeit to the seal of the Holy Spirit. We are marked with the Holy Spirit, which is a guarantee that we have eternal life with Jesus. As we'll see in chapter 14, the mark of the beast is a guarantee of eternal condemnation.

The mark that will be visible is not a bar code. It isn't an implanted microchip. It is the name of the beast or the number of his name. We shouldn't read into Scripture what isn't there. If the Antichrist's name were Smith, then each person would be forced to have Smith or the number of Smith branded in some way on his hand or forehead.

I have a sweatshirt that says "Property of Jesus of Nazareth." The sweatshirt doesn't belong to Jesus, but the person wearing it does. In the same way, the mark of the beast doesn't enable a person to buy or sell because it identifies the person's bank account, but the fact that the person now belongs to the Antichrist. It is the counterfeit of the seal that Christians receive from the Holy Spirit.

> How is worshiping the beast tied to this mark?

There is an emphasis on the fact that the beast has the ability to force people to accept the mark. Just as they are killed if they refuse to worship the beast's image, I wouldn't doubt that anyone caught without the mark would be killed if they refused to accept it. It is tied even more directly to worshiping the beast in Revelation 14:9. In God's eyes, receiving the mark is the same as worshiping the beast.

> How do we calculate the number?

The number 666 is the number of the beast's name. It isn't some serial number that identifies each of us. One way to calculate his number would be to take the numerical value of each letter in the order it appears in the alphabet and add them together to get the number. This is what I thought it was for many years. However, I visited a web site that shed a lot of light on how this should really be done. The concept is based on the fact that Hebrew and Greek don't have numbers but each letter represents a number. You can search for this on the internet if you would like to see some exhaustive research that others have done on the "Beast" and his number.

Hank Hanegraaaff and Sigmund Brouwer used this or similar method in their novel, *The Last Disciple*, to come up with the name of the beast being Nero Caesar. However to come up with 666 they had to write it in Hebrew without the vowels.[56] While I believe they did a lot of research and were very accurate in what they did for

---

[56] Hank Hanegraaaff and Sigmund Brouwer, *The Last Disciple* (Wheaton: Tyndale House Publishers, Inc, 2004), 336-334

the book, it is evident that by using different methods, you can come up with what you want.

You can also find detailed explanations for calculating his number, barcodes, and microchips. In addition, there are recent news articles that are pretty scary. Be careful, however. I originally recommended a web site and later found out it was cultish and some are simply crackpots.

Buy or Sell

This is a little bit of a side trip regarding modern technology and how it fits with the mark of the beast. When debit cards came out, many Christians were concerned about using them instead of cash or checks. They thought it was a first step in providing the technology that would enable the beast to gain power and issue his mark. At that time, grocery stores didn't accept credit cards but started accepting debit cards.

Now, it is an accepted business practice to accept credit and debit cards. Anyone can accept them though online companies like PayPal. You can connect a card swipe cube or triangle to your smart phone and process someone's card.

Many credit cards and some "customer loyalty" cards have microchips in them. You don't need to swipe the card, only hold it near the reader. Smart phone apps promise the ability to buy from your phone as you walk through a store without going through a checkout line.

> Why would banks and even the IRS want to have a cashless society?

Clearly, banks want to stop handling pieces of paper, either cash or checks. It takes time and money to do so. Ages ago, I worked at Peoples Bank in IT. At that time it was obvious that they were a long way from being able to do this, but they have come along a lot faster than I would have thought possible. The IRS would also love a cashless society. Think about how much easier it is to audit people when they have all their financial transactions recorded and tied back to their social security number. You cannot open a bank account without a social security number because there are certain transactions that a bank must report, such as any transaction over $9,999.99. With all of this in place, think how easy it would be for the government to prohibit the use of cash in the interest of reducing crime. No more laundering money, under the table transactions, can't buy a gun or drugs without knowing who or when. There are many positive reasons to do this.

Greed is probably another factor in going cashless. Banks that issue credit cards receive up to 3% or more of each credit card transaction. Some also have authorization fees of $0.25 or more just to verify that your card is valid. Debit cards used to have the same fees until recently when laws were passed to reduce them. And those rewards, airline miles or cash back, are also taken out of the proceeds of the transaction. Merchants say nothing and just pass the increased business cost on to customers. Since few people pay cash, businesses can't complain. Consumers are motivated to get some of that cash back by using a cash-back reward card.

The next logical step is to say that everyone must tattoo their number on their body since you can't do anything without the number, so why carry a card? For the vain, it could only be visible with ultraviolet light. Better yet, why not simply insert a microchip under your skin, since that technology would be even more foolproof? I've read about the military trying this rather than using dog tags.

> If a bank came up with an implant that would allow you to buy your groceries simply by waving your hand over the counter, would you take it?
>
> How is it any different from a card in your pocket?
>
> Would you refuse it because it would be too much like receiving the mark of the beast?
>
> What if the government insisted that all citizens received a chip implant, whether on your hand, forehead or anywhere else. Why would you accept it or reject it?

All this technology would make it easier for the beast to keep track of people who had his mark. But I want to emphasize that this technology is not the mark of the beast. It can be used for good or evil. We can't base our rejection of an implant based on Revelation 13:16-17 unless the implant also included an outward visible sign that included his name or the number 666.

Don't get me wrong, I'm not advocating microchip implants. I think they would be a huge violation of our privacy beside the ability for someone to steal your identity with the shake of your hand. We need to understand that the mark of the beast is a mark of ownership. It is just as bad as setting priorities in our lives that dethrone God from His rightful place in our lives. It's called idolatry. The difference is that we can repent of our idolatry.

My short answer to these questions is that accepting a tattoo or implant would not be wrong but it would be stupid. Perhaps that's why Revelation 13:18 says it calls for wisdom.

Wisdom

> How do wisdom and understanding work together regarding this number?

Most of the speculation about the name or the number of the beast is not wisdom but an attempt to gain understanding without wisdom. We are admonished to do the calculation; however, I fear that it isn't done with wisdom. We are relying on our own methods and not God's. I readily admit that I don't have the wisdom to do the calculation; however, I think that if we do seek wisdom, we won't need to calculate the number to verify the name of the beast.

> And unto man he said, Behold, the fear of the Lord, that is wisdom; and to depart from evil is understanding. (Job 28:28)

Both wisdom and understanding are tied together in this passage. A wise person is one who has recognized God for who He is. This fear must be that which brings us to our knees in the presences of a holy, almighty, merciful God. Depart from evil. If we know God, it results in understanding, which is to shun evil. The results of wisdom and understanding should result in a holy life. By refusing the mark, a person would be departing from evil. We can know the mark of the beast, probably not before it appears, but when it does because we will have known the true God.

> I thought, "Age should speak; advanced years should teach wisdom." But it is the spirit in a man, the breath of the Almighty, that gives him understanding. It is not only the old who are wise, not only the aged who understand what is right. (Job 32:7-9 NIV®)

It is clear that it isn't growing old and learning about things that bring on wisdom. It is the Holy Spirit within us. He gives us the understanding and then we can get on about the business of knowing God. Just as the mark keeps people from receiving the Holy Spirit in their lives but signifies their alliance to the beast, so the Holy Spirit keeps us from the beast because we know the true God. The ability to know God comes from the Holy Spirit but He expects us to find out most things from His Word.

What should we be looking for when we apply the **idea** of calculating the number of man?

> For though by this time you ought to be teachers, you have need again for someone to teach you the elementary principles of the oracles of God, and you have come to need milk and not solid food. For everyone who partakes *only* of milk is not accustomed to the word of righteousness, for he is a babe. But solid food is for the mature, who because of practice have their senses trained to discern good and evil. (Heb 5:12-14 NASB)

We continually have to train ourselves. We can't just read the Bible once and expect to know His Word and thus, good and evil. That is why the wise are the ones who are to look at the number of man. We are to examine things men come up with, whether they are new religions, new methods of controlling our cash, or forms of education. We need to look at each and try to determine what there is in them that take us away from Jesus or bring us closer to Him. In this case the mark will not be obvious to people. They will say, "What harm could having this sign tattooed on me do? It only allows me to use my credit card or pay my bills." What harm does teaching evolution do in schools? It is the same for this and other ideas that are contrary to God's wisdom.

I don't think that the biggest challenge will be in taking someone's name and calculating a number that comes up to 666, but in recognizing the underlying motives and consequences of taking the number. This is what we are expected to do. Even so, it appears that God has so devised it so that the name will add up to 666 just in case we have any doubts.

Who has his seal on you? Jesus or Satan?

Let's make our top priority to love, honor, worship, and obey Jesus. If we do this, we won't have to worry about being deceived by Satan before or after these beasts appear. We will also love our neighbors as ourselves as we live out what Jesus has put into us, the Holy Spirit – His seal on our lives.

Lesson 13 – Revelation 14:1-20

Revelation 14:1-13

Then I looked, and behold, on Mount Zion stood the Lamb, and with him 144,000 who had his name and his Father's name written on their foreheads. And I heard a voice from heaven like the roar of many waters and like the sound of loud thunder. The voice I heard was like the sound of harpists playing on their harps, and they were singing a new song before the throne and before the four living creatures and before the elders. No one could learn that song except the 144,000 who had been redeemed from the earth. It is these who have not defiled themselves with women, for they are virgins. It is these who follow the Lamb wherever he goes. These have been redeemed from mankind as firstfruits for God and the Lamb, and in their mouth no lie was found, for they are blameless.

Then I saw another angel flying directly overhead, with an eternal Gospel to proclaim to those who dwell on earth, to every nation and tribe and language and people. And he said with a loud voice, "Fear God and give him glory, because the hour of his judgment has come, and worship him who made heaven and earth, the sea and the springs of water."

Another angel, a second, followed, saying, "Fallen, fallen is Babylon the great, she who made all nations drink the wine of the passion of her sexual immorality."

And another angel, a third, followed them, saying with a loud voice, "If anyone worships the beast and its image and receives a mark on his forehead or on his hand, he also will drink the wine of God's wrath, poured full strength into the cup of his anger, and he will be tormented with fire and sulfur in the presence of the holy angels and in the presence of the Lamb. And the smoke of their torment goes up forever and ever, and they have no rest, day or night, these worshipers of the beast and its image, and whoever receives the mark of its name."

Here is a call for the endurance of the saints, those who keep the commandments of God and their faith in Jesus.

And I heard a voice from heaven saying, "Write this: Blessed are the dead who die in the Lord from now on." "Blessed indeed," says the Spirit, "that they may rest from their labors, for their deeds follow them!" (ESV)

The Lamb And 144,000

How did these 144,000 people get to Mount Zion? What does their presence there reveal about God?

The 144,000 are found on Mount Zion, the city of David, which is Jerusalem. Have you ever wondered how they got there? After all, this is the end times and if they were super evangelists as described by some, the Antichrist would certainly not allow them free travel. He would rather kill them on sight. Why would they all head for Mount Zion? I know they follow the Lamb wherever He goes, but why here and now?

> For the LORD hath chosen Zion; he hath desired it for his habitation. This is my rest for ever: here will I dwell; for I have desired it. I will abundantly bless her provision: I will satisfy her poor with bread. I will also clothe her priests with salvation: and her saints shall shout aloud for joy. (Ps 132:13-16)

I think Jesus is marking out His territory, God's chosen place for His dwelling. In Revelation 12:10, it says that the authority of Christ has come. Chapter 13 describes the opposition to His authority and now we can see Jesus making His presence known in the spiritual realm.

Why would this be a spiritual or symbolic visit and not a physical visit?

It is spiritual or symbolic because His physical return will be accomplished with a much different effect.

> And his feet shall stand in that day upon the mount of Olives, which is before Jerusalem on the east, and the mount of Olives shall cleave in the midst thereof toward the east and toward the west, and there shall be a very great valley; and half of the mountain shall remove toward the north, and half of it toward the south. (Zech 14:4)

> Which also said, Ye men of Galilee, why stand ye gazing up into heaven? this same Jesus, which is taken up from you into heaven, shall so come in like manner as ye have seen him go into heaven. (Acts 1:11)

The next few verses in Zechariah describe the day that Jesus comes back physically, and it simply doesn't match up with this encounter with the 144,000. Another reason that I think this appearance is spiritual or symbolic rather than physical is that within the next couple of verses, they are singing before the throne and in front of the twenty-four elders and four living creatures. This couldn't happen if Jesus came back physically to the Mount of Olives as described in Acts 1:11. Mount Zion and the Mount of Olives are two different places.

Since the 144,000 are all Jews, what could their arrival on Mount Zion symbolize?

And so all Israel shall be saved: as it is written, There shall come out of Sion the Deliverer, and shall turn away ungodliness from Jacob: For this is my covenant unto them, when I shall take away their sins. (Rom 11:26-27)

This prophecy could be fulfilled by Jesus' appearance on Mount Zion. This could be the point in the tribulation when all of Israel is saved and they turn to Jesus as their Messiah.

But ye are come unto mount Sion, and unto the city of the living God, the heavenly Jerusalem, and to an innumerable company of angels, To the general assembly and church of the firstborn, which are written in heaven, and to God the Judge of all, and to the spirits of just men made perfect, And to Jesus the mediator of the new covenant, and to the blood of sprinkling, that speaketh better things than that of Abel. (Heb 12:22-24)

Mount Zion is also referenced as the heavenly Jerusalem, the city of the living God. All of us who have been born again have already come to Him in the spiritual realm (Eph 2:6). The 144,000 that now appear with Him have come to Jesus as well, which simply means they are seated with Christ and God or they are all dead. Considering the persecutions, they very likely represent all those who have been martyred and have completed the number of the fellow servants who are to be killed in Revelation 6:9-11. With this, God no longer has any reason to hold back His wrath.

How can these 144,000 be so pure?

And it shall come to pass, that he that is left in Zion, and he that remaineth in Jerusalem, shall be called holy, even every one that is written among the living in Jerusalem: When the Lord shall have washed away the filth of the daughters of Zion, and shall have purged the blood of Jerusalem from the midst thereof by the spirit of judgment, and by the spirit of burning. And the LORD will create upon every dwelling place of mount Zion, and upon her assemblies, a cloud and smoke by day, and the shining of a flaming fire by night: for upon all the glory shall be a defence. And there shall be a tabernacle for a shadow in the daytime from the heat, and for a place of refuge, and for a covert from storm and from rain. (Isa 4:3-6)

There seems to be even more in store for the future of Zion. The correlation I see here is that all who remain in Jerusalem will be called holy. It isn't something that they have done, but they are washed clean and then protected by the Lord. Notice that the 144,000 haven't been defiled by sexual impurity and no lie was found in their mouths. How can you find that many men on earth that would meet these standards whether they are Jewish or not? No, this can only come because they have been washed clean by the blood of the Lamb. They are in this sense just like any Christian who is in the presence of the Lord after death. See Lesson 6 for previous discussions about the 144,000.

Two Names on Their Foreheads

Why would there be both the names of Jesus and the Father on their forehead?

When we last saw these people being sealed, it wasn't specified how they were being sealed, just that it was on their forehead. Here we see that it is the name of Jesus and of God the Father. Some people have a concern with the concept of the trinity. They are a little worried that by worshiping Jesus, they are not worshiping the Father. Some are concerned that they aren't giving proper time to the Father if they worship Jesus. Among Jews who don't know Jesus, it is more than a little problem; it is blasphemy to worship Jesus. These names let us know that to worship one is to worship both. The beautiful thing is that these are all Jews and they have come to the realization that Jesus and God are one and the same.

How are all Christians like the 144,000?

For you know that it was not with perishable things such as silver or gold that you were redeemed from the empty way of life handed down to you from your forefathers, but with the precious blood of Christ, a lamb without blemish or defect. He was chosen before the creation of the world, but was revealed in these last times for your sake. Through him you believe in God, who raised him from the dead and glorified him, and so your faith and hope are in God. (1 Peter 1:18-21 NIV®)

The Gospel is presented clearly in these verses. Like the 144,000, we have been redeemed by the blood of Jesus. It was established to happen this way before the creation of the world. When we finally believe in Jesus to be our God and Savior, it is only then that we truly believe in God. Nothing other than this is a true (or saving) belief in God. It isn't Jesus or the Father. It is both as represented by the seal on the foreheads of the 144,000.

First Fruit

What is the meaning of the first fruits in the Old Testament and how are these 144,000 first fruits?

Then the Lord spoke to Moses, saying, "Speak to the sons of Israel and say to them, 'When you enter the land which I am going to give to you and reap its harvest, then you shall bring in the sheaf of the first fruits of your harvest to the priest. He shall wave the sheaf before the LORD for you to be accepted; on the day after the sabbath the priest shall wave it. Now on the day when you wave the sheaf, you shall offer a male lamb one year old without defect for a burnt offering to the LORD.'" (Lev 23:9-12 NASU)

The first fruit is a sample of that which is about to be harvested. The lamb to be sacrificed at the same time was to be without defect. The offering was presented openly and visibly, waved before the Lord. Unger tells us that it became a tradition and the harvest could not start until the ceremony of the first fruit had first taken place.[57] The first fruit was brought in a basket and presented to the priest who placed it before the altar of the Lord.

Here we see the 144,000 with the high priest, Jesus who is also the Lamb without defect. Then we see them before the altar. Unger also tells us that when the whole village could not make the trip, they sent representatives with the first fruit, at least 24 people.[58] Only the ones that follow the Lamb can come into the city singing the new song. When the Jews went to Jerusalem with the first fruits, they also sang songs along the way. Psalm 122 and Psalm 150 are two examples of the songs they sang. Understanding the importance of the first fruits in the Old Testament shows us that this scene from Revelation indicates that the rest of the harvest can now take place.

These last two chapters of Revelation appear to be pauses in the timing of the tribulation. What clues help us re re-establish the time-line?

Three Angels

Another angel appears. The previous angel appeared in chapter 11. This shows that chapters 12 and 13 are parenthetical chapters. They do not occur in the same time sequence but are a "time out" to explain some things that have already happened as well as to introduce more information about the beast and his origin. We are now picking up again with the last of the three woes.

Eternal Gospel

We have been commanded to spread the Gospel. Why would God now use an angel to proclaim the Gospel?

The first thing of interest to note is that the beast has authority over the people who will hear the first angel's proclamation of the Gospel. God is not going to leave anyone with an excuse. Nor is He going to leave anyone who earnestly seeks Him

---

[57] Unger, s.v. "First Fruit."
[58] Ibid.

without an opportunity to come to Him (Heb 11:6). The harvest will not start without fair warning.

We have been told to go to all of the nations and make disciples (Matt 28:19). This is more than just preaching the Gospel. We are to teach those who believe to observe what they have been taught. It is a long-term commitment. This is not the case with the proclamation from the angel. He is proclaiming a last chance to declare allegiance to God. He will announce this to people who we have not reached and will not be able to reach in the time left. By this time, most people will have already made up their minds.

> What is the difference between seeking a sign versus understanding the signs and how does this relate to the angel?

> A wicked and adulterous generation seeketh after a sign; and there shall no sign be given unto it, but the sign of the prophet Jonas. And he left them, and departed. (Matt 16:4)

The religious leaders were looking for a sign, but they had already made up their minds that Jesus wasn't the Messiah. The only sign that they were given was Jesus' resurrection and they even refused to believe that. When this angel appears in the heavens and broadcasts the message, most people will reject it also.

> And as he sat upon the mount of Olives, the disciples came unto him privately, saying, Tell us, when shall these things be? and what shall be the sign of thy coming, and of the end of the world? (Matt 24:3)

There is a big contrast between Jesus' response to this question from His disciples and His response to the Pharisees. He went on for two chapters explaining the signs of the end of the age. He wants us to be looking for signs of His coming. We should inquire about the signs we have already seen but we shouldn't be asking for signs when we've already made up our minds that we will ignore them – especially when Scripture is already clear as it was for the Pharisees.

> And this Gospel of the kingdom shall be preached in all the world for a witness unto all nations; and then shall the end come. (Matt 24:14)

This is one of those signs. Many assume that our task is to preach the Gospel to every nation before Jesus will come back again. However, if you look carefully at the task and the weakness of men, we cannot do it.

> But when they persecute you in this city, flee ye into another: for verily I say unto you, Ye shall not have gone over the cities of Israel, till the Son of man be come. (Matt 10:23)

That doesn't mean we shouldn't try because He has commanded us to go to all nations.

> Why or why not would this angel be a technological advance of mankind that would enable us to fulfill the sign?

Some think that the angel that John saw was actually a satellite transmitting the Gospel by radio or TV There is always that possibility, but the text says that the angel flew in midair, which is a pretty specific phrase. If John did see a satellite, I would think that he would describe it as something other than an angel, which generally looks like a person, and would have said in the heavens rather than midair. The other thing is that the angel proclaims this with a loud voice. It is audible to people whether or not they have radios or TVs Sometimes we forget that there are still many people in the world without radio, TV, internet, and smartphones.

> Why is it called an eternal Gospel?

As was stated in 1 Peter 1:20, Jesus was chosen before the creation of the world. The plan of salvation is eternal. It is also called the eternal Gospel because this is what God has been saying all along. The following passages from the Old Testament demonstrate the consistency of the message that the angel is proclaiming.

> And now, Israel, what doth the LORD thy God require of thee, but to fear the LORD thy God, to walk in all his ways, and to love him, and to serve the LORD thy God with all thy heart and with all thy soul, To keep the commandments of the LORD, and his statutes, which I command thee this day for thy good? (Deut 10:12-13)

We are to fear Him, to walk in all His ways and to love Him. How can you both fear and love someone at the same time? Isn't this fear our awesome response when we finally realize who He is and who we are not? Isn't it the knowledge that, if He wanted to, He has the ability to cancel everything and start over? Yet He loves us! Our love and service are based on an awareness of who He is and what He has done for us, not a fear of eternal damnation. This love certainly isn't a result of our efforts to be good enough for Him so He won't punish us. Jesus has already taken our punishment for us.

> Now therefore fear the LORD, and serve him in sincerity and in truth: and put away the gods which your fathers served on the other side of the flood, and in Egypt; and serve ye the LORD. (Josh 24:14)

This kind of fear causes us to toss everything out that comes before Him because we have a desire to serve Him. Solomon echoed Joshua's words many years later.

> Let us hear the conclusion of the whole matter: Fear God, and keep his commandments: for this is the whole duty of man. (Eccl 12:13)

Solomon clearly stated that our purpose is to fear God and keep His commandments. Of course, the only way to do that is through Jesus.

> This fear God commanded doesn't sound like the Gospel that we usually understand. How does it relate to Jesus and the fact He paid for our sins?

> For the Father judges no one, but has committed all judgment to the Son, that all should honor the Son just as they honor the Father. He who does not honor the Son does not honor the Father who sent Him. (John 5:22-23 NKJV)

> Whoever denies the Son does not have the Father either; he who acknowledges the Son has the Father also. (1 John 2:23 NKJV)

If anyone truly fears God, then he will honor Jesus; he will accept Jesus because the Father has sent Him. If the true motive of people's hearts is not a loving fear of God, then they will reject Jesus.

> For I delivered unto you first of all that which I also received, how that Christ died for our sins according to the scriptures; And that he was buried, and that he rose again the third day according to the scriptures: And that he was seen of Cephas, then of the twelve: (1 Cor 15:3-5)

This is the Gospel that Paul preached. Since Christ died for our sins, our fear of Him is not a fear of rejection or condemnation. The fact that this is not that kind of fear is proved by His resurrection and appearance before others.

> And as we live in God, our love grows more perfect. So we will not be afraid on the day of judgment, but we can face him with confidence because we live like Jesus here in this world. Such love has no fear, because perfect love expels all fear. If we are afraid, it is for fear of punishment, and this shows that we have not fully experienced his perfect love. (1 John 4:17-18 NLT)

If anyone fears God only because he is afraid of being punished, then he doesn't really know Jesus or His love. If they did, they would have confidence that there would be no punishment for them on the Day of Judgment, but rather open loving arms.

Fallen Babylon

> How does the second angel declaring that Babylon has fallen tie in with the eternal Gospel?

For the wrath of God is revealed from heaven against all ungodliness and unrighteousness of men, who hold the truth in unrighteousness; Because that which may be known of God is manifest in them; for God hath shewed it unto them. For the invisible things of him from the creation of the world are clearly seen, being understood by the things that are made, even his eternal power and Godhead; so that they are without excuse: Because that, when they knew God, they glorified him not as God, neither were thankful; but became vain in their imaginations, and their foolish heart was darkened. Professing themselves to be wise, they became fools, And changed the glory of the uncorruptible God into an image made like to corruptible man, and to birds, and fourfooted beasts, and creeping things. Wherefore God also gave them up to uncleanness through the lusts of their own hearts, to dishonour their own bodies between themselves: Who changed the truth of God into a lie, and worshipped and served the creature more than the Creator, who is blessed for ever. Amen. (Rom 1:18-25)

Because God has created all things, because it is evident to men that there is a Creator, He is to be worshiped. This is part of the eternal Gospel. We get into trouble when we turn to other things than Him. It doesn't matter if it is an image of the beast or an image of any beast. We are without excuse, yet God loves us so much that He is willing to give us every chance. He has sent His messengers, and then He sent Jesus to tell us. Now He sends these angels. Yet these verses say that the desire of men's hearts is sinful, therefore He will finally give them over to their sin. Babylon is synonymous with sin, especially with the degrading downward spiral described in the verses above and those that follow them in Romans 1:26-32. This lends meaning to why the angel declares that Babylon has fallen. Sin is going to end!

What else does Babylon symbolize?

The root word of the name Babylon comes from the Hebrew, which means to confound and refers to the confusion at the tower of Babel. As used symbolically here and other places in Revelation, Babylon has confounded the nations again. This time it has come with false religion and political power.

God's order for the future is Jesus as King and the center of all things. Everything will revolve around Him. The Gentile nations are blessed because of Him (Isa 11:10-12). However, before that time comes, Jesus tells us that the time of the Gentiles will come and they will rule.

And they shall fall by the edge of the sword, and shall be led away captive into all nations: and Jerusalem shall be trodden down of the Gentiles, until the times of the Gentiles be fulfilled. (Luke 21:24)

In the Old Testament, Babylon was the first to take Judah into exile and Nebuchadnezzar basically set himself up as God. It was the center of political power and false religion. So the Babylon of Revelation is a religious (Rev 17:3-6), political, and economic force (Rev 18:3). This angel has announced the destruction of this false religion and political system that has been opposing Jesus for centuries.

> How is Babylon's evil sexual influence related to its false religion?

From the NIV® translation we get a sense of the power of the false religion represented by Babylon. It states that Babylon made the nations drink the maddening wine of her adulteries (Rev 14:8). The idea of maddening adulteries refers back to God's concept of what a person or nation does when they leave Him to look for other gods.

> And yet they did not listen to their judges; for they played the harlot after other gods and bowed down to them; they soon turned aside from the way in which their fathers had walked, who had obeyed the commandments of the LORD, and they did not do so. (Judg 2:17 RSV)

There is a long chain of references from this verse that show that this is what Israel did over and over again. Judges 8:27 shows that even Gideon, who had served the Lord mightily, was susceptible and prostituted himself after his conquests. There are many more Old Testament references, but the most common thing about them is that they usually refer to idol worship, which is now related to occult activity. Astrology is often related to Babylon, the tower of Babel, and is thought to have developed in that area of the world. The Lord is fed up with this junk and has sent His angel to declare that this system is about to fall.

Final Warning

> How do we know that a person who doesn't worship the beast but receives the mark will suffer God's wrath?

The third angel gives a double warning about receiving the mark of the beast. The first warning makes it sound as if a person must both worship the beast and receive the mark for God's wrath to be poured out on him (Rev 14:9). But the second warning clarifies that there will be no rest for him if he does either (Rev 14:11). Again, it appears that by receiving the mark, a person is identifying himself with the beast and thus worshiping him.

> What is the difference between God's wrath and His anger?

In Revelation 14:10, we have two different words that appear almost the same, God's wrath and anger. "He also shall drink the wine of God's wrath [*thumos*], poured unmixed into the cup of his anger [*orge*] (RSV). To confuse the issue, some translations reverse the use of the two words or use fury instead of wrath.

> *Thumos* (thoo-mos'); passion (as if breathing hard): KJV-fierceness, indignation, wrath.[59]

This Greek word for wrath or fury is something that describes a passionate or sudden outburst. In the New Testament, this is the first time it is used to describe God's wrath. Every previous reference is used to describe man's wrath or anger and is never used to describe a positive attribute. It is used again in the next few chapters to describe God's wrath.

> *Orge* (or-gay'); properly, desire (as a reaching forth or excitement of the mind), i.e. (by analogy,) violent passion (ire, or [justifiable] abhorrence); by implication punishment.[60]

This word is translated as anger and is something that has been thought over, considered, and more consciously dealt with, including punishment. It is very odd to have both of these words in the same verse related to attributes of God. Since both are used, this angel is describing something more than His contemplated, anger.

Even Christians can experience His anger when we disobey and He has to discipline us. It appears that His wrath is in subjection to His anger for it isn't until one is poured into the other that it is full strength and not diluted. It can be seen that those who taste these combined attributes of God are not His children.

> What does the Bible say about a person always having the ability to repent regardless of his sin?

There are many verses in the Bible that are intended to assure us that we can repent and be saved. We have Jesus' words in John 3:16 that promise anyone who believes will have eternal life. We have numerous verses about repentance. Peter's sermon on the day of Pentecost (Acts 2:38) or after healing the cripple at Solomon's Portico (Acts 3:19) promise salvation. However, there are also a few verses that make it clear, from early on, people make choices that are final in God's book.

> But they rebelled, and vexed his holy Spirit: therefore he was turned to be their enemy, and he fought against them. (Isa 63:10)

> Wherefore I say unto you, All manner of sin and blasphemy shall be forgiven unto men: but the blasphemy against the Holy Ghost shall not be forgiven unto men. (Matt 12:31)

Both of these verses talk about a sin against the Holy Spirit that turns God against them. Jesus even says that if someone is to blaspheme against the Holy Spirit, then he

---

[59] *Strong's*, s.v. "NT:2372."
[60] *Ibid.*, s.v. "NT:3709."

or she can never be forgiven. A conscious decision to take the mark of the beast is doing just this. Understanding what the mark signifies, worship of Satan and his cohorts as an unholy trinity reveals that taking the mark as a seal of ownership to Satan closes the door for salvation forever.

> What is hell's purpose and what is it like?

Jesus made it clear that the original purpose of hell was for Satan. If it were not a place of eternal fire, then He would not have used these words:

> Then shall he say also unto them on the left hand, Depart from me, ye cursed, into everlasting fire, prepared for the devil and his angels: (Matt 25:41)

> And in hell he lift up his eyes, being in torments, and seeth Abraham afar off, and Lazarus in his bosom. (Luke 16:23)

Hell is also a place of torment. Many say that Luke 16:23 is only in the context of a parable so that it is to be discounted. But we know that Jesus always used real situations in His parables. This was not something that couldn't happen, but was very possible.

People often say that the reason for the torment in hell is that God is not there. They also say that people who don't want to be with God get their wish and God lets them go to hell.

> Are these views of hell true? Explain why or why not.

Again, the parable in Luke helps us understand. This description of hell puzzled me because they could see Abraham even though he was far away. I had always thought of hell as a place where there would be no visibility of God or for that matter, anyone else in heaven. But Revelation 14:10 affirms the fact that those who do perish will see God. They will be tormented in the presence of the Lamb. This will make their torment even greater since they will continually see what they missed.

> How do we know that hell is eternal? Will there be any relief?

The smoke rises day after day for eternity. There will be no coffee breaks as some joke. There will be no rest.

People just don't want to believe and accept the reality of hell. They tell jokes about it. They draw cartoons about it. All of these things are designed by Satan himself to ridicule and make the idea of eternal punishment in a hot fire ludicrous. If they can get eternal punishment out of their minds, then they don't have to make a decision about Jesus. I've talked to people about heaven who have stated that since they don't believe in hell there is no reason for them to believe in heaven or anything else either. They should read these passages.

Patient Endurance

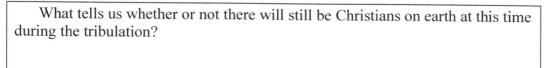

What tells us whether or not there will still be Christians on earth at this time during the tribulation?

Again, we are warned that it will require any saints who are still alive to have patient endurance. There will be great temptation to succumb to the beast and receive his mark so that they can have the physical pleasures of the world or to escape torture and persecution (1 Peter 1:6-7). They are the ones who keep their faith in Jesus. It is obvious from Revelation 14:12 that there are still believers on earth. They will die rather than receive the mark. But when they die in the Lord, they will be at rest in contrast to those who have no rest in the fires of hell; believers will rest and the rewards of their deeds will be given to them.

Anyone who dies in the Lord from this point on will be blessed. Again, this shows that there are still Christians or perhaps, that some who have not made a choice to follow the beast will turn to Jesus in faith.

Those who had previously "accepted" Jesus but didn't have genuine faith will take the mark. This will be in spite of the eternal displeasures that it will reap. They have a choice.

If you were in their place, would you endure? How are you enduring right now?

Receiving the mark of the beast seems black and white to us on this side of the tribulation. Our choices aren't always as black and white. Our marks may be slowly etched on our forehead as we neglect little things in our lives. They may come in horrendous pressures when a loved one suddenly dies or financial ruin crashes in the roof. Haven't we all known someone who walked with the Lord and then has become angry with God? Do you ever get tired of resisting sin in your live? It isn't anything like our brothers and sisters in the future will face. The message is the same for us as it is for them. Don't give up.

I am tired of resisting temptation
I am weary
I don't feel good
I need a rest.
This calls for patient endurance for the saints
Don't give up!
Don't do it!
This one small sin won't matter
Life will be better
Who is your master?
You could regret it forever.
This calls for patient endurance for the saints
Don't give up!
Don't do it!
There is no relief in sight
I can't continue to resist
The pain won't let up
I just want to give up.
This calls for patient endurance for the saints
Don't give up!
Don't do it!
You will not be tempted beyond what you are able
You will be blessed
With every temptation, there is a right way out
He will provide the rest.
This calls for patient endurance for the saints
Don't give up!
Don't do it!

Revelation 14:13-20

And I looked, and behold, a white cloud, and sitting on the cloud was one like a son of man, having a golden crown on His head, and a sharp sickle in His hand. And another angel came out of the temple, crying out with a loud voice to Him who sat on the cloud, "Put in your sickle and reap, because the hour to reap has come, because the harvest of the earth is ripe." And He who sat on the cloud swung His sickle over the earth; and the earth was reaped.

And another angel came out of the temple which is in heaven, and he also had a sharp sickle. And another angel, the one who has power over fire, came out from the altar; and he called with a loud voice to him who had the sharp sickle, saying, "Put in your sharp sickle, and gather *the clusters from* the vine of the earth, because her grapes are ripe." And the angel swung his sickle to the earth, and gathered the clusters from the vine of the earth, and threw them into the great wine press of the wrath of God. And the wine press was trodden outside the city, and blood came out from the wine press, up to the horses' bridles, for a distance of two hundred miles. (NASB)

The First Harvest

How can we identify the first harvester?

He was still speaking when, behold, a bright cloud overshadowed them, and a voice from the cloud said, "This is my beloved Son, with whom I am well pleased; listen to him." (Matt 17:5ESV)

Behold, he is coming with the clouds, and every eye will see him, even those who pierced him, and all tribes of the earth will wail on account of him. Even so. Amen. (Rev 1:7 ESV)

And in the midst of the lampstands one like a son of man, clothed with a long robe and with a golden sash around his chest. (Rev 1:13 ESV)

I saw in the night visions, and, behold, one like the Son of man came with the clouds of heaven, and came to the Ancient of days, and they brought him near before him. And there was given him dominion, and glory, and a kingdom, that all people, nations, and languages, should serve him: his dominion is an everlasting dominion, which shall not pass away, and his kingdom that which shall not be destroyed. (Dan 7:13-14)

As we look at all these verses, we can see that Jesus is the first harvester. Jesus was enveloped in a white cloud from which God spoke. The cloud is a symbol of the glory of the Lord and it represents His presence. Since the first harvester is sitting on this cloud, it indicates that the harvest is in the Lord's control and He chooses when it will occur. When we studied chapter one, it was clear that these references were about Jesus. He is portrayed as the Son of Man who will be coming with the clouds. We have also studied the verses in Daniel before with the conclusion that the Son of Man who is worshiped clearly refers to Jesus.

For as the lightning cometh out of the east, and shineth even unto the west; so shall also the coming of the Son of man be. Immediately after the tribulation of those days shall the sun be darkened, and the moon shall not give her light, and the stars shall fall from heaven, and the powers of the heavens shall be shaken: And then shall appear the sign of the Son of man in heaven: and then shall all the tribes of the earth mourn, and they shall see the Son of man coming in the clouds of heaven with power and great glory. And he shall send his angels with a great sound of a trumpet, and they shall gather together his elect from the four winds, from one end of heaven to the other. (Matt 24:27, 29-3,)

... so shall also the coming of the Son of man be. Then shall two be in the field; the one shall be taken, and the other left. Two women shall be grinding at the mill; the one shall be taken, and the other left. Watch therefore: for ye know not what hour your Lord doth come. (Matt 24:39-42)

For if we believe that Jesus died and rose again, even so them also which sleep in Jesus will God bring with him. For this we say unto you by the word of the Lord, that we which are alive and remain unto the coming of the Lord shall not prevent them which are asleep. For the Lord himself shall descend from heaven with a shout, with the voice of the archangel, and with the trump of God: and the dead in Christ shall rise first: Then we which are alive and remain shall be caught up together with them in the clouds, to meet the Lord in the air: and so shall we ever be with the Lord. (1 Thess 4:14-17)

Behold, I shew you a mystery; We shall not all sleep, but we shall all be changed, In a moment, in the twinkling of an eye, at the last trump: for the trumpet shall sound, and the dead shall be raised incorruptible, and we shall be changed. (1 Cor 15:51-52)

> What are the common elements between 1 Thessalonians 4:14-17 and 1 Corinthians 15:51-52 that describe the rapture and Jesus' coming in Matthew 24:39-42?
>
>
> What are the differences?

Coming of the Son of Man (Matthew 24:27, 29-31, 24:40-42)	Rapture (1 Thessalonains 4:14-17 and 1 Corintians 15:51-52)
Commonality	
Coming of the Son of Man	Coming of the Lord
Jesus' words	Lord's own words
Great trumpet sound	Trump of God
Quick (flash of lightning)	Quick (twinkling of the eye)
In the clouds	In the clouds
Gathered together	Caught up to Him
Elect gathered, other left behind	Believers will be gathered implies other left
Differences	
Lightning	No mention
After the tribulation	No mention
Sun, moon, stars darkened	No mention
Sign of Son of Man will appear in heaven	No mention
People will see Him and mourn	No mention
Angels do the gathering	No mention
No mention	We will be changed
No mention	Dead raised

> What is your conclusion? Are these the same events or not? How does this affect the time-line of the rapture?

By comparing these two accounts, it appears that it is more likely the same rather than different events. Just because a verse does not mention something does not mean that it doesn't apply. Just as two witnesses testify to something they have seen, one may leave out some details. It doesn't mean that an investigator should conclude those details didn't happen.

Many people believe the rapture and the "coming of the Lord" are two different events because the rapture is a secret return of the Lord and only occurs in the air while the "coming of the Lord" is when Jesus sets foot on the earth. However, the description in Matthew 24 seems to support a public appearance in the air rather than the time when He will actually set foot on the Mount of Olives. As we study further, we may discover if or how much time takes place between the rapture and when Jesus does touch the earth again.

People who believe that the rapture is a different event from the harvest agree that only the saved will see Jesus at the rapture. By examining the passages as we have, it is apparent that we can't separate these two events based on this criteria. It is apparent that the whole world will see the harvest and Jesus coming with the clouds, with power and great glory.

At this point, it looks like the harvest mentioned in Revelation 14 and Matthew 24 refer to the rapture. Jesus says that it will occur immediately after the distress of those days. If we believe that the persecution described in Revelation is the "distress of those days" and the events in Revelation 8 describe the time when the sun and moon are darkened, then this harvest is placed near the end of the tribulation. This is at a different time than when we normally consider the rapture to take place.

Those who support the rapture coming before the tribulation explain that this harvest is only for those people who became Christians during the tribulation. If that is true, then we actually see Jesus coming back three times. Once for the rapture, once for the harvest, and then on the Mount of Olives.

> Why will people mourn when the rapture occurs?

When the harvest happens, the elect will be gathered and the nations will mourn. They will mourn because they will know without any doubt what just happened. People will not scratch their heads and wonder why millions have disappeared. They will know because they will be able to see Jesus in the clouds. Jesus clarifies this when He says one will be taken and one left. They will be working together or doing whatever happens from day to day.

And when these things begin to come to pass, then look up, and lift up your heads; for your redemption draweth nigh. (Luke 21:28)

> What does it mean for us to watch (Matt 24:42) or look up?

To keep watch is not to see try to see Jesus ahead of time in the clouds and then to shout to people to get ready. We are to watch the signs of the times, the sinfulness of mankind, and the problems sin has caused in the world. We need to be continually shouting to everyone that He is coming, He is coming soon, be ready. When He shows up, there will be no time to get ready. When Jesus comes to us in a cloud, it will be for our redemption. It will not be for punishment, but reward. We will need to pray that we are ready, having the right attitude, and that we have done what we can to prepare others.

> When the Son of man shall come in his glory, and all the holy angels with him, then shall he sit upon the throne of his glory: And before him shall be gathered all nations: and he shall separate them one from another, as a shepherd divideth his sheep from the goats: And he shall set the sheep on his right hand, but the goats on the left. (Matt 25:31-33)

Explain why these verses do or do not refer to the rapture as well.

Even though Matthew 25 is part of Jesus' discourse on end times, this is clearly a different time than the harvest. It occurs at an unspecified time after the harvest. This verse is talking about the judgment and is clearly distinguished from the harvest because Jesus is sitting on His throne at this time. If we are to keep things in time order, then this is a thousand years after the harvest. Many people try to reconcile this with the rapture and get confused. I have even heard a person who used these verses to "prove" that at the rapture the wicked are actually taken and the saints left on earth for a thousand years.

Why does an angel need to announce the timing of the harvest?

> But of that day and hour knoweth no man, no, not the angels of heaven, but my Father only. (Matt 24:36)

While Jesus was on earth, He said that He didn't know when the harvest would take place. I can't prove it, but I think that after Jesus ascended to the Father, that He knew the time. You will notice that the Son of Man is already on the cloud. He may not know the exact time, but He is ready, He has seen the times or at this point, He does know. However, that is beside the point. This other angel has come out of the temple, from the presence of the Father. Of this I am positive, as soon as the Father revealed the time to the angel, Jesus knew also. The angel announces it to demonstrate to us that this is the Father's decision.

> Do you not say, "Four months more and then the harvest"? I tell you, open your eyes and look at the fields! They are ripe for harvest. Even now the reaper draws his wages, even now he harvests the crop for eternal life, so that the sower and the

234